LARRY MATTIE
Korea Jan. 195
987 F.A. H.Q. Co.

'3

WISCONSIN
KOREAN
WAR
STORIES

W. O. Wood

Veterans Tell Their Stories from the Forgotten War

Sarah A. Larsen and Jennifer M. Miller

Introduction by Jeremi Suri

*Foreword by John Scocos, Secretary,
Department of Veteran Affairs*

Wisconsin Historical Society Press

Published by the Wisconsin Historical Society Press
Publishers since 1855

© 2008 by the State Historical Society of Wisconsin

Wisconsin Korean War Stories is a partnership of the Wisconsin Historical Society and Wisconsin
Public Television, in association with the Wisconsin Department of Veterans Affairs.

Publication of this book was made possible, in part, by gifts from
• Sherry and John Stilin in memory of Robert Kossoris
• Todd I. and Betty J. Berens

For permission to reuse material from *Wisconsin Korean War Stories* (ISBN 978-0-87020-394-7)
please access www.copyright.com or contact the Copyright Clearance Center, Inc. (CCC),
222 Rosewood Drive, Danvers, MA 01923, 978-750-8400. CCC is a not-for-profit organization that
provides licenses and registration for a variety of users.

www.wisconsinhistory.org

Photographs identified with PH, WHi, or WHS are from the Society's collections;
address inquiries about such photos to the Visual Materials Archivist at the above address.

Front cover photo courtesy of Ray Hendrickse
Back cover photo courtesy of Robert Strand

Printed in the United States of America
Designed and composed by Jane Tenenbaum

12   11   10   09   08   1   2   3   4   5

Library of Congress Cataloging-in-Publication Data
Larsen, Sarah A.
Wisconsin Korean War stories : Veterans tell their stories from the forgotten war / Sarah A. Larsen
and Jennifer M. Miller; introduction by Jeremi Suri ; foreword by John Scocos. — 1st ed.
p. cm.
Includes bibliographical references and index.
ISBN 978-0-87020-394-7 (pbk. : alk. paper) 1. Korean War, 1950–1953 — Personal narratives,
American. 2. Korean War, 1950–1953 — Veterans — Wisconsin. 3. Soldiers — United States.
I. Miller, Jennifer M. II. Title.
DS919.L37 2008
951.904′20922775—dc22

2007037326

*For all of the men and women who courageously
serve their country in the Armed Forces*

Contents

Acknowledgments

Thank you to the Wisconsin Historical Society's Kathy Borkowski, Kate Thompson, and Sara Phillips. My work on this book would not have been possible without their patient guidance and thoughtful insights. My gratitude also goes to Wisconsin Public Television's *Wisconsin Korean War Stories* producer Mik Derks whose care for the veterans' stories and knowledge of the transcripts was invaluable to me in arranging them. His respect for the veterans' words enriched my appreciation of how important this project is. Thank you, Mik for answering all my calls. I would like to extend my deepest appreciation to the veteran men and women who shared their stories with the people of Wisconsin for this book — I am honored to have had the opportunity to learn from your stories of bravery, selflessness, and honor. It is to all of you I dedicate this book. — S. L.

I would first like to extend thanks to my advisor at the University of Wisconsin, Professor Jeremi Suri, who suggested me for this project and offered vital support and suggestions throughout. During my time at the UW–Madison History Department, Jeremi has acted as a valuable guide, mentor, and friend, and I look forward to our continued collaboration. I would also like to extend my appreciation to my editors at the Wisconsin Historical Society Press, Sara Phillips, and Kathy Borkowski, who were always patient, cheerful, and helpful. I am proud to have taken part in an organization and a publication that does so much to preserve and interpret our past. Finally, thanks to my friends and colleagues who provided suggestions and edits to these introductions, particularly Christine Lamberson and Heather Stur. They encouraged me to pare down wordy prose and provided invaluable insights and humor as I strove to make sense of the mysteries of war and do justice to the experiences of Wisconsin veterans. Part of what I love about history is that it is always a collaborative process, whether this is between colleagues, authors and subjects, or authors and readers. In the end, I hope readers will enjoy reading about the experiences of these veterans as much as I enjoyed writing about them. — J. M.

Foreword
KOREA: CAPTURED BY THE COLD WAR

The Korean War has been called the "forgotten war," but not by its veterans. More than 132,000 Wisconsinites served during the Korean War, alongside 1,789,000 other American military personnel who took part in the conflict. They endured severe hardships as well as significant casualties. 747 Wisconsin citizens died, 84 are still listed as missing, 4,286 were wounded, and five received the Medal of Honor for conspicuous gallantry "above and beyond the call of duty" (four of whom were killed in action).

The Wisconsin Department of Veterans Affairs is pleased to be associated with the production of the high quality TV documentary as well as its companion book publication, *Wisconsin Korean War Stories*. After all, promoting an appreciation of the experiences of Wisconsin veterans is part of the agency's important educational mission. Our mission is enhanced by our valued partners, Wisconsin Public Television and the Wisconsin Historical Society.

In the pages that follow, a number of our state's veterans tell their own experiences of the Korean War. Their first hand accounts of service and sacrifice appear next to photographs from these men's and women's tours of duty in Korea, and expand on the stories told in the television production.

Some historical background and contextual information from the perspective of Korean veterans is in order here. Following World War II, the United States and the Soviet Union agreed to temporarily divide Korea into North and South, but as tension between the superpowers rose, the division of Korea hardened. The Soviets had installed a Communist ruler in North Korea while South Koreans chose a western-oriented president. Neither recognized the other. Both sought to unify Korea at the earliest opportunity, by force if necessary. Remote areas like Korea, which bordered on Communist China and the Soviet Union and which few Wisconsinites probably knew anything about, became more important in the eyes of American leaders as disputes arose between the United States and the Soviets. These long term tensions formed the basis of the Cold War.

The development of the Cold War foreshadowed the Korean conflict. The United States, as the leader of the Free World, struggled to counter Communist advances by political, economic, and military means in both Europe and Asia. Americans hoped that the recently created United Nations would bring collective security to a world recovering from the effects of the Second World War by preventing future aggression. The Soviet-backed North Korean invasion of South Korea in June 1950, however, invited an American response.

The apparent lack of American military readiness to rapidly defeat the North Korean invaders led to important changes. The U.S. military command adapted to the initial setbacks by introducing improved antitank weapons and new troop training methods, reintroducing the draft, increasing firepower of infantry units, deploying first line aircraft to the Far East, and greatly increasing the allocation of artillery. Rapid medical evacuation for the wounded, specialized clothing to meet the challenges of Korea's extreme climactic conditions, and better food were also provided. Perhaps most important, however, was the selection of a theater commander who appreciated President Harry Truman's goal of limiting the war.

When peace negotiations began in July 1951, the combatants dug in and reinforced their front line positions near the 38th parallel. Although extensive trench networks were constructed, active patrolling generated numerous bloody clashes along with massive artillery bombardments. Deadly struggles took place, often during the night, at insignificant spots made famous by fierce combat, like Bloody Ridge, Heartbreak Ridge, Old Baldy, the Punchbowl, and Pork Chop Hill. The U.S./U.N. forces demonstrated resolve on the battlefield in spite of an anticipated ceasefire, while the North Koreans and Chinese saved face by not appearing to be defeated. Ultimately, despite high casualties, neither side was able to unify Korea. Negotiators reached an agreement to establish an armistice in July, 1953. The demilitarized zone separating North and South Korea remains close to the original line of demarcation along the 38th parallel.

The most difficult challenges facing American troops in Korea were ideological. The idea of a limited war disturbed Americans, particularly its veterans. Why should American soldiers be expected to risk their lives in Korea if the nation's leaders had no intention of achieving victory there? The goal of total victory, so plainly evident in the outcome of World War II, was simply not part of the strategy for Korea.

The consequences of the Korean War also convinced American leaders that the country needed to improve its military readiness in order to deter Communist aggression into the protracted future. How could deterrence through readiness be justified as a policy if it went against the American conception of using military forces for offensive purposes so that wars could be ended as quickly as possible? Some veterans could indeed say that Korea and the seemingly contradictory issues generated by the Cold War have captured American thinking into the twenty-first century.

John Scocos, *Secretary*
Wisconsin Department of Veterans Affairs

Introduction

The Korean War redefined American society and power. It brought the Cold War home, and it brought Americans to the Cold War. Before 1950, Americans could hope for a return to some degree of separation from foreign conflict; after the shock of the North Korean attack and the suffering of prolonged combat, Americans could only expect more violence, more suffering, and more warfare with Communist adversaries. The Korean War forced citizens all across the country to prepare, yet again, for uncertainty and sacrifice.

This extraordinary book tells this story in the words of the men and women who know it best — those who lived through the period and participated in various dangerous and difficult roles. It is a narrative of war and society. It is a reflection on combat and family. It is, above all, an emotional — and sometimes tearful — reconstruction of what the war meant to people who found themselves caught in it. Many died and many more survived, but all who served left a part of themselves on the cold and bloody Korean terrain. Sandwiched between the Second World War and the Vietnam War, the events in Korea are often overlooked by later observers, but this book will help to change that. Reading these heartfelt accounts, the Korean War will never again be a "forgotten war."

A focus on Wisconsin stories from the conflict is appropriate and necessary. It shows how deep the war penetrated American society, transforming lives far removed from the Far East. The voices in this volume are racially and ethnically diverse, as well as rural and urban, but they are all middle American. None of the people who appear in this book had any personal economic or political interest in the war. Few had any familiarity with the region. All of them, however, shared a deep faith in the righteousness of American ideals and a strong commitment to serve their nation when called. They fought in Korea, therefore, not for any particular territorial or strategic aims, but for a larger purpose. They fought to defeat what they viewed as an aggressive Communist threat to the American way of life — a threat exposed by the North Korean attack that promised to grow, like Fascism had a decade earlier, if no one did anything to stop it. This was the middle American view of the Cold War, often caricatured in retrospect. It was anticommunist and patriotic, but it was not extreme. The veterans in this book fought to preserve their lifestyles in perilous times; they did not fight with an imperialist mission to remake the world. They reflected the attitudes one would expect to find in Wisconsin and other parts of the country at the time.

As with other wars, the experience of combat in Korea challenged these attitudes. Were Americans really preserving their lifestyles as they fought in proximity to the Chinese border, yet so far from home? Could they defeat the enemy in this terrain and return to their normal lives? Could they ever "win" this new conflict with a numerous and seemingly fanatical adversary?

Personal confrontation with these questions, experienced in different ways by almost every veteran, made the Korean War a turning point for American society. Many began to doubt whether the extreme suffering of combat contributed to peace and prosperity for the United States. In some ways, it appeared that enemy forces fought harder in response to American intervention. The North Korean and Chinese combatants whom Americans confronted were not intimidated by the larger, wealthier U.S. soldiers coming to the peninsula. The veterans in this book did not lose faith in American ideals, but they began to question American capabilities — at least in this part of Asia.

As the war diminished the image of American might, it also contributed to an exaggerated view of Communist strength and determination. North Korean, Chinese, and Soviet cooperation in the war convinced many Americans — especially those fighting on the ground — that they were face-to-face with a brutal, monolithic enemy who would seize every opportunity for expansion. The United States was not prepared to fight such a determined foe. The Korean War, as a consequence, inspired a broadened nationwide effort to contain Communism at virtually all points across the globe. To do otherwise, many observers thought, would encourage continued Communist expansion and require more wars like this one.

After 1950, the United States implemented policies to prevent Communist aggression before it occurred. These policies included increased aid to undemocratic but firmly anticommunist regimes, such as the French colonial government in Vietnam and the Guomindang government in Taiwan. Washington embarked on a permanent buildup in American nuclear forces that respected figures, including General Dwight Eisenhower, hoped would partially substitute for a large standing Army. Inside the United States, the looming, all-pervasive image of Communist danger encouraged the persecution of alleged enemy sympathizers. This wave of intolerance, perpetuated by Wisconsin Senator Joseph McCarthy, swept up good middle Americans as both prosecutors and victims. The Korean War, in this sense, brought the fighting from the Asian battlefields to Midwestern towns.

The worst moments of McCarthyism passed after direct combat ceased on the Korean peninsula in the summer of 1953. The Cold War, however, only increased in intensity at home and abroad. Middle Americans remained mobilized in high numbers for renewed combat in Korea and other areas of conflict. They contributed unprecedented time and treasure to the development of new destructive weapons to deter enemy aggression. Most significant, they came to fear both the expansion of a monolithic Communist threat and the weakness of its opponents in virtually all regions of the world. Americans prepared, as they never had before, to fight a global struggle through war by other means. This, of course, is exactly how the three presidents who led the country after the Korean War — Dwight Eisenhower, John Kennedy, and Lyndon Johnson — described the emerging struggle in Vietnam. The experiences of Wisconsin men and women during the Korean War were the experiences of a nation entering a long, costly, and difficult global struggle. The Korean War defined the Cold War.

Professor Jeremi Suri
Department of History
University of Wisconsin–Madison

North and South

"Carry the battle to them. Don't let them bring it to you."
— Harry S. Truman

Located on a small peninsula that extended from China's northeastern border, Korea was little more than a name on the map to most Americans in the early 1950s. As historian Lisle Rose notes, in July 1950, "everyone was vaguely aware that the U.S. was committed to Korea, but only vaguely committed." Yet the situation on the divided peninsula had slowly been building since the end of World War II, when the country was divided into North and South Korea. It culminated in North Korea's attack on South Korea on July 25, 1950. The United States, with the authorization of the United Nations, rushed to South Korea's aid, beginning a "police action" that escalated into a three-year war. As the post–World War II era's first "hot war," the Korean War changed the tone of the Cold War. It solidified, intensified, and militarized existing Cold War divisions, beginning an era of big defense budgets and international military commitments. Korea transformed the fight against Communism into a global crusade; as historian Bruce Cumings has noted, "We are all a product of Korea, whether we know it or not."

Prior to the twentieth century, Korea had a long history of independence. This changed in 1910 when Japan formally claimed Korea as a colony during its rise to dominance in East Asia. When the Allies defeated Japan in 1945, however, they did not have a formal plan for Korea. The country was therefore hastily divided between the Soviet Union in the North and the United States in the South, with an arbitrary line established at the 38th parallel. This solution, however, did not take into account the hopes of the Korean people, emerging from half a century of colonization, or the political and social disorder that remained after the war. Politics along the peninsula quickly became polarized between the left and the right, as different political parties offered their own visions of the future, centered on an independent Korea. As growing Cold War suspicions between the United States and

UW–Madison, Dept. of Geography, Cartography Lab

the Soviet Union combined with these deep political divides in Korea, however, the chances for a unified, independent Korea quickly diminished.

Struggling to deal with a politically and territorially divided country, the Truman administration helped pass a United Nations resolution calling on the United States and the Soviet Union to hold elections in their respective zones in May 1948. In South Korea, this resulted in the election of U.S.–supported Syngman Rhee as president. Rhee, a Korean nationalist educated in the United States, was also strongly anticommunist; his election was met with widespread protests by South Korean leftists and Communists. Rhee began a program of martial law to quell the political unrest, but this only led to widespread popular revolts and increased guerrilla activity, especially in mountain regions. Despite the potential for serious conflict, the United States, faced with budget restraints, saw Korea as less militarily important than other East Asian states and began to withdraw from the country. In contrast, the American military occupied Japan until 1952 and, throughout the Cold War, valued the strategically located island state as the keystone of an American defense perimeter in Asia.

In North Korea, the Soviet Union moved to secure its position, hoping to regain Russia's pre–twentieth century status as a power in East Asia. In February 1946, the Soviets approved the creation of a provisional government in North Korea, led by Kim Il-sung and North Korean Communists. Kim had spent most of World War II in the Soviet Union, and his rise to power reflected the Soviet Union's desire to maintain influence in the peninsula. Unlike the United States, the Soviet Union continued to offer extensive military training and weaponry to the North Korean military. Though Korea was now firmly divided between North and South, both Rhee and Kim claimed authority over the whole peninsula, creating an increasingly tense situation.

The division of Korea into North and South took place against a backdrop of growing Cold War unease in the West. Based on growing conflicts in Europe, the relationship between the United States and the Soviet Union had become plagued with suspicion. In Asia, the 1949 victory of the Chinese Communists over the Chinese Nationalists brought Mao Zedong to power, increasing American fears about Communist aggression and global Communist domination. North Korea's surprise attack on South Korea on the morning of June 25, 1950, tapped into these fears, causing a strong response from the United States. Most Americans believed that the war was a Soviet ploy for global dominance and that North Korea was under Soviet control.

The American public therefore supported President Harry S. Truman's decision to send U.S. troops to the region. Telegrams to President Truman called on the United States to "Stop the Russians in Korea now rather than here later," claiming, "Americans want Russia stopped now. Get there fastest with the mostest." Speaking to Congress, Truman himself described the invasion as "naked, deliberate, unprovoked aggression" and argued that American action "was undertaken as a matter of moral principle." In reality, Kim Il-sung conceived the invasion as a chance to reunite the peninsula as a Communist state under his own leadership, yet acted with the support of both the Soviet Union and the People's Republic of China.

With its bold and swift attack, North Korea had caught both South Korea and the United States by surprise and quickly began moving down the peninsula. Rather than take on North Korea by itself, however, the United States brought the situation to the newly established United Nations. Pressured by the United States, the U.N. passed a resolution calling for an immediate halt to the fighting. This failed to change the situation in Korea; a second resolution followed calling for military intervention by U.N. member states on behalf of South Korea. The United States quickly dispatched weapons to the beleaguered South Korean Army, yet it was unable to prevent the North Korean capture of Seoul, South Korea's capital city, in June 1950. It was soon clear that it would take the involvement of the American military to stop the North Korean Army. Though American and South Korean troops bore the brunt of the U.N. fighting, U.N. troops came from countries as diverse as Canada, Australia, Ethiopia, Thailand, and Turkey, while countries such as Norway and Sweden offered medical support. China's entry into the war in October 1950 dramatically lengthened the conflict, transforming it into a true clash between the Western and Communist blocs.

By the time the armistice was signed in July 1953, 1.8 million Americans had served in Korea, with 35,000 never to return. Of these, 8,100 were never accounted for. Of those killed, 747 came from Wisconsin. For the Koreans themselves, the Korean War was a total war; approximately 10 percent of the Korean population was killed, wounded, or missing by the end of the war. Over the course of three years, the Korean War claimed 2.5 million lives. Though officially termed a "police action" by the United States, the Korean War was, in reality, both a civil and an international war. Its repercussions touched the entire globe, changing the course of the twentieth century.

Dale Aleckson, Mosinee (Army, 24th Corps)
Eui Tak Lee, McFarland (Army, 25th Division)

DALE ALECKSON When I graduated from high school in 1947, the Army was recruiting pretty heavily to fill in replacements for the GIs who were coming out of World War II. They came around with a program of eighteen months' enlistment and the carrot was that you could still get in on the GI Bill. You were guaranteed one year of the GI Bill plus every month that you put in the service. So when I added that up, it was thirty months. I joined the Army, much to my mother's consternation, when I was seventeen years old. I was excited about being in the service because I was slightly disappointed that World War II had ended, which seems rather strange. As I think back, I didn't know what war was but thought it was a glorious, patriotic thing to give back in the service.

I was certain that I was going to go into the paratroopers at Fort Campbell, Kentucky, and I was excited about that. I remember sitting on the ground on the company street and Captain Bartholomew got up on the stand. I'm thinking, "Well, I'm going to Fort Campbell." He announced, "The following soldiers will go to cold Korea," and I'm thinking, "Where is that?" I'd never heard of it. The first name he called off was "Dale Aleckson." I was sent out to Camp Stoneman, California, and put on an old victory ship, which was about as ugly a way to traverse the Pacific Ocean as you could find. There was no transition yet really from World War II equipment. When we landed at Inchon, the tide was unbelievable and we had to go over the side of this victory ship on cargo nets. We had no training on that. I remember carrying the seventy-pound pack, going over and thinking, "I'm never going to see that landing craft down below." But I made it along with everybody else.

I spent about twelve months in Korea. It was a very destitute, desolate country when I was there. The Japanese had occupied the country for thirty-five years. From what I heard and saw, the Japanese had a pretty brutal reign over that country. The poor people were just living in the streets. Japan stripped that country of everything; it was ravaged. When I'd stand on the roof of my hotel that I lived in, we'd look across Seoul, and it was a city of two or three million people with little huts attached one to the

Dale Aleckson served with occupation forces in Korea after World War II from 1947 to 1948. *Dale Aleckson*

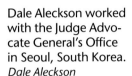

Dale Aleckson worked with the Judge Advocate General's Office in Seoul, South Korea.
Dale Aleckson

other with tin roofs and cardboard. The city was squalor. The sanitation was unbelievably bad.

EUI TAK LEE I was born in 1932 under Japanese rule. Military Japan had a policy toward the Koreans of assimilation, so I was in primary school and every morning, all the students would gather in the school grounds and bow toward the emperor's palace in Tokyo. They banned the Korean language. I spoke Korean at home, but in school, I had to use Japanese. They only allowed us to use Japanese and to learn in Japanese. I still use the Japanese multiplication table after all these years because I learned it so young. They also had a policy about changing the Korean names into Japanese. My name is Eui Tak Lee. My family name had to change to Nyshimura. The Japanese motto was "Japan and Korea, one body."

DALE ALECKSON Here's this little peninsula that had been occupied for thirty-five years but at one time was a country by itself. We just didn't seem to learn that all the partitioning that was done after World War I really didn't work very well and here we were party to the partitioning of another country.

Eui Tak Lee, pictured far right, worked in Taegu for the 55th Military Police as a translator. *Eui Tak Lee*

EUI TAK LEE The Republic of Korea was established in the South through the free election in 1948. The United Nations observed and it was really a democratic process. In the North, the Russians built a North Korean Communist regime. They gave tanks, artilleries, and cannons to North Koreans.

DALE ALECKSON I was assigned to Judge Advocate, which put me in Seoul with the 24th Corps Headquarters. Because I was the only enlisted man with Judge Advocate, I was billeted in with G-2. G-2 is the intelligence arm of the Army. They were doing the undercover, secret stuff in Seoul. This was 1948, and we talked weekly about the North Koreans and the Russians coming south. About two or three times a week, Russia would turn off the electricity in Seoul. They had all the power in North Korea. We'd be sitting there and the lights would go out. The U.S. Army functioned with a lot of generators. They did not have control of the electrical power. I thought, "The Russians have all the manufacturing and heavy industry and we took all the agriculture to the South."

We were reasonably sure there was going to be armed conflict in 1947 and '48. There was a saying, among the Army guys, "Golden Gate in '48, salt mines in '49." That referred to the salt mines in Siberia. GIs like to get a lot of those things going, but that was a reflection of what we, as enlisted men,

The division along the line of the 38th parallel was the result of a hasty administrative decision made in mid-August 1945 by the United States and the Soviet Union as a means of dealing with Japan's surrender to Allied forces. Today, the two countries remain separated by a demilitarized zone running along the 38th parallel. *Courtesy U.S. Army*

saw. And in 1948 when I was there, the United Nations had a lot of representatives in Seoul trying to set up a one-country government, North and South. The Russians said, "Nix, you're not even coming up here north of the 38th." The United Nations couldn't bring about the unification. Had the U.S., Soviet Union, and Britain not agreed to partition this country, none of this would have happened. I guess we can always look back and see those things, but what a terrible, terrible decision. Those people didn't want to be partitioned; they didn't want there to be Communism in the North and democracy in the South.

In my mind, I always thought it would be the Russians that would invade South Korea because they were training the North Korean Army. They trained armies to fight. We trained an army in the South, but it wasn't really very much. I mean, we really didn't put a lot of effort into making it a fighting force. It was going to be more of a home security kind of thing. At the time, it was pretty clear that Russia wanted to use the North Koreans as a means of controlling the full Korean peninsula. They wanted to say they unified it. There is no doubt in my mind that the Russians were very much interested in spreading Communism.

When I got home, I told some of the people in my little community that we were going to be in war again. Most of them had never even heard of Korea, and thought, "What does this eighteen-year-old kid know?" I was stunned when the Truman administration pulled most of the troops out in

1949. It was part of the effort to let the U.N. establish this new government when they put Syngman Rhee into the presidency of South Korea. At that time I don't think there was any way of unifying those two nations. That should have happened in 1945 and we'd have a different situation today. It was not a fair fight when the North Koreans decided to invade in 1950.

EUI TAK LEE After the South Korean government was established, the U.S. forces withdrew. The Communists wanted to make everybody Communist, so North Korea invaded the South and the Korean War started. The South Korean Army was only lightly equipped: no tanks, no armored vehicles, and no heavy artilleries. The North Koreans had huge armored divisions and they were well trained. The South Korea troops, with their patriotic zeal, fought back with rifles.

DALE ALECKSON When I was there, I often thought about what I would do if the North Koreans came across the [38th] parallel. We weren't trained to fight. We had pretty decent training in Fort Knox, but we had no equipment. I had a little .38-caliber carbine; each of us had one in our room, but if they had come over, I think we would have been overrun or we would have retreated immediately. We were not a fighting force.

I'm a seventy-five-year-old guy now, getting to the end of the line. But I still look back and think, "Oh...that could have all been avoided." That could add to the bitterness for the veterans that fought, and to this day, the general public doesn't have much appreciation for what happened. Just that they would call it a "conflict" reflects the lack of understanding. It was terrible. I don't have that bitterness because I wasn't laying in a foxhole someplace, getting shot at or marching back and forth, but for the guys that went through it...Saying some good came out of it, that would get thin for the guy that was there.

Taejon

"We didn't have much to hold them back with as far as big guns or anything like that, and we just had to retreat. That was our life for the next three or four weeks: dig in, retreat, run and try to survive. We were outnumbered and outgunned."
— *Valder John*

The North Korean invasion of South Korea had taken both the United States and South Korea by surprise. American soldiers, who only a day earlier had been enjoying occupation duty in Japan, suddenly found themselves in combat. These soldiers were not prepared for battle; armed with old, World War II–era weapons and sparse in number, they were simply unable to resist North Korea's quick advance down the peninsula. Indeed, by June 29, 1950 — only four days after the start of the war — the North Korean Army had already captured the South Korean capital of Seoul, destroying half of the South Korean Army. At the start of the war, American soldiers believed they would make quick work of North Korean forces. They were shocked to discover that the opposite was the case. As Wisconsin veteran Darrell Krenz put it, the U.S. military "figured the North Koreans would see the United States soldiers and run like hell, but they didn't. They ran all right — right over us."

Desperate to stop the North Korean advance, the U.S. Army created Task Force Smith, a group of 540 soldiers drawn from various units. These soldiers, These soldiers, including Darrell Krenz, arrived in Taejon, a city and railroad center one hundred miles south of Seoul, in early July. Deployed in nearby Osan on July 5, Task Force Smith consisted of two underarmed, understaffed, and understrengthed rifle companies. With only these weapons, American troops were unprepared to resist the North Korean Army, which used heavy T-34 tanks to crush American lines. In the span of a few short hours, Task Force Smith lost nearly one-third of its soldiers. These early difficulties led the magazine *The New Republic* to comment that the United States was "fighting a World War III army with World War II weapons."

Exploiting the United States' lack of equipment and troops, the North Korean Army continued its push down the peninsula. On July 14, U.N. forces again tried to stop the North Korean offensive at Taejon. American forces, led by the 24th Infantry Division, took up positions along the Kum River, determined to protect the city. The U.N. forces managed to hold on to Taejon for a week, giving the military time to bring in reinforcements and heavier weaponry. The North Korean Army, however, was able to surround the town, and after a horrific and bloody seven-day battle, Taejon fell on July 20, 1950. American casualties were almost 30 percent; many other soldiers were taken prisoner of war (POW) by North Korea and forced to embark on a brutal march north behind North Korean lines.

The battle at Taejon was intense and confused. In perhaps the biggest blow to American forces, North Korea captured Major General William F. Dean, commander of the 24th Division; the general had lost his way after withdrawing into the mountains surrounding the city. Dean, the highest-ranking American officer captured by North Korea, was held as a POW through the rest of the war, finally released in September 1953. By July 26, 1950, the Korean War was only one month old, yet the American military had already lost six thousand troops. South Korea, which bore the greatest hardships, had lost seventy thousand soldiers and countless civilians. By September, the North Korean Army had trapped U.N. forces at the tip of the peninsula in the area surrounding the southeastern city of Pusan. Only a major offensive could change the course of the war.

Valder John, Green Bay (Army, 24th Infantry Division)
Darrell Krenz, Madison (Army, 24th Infantry Division)
Stewart Sizemore, Lake Geneva (Army, 24th Infantry Division)

VALDER JOHN I joined the military from Milwaukee, Wisconsin, in 1948. I finished my training and wanted to go overseas but I was too young. I had to come home to get my parents' permission to go. They signed the paper and I went back and got orders. I was going to Japan for occupation duty there. It was nice, good duty and I liked it. Everything was going smooth. I came in one day, on the 25th of June, 1950, and the U.S. guards stopped me and told me to go straight to this one building in the camp. I got over there and there were a bunch of people lined up getting shots. I had to get in line. They didn't tell us what the shots were about. From there we went back to another assembly area and they said, "Just pack up your belongings in the footlocker and lock them up." And we were just to take our field gear and packs. I think it was the Japanese barber who said, "Oh, you're going to Korea." That's how I found out.

Darrell Krenz shipped out to Korea in early July 1950 with Task Force Smith, the first Army troops to enter the war in North Korea. *Darrell Krenz*

DARRELL KRENZ I grew up in McFarland. My father and mother were divorced. We didn't have a high school in McFarland and my dad didn't have a quarter for the bus, so I rode my bicycle to East High School. I graduated from tenth grade and said, "That's it. I'm seventeen years old and I'm going into the service." I went to Breckenridge, Kentucky. I was training with the 101st Airborne at that time. I graduated and they wanted me to go for advanced training, but I said, "No, I joined the Army; I want to go overseas." I was in Japan trying to get my high school diploma. I qualified on the new bazooka they had, the 3.5 bazooka. I was on machine guns. There were three sniperscope rifles given out to a battalion and I had one of them. I was there fourteen months when the Korean War broke out.

STEWART SIZEMORE I was raised in an orphanage in West Virginia. All the veterans came back from the Second World War, which made the jobs few and far between. When I got out of high school I had two options, either digging coal or running moonshine. I elected to go into the service because they had more options.

DARRELL KRENZ We went on alert immediately on the 25th of June, 1950. On the Fourth of July we were shipped to Korea. I was a private first class and part of Task Force Smith at that time. It was only a couple of platoons. They figured the North Koreans would see the United States soldiers and run like hell, but they didn't. They ran all right — right over us.

VALDER JOHN We were told that there weren't going to be many fighting forces, that the fighting forces weren't that strong, that they were farmers who weren't armed with anything but pitchforks and clubs. They didn't think that there was going to be any opposition and so we went marching up into the hills. We were digging in and I think it was the next day that we

Raised in an orphanage in West Virginia, Stewart Sizemore joined the army after high school as veterans were coming back from World War II. Jobs were scarce and the military was a heroic alternative to digging coal or running moonshine.
Stewart Sizemore

came into contact with North Koreans. There were quite a few of them. I thought they were going to go back across the 38th parallel. We dug in anyway. The next thing we knew, we were surrounded by them. Thousands and thousands of them. They came down and started attacking us. We didn't have much to hold them back with as far as big guns or anything like that, and we just had to retreat. That was our life for the next three or four weeks: dig in, retreat, run, and try to survive. We were outnumbered and outgunned.

Little by little, our division came over. We were getting heavy equipment, guns, and tanks, but that didn't seem to do much good against them because there were just too many of them. When they came at us they looked like ants coming over a hill. You couldn't stop them. It was just a slaughter from the time that we got there. Sometime in July they told us that we were going to go back north to Taejon. We didn't understand that because the North Koreans were occupying that area. The day we walked in there, we didn't know it, but the division was already surrounded. We got there, and a day or so later we got word back from Dean, the commanding general, saying that we were going to be there at Taejon, that we were going to hold it at all costs. There would be no retreating. We were going to fight to the last man.

STEWART SIZEMORE We weren't really qualified to go into combat. All of our regiments were understrength. We were supposed to have three battalions and we only had two. Our weapons were from World War II. A lot of them weren't very good; the barrels were worn out. We didn't have the amount of weapons we were supposed to have. At the time we were packing up our footlockers, everybody said, "Well, we'll be back!" That's why we had very little training. When the war broke out, we were saying, "Well, wait until they see the Americans...We'll be back in Japan in three days." Unfortunately, that wasn't true. That never happened.

In the meantime, our sister regiment, the 24th, had sent over Task Force Smith. They were ahead of us for about three days. They'd met up with the North Koreans already and they didn't last very long because they had no armor. The T-34s, probably one of the finest tanks ever made, just ran right through them. They did the same to us. It was pouring down rain so that when we dug our positions, the holes were full of water. We didn't stay there

Task Force Smith, of which Darrell Krenz was a part, showed courage in the face of formidable North Korean opposition. Darrell pictured with bazooka. *Darrell Krenz*

long because the North Koreans just ran us out of it. We weren't going to stop two North Korean divisions of roughly twenty or thirty thousand men. They just engulfed us to the right and to the left. We weren't expected to stop them because we had nothing to stop the T-34s with. We had the old 2.36 rocket launchers, which were totally worthless. They just bounced off and the T-34s just kept coming. We found out after that battle that we weren't there to win a war. We were there to delay. We were buying time with blood.

VALDER JOHN We didn't have too much left in Taejon as far as support goes but fought on there for days. Each day we'd lose more people, more equipment. And they kept getting closer and closer, surrounding us. I thought we were really going to get support. Early one morning I woke up and saw this big tank coming down one of the main streets behind our headquarters in Taejon. I saw these big English numbers on the side and I thought it was one of ours. It was just monstrous. The tank went by me and went around the corner where our aid station was and it just started shooting at all the wounded. The North Koreans had captured that tank when it ran out of gas.

A major came up to me wanting to know if I ever fired a bazooka. I said that I had fired a bazooka in basic, so he said, "Come with me." I went with him and they showed me how to operate this new 3.5 bazooka. There were some tanks at the air base at the north end of Taejon that the Air Force had spotted coming our way. Ten or fifteen of them, they weren't quite sure. Three teams were sent out to protect the road from the airport into Taejon.

The tanks came down, and the road was high enough off the rice paddies that only one tank could go one way. They couldn't turn around and so we fired on them. We took five or six prisoners. They were burned pretty badly, so two or three of us escorted them back into Taejon and turned them over to the South Koreans. We'd stopped the tanks from coming into Taejon by blocking the whole road off. That stopped them for a few days.

By the 19th or 20th of July, there was nothing left of Taejon. Everything was mostly flattened out. There weren't very many of us left, so General Dean said we were going to try to break out. Every man was for himself, to get out the best he could. I think it was about two o'clock in the afternoon, and we started breaking out of the city. No matter which way we went, we were surrounded. They were just machine-gunning everybody. You'd try to get under a truck, and you got shot out. I don't know how many vehicles I got on and was knocked off of, or the driver was shot, or we fell off the road. I got run over by one of our own jeeps and broke my leg. Not completely, but one of the bones in my leg. I got hit in the hip by small-arms fire.

I managed to fall into a rice paddy. I saw the North Korean soldiers just picking our troops off left and right. I lay there as they were taking potshots at me all afternoon. I guess whoever was doing that finally got tired or convinced that I was dead, so he stopped shooting. I lay there until it got dark, I guess. I could see them bayoneting and shooting people that were still alive and wounded. I saw them coming, so I just curled up and they went around me.

STEWART SIZEMORE One of the problems we had going over there was that we were thrown in piecemeal. We didn't have the right amount of artillery pieces. You don't fight T-34 tanks with rifles and grenades. There were replacements coming in and they sent me to bring them back. We usually brought them up at night. If they lived to see the next morning, we classified them as veterans. I remember one time where I went to pick up three replacements and the North Koreans had T-34s dug in on the Naktong [Bulge], and they were shelling us. One of the replacements was so rattled, he beat his head against a cement wall until there was nothing but a bloody pulp. He never did get there because he wasn't fit. The replacements didn't last very long and those casualties were pretty high.

DARRELL KRENZ By the 20th of July, the whole 24th Division was surrounded in Taejon. General William Dean was my commanding general. He was on the road looking at a map on a jeep. He had it all spread out and we started getting hit really badly. He took off that way and I took off this way. He held out in the weeds but got captured about a week later. It was a big thing to have the general captured. It was chaos for us. Nobody knew what they were doing. We found rifles just lying around. GIs had left them and run. We could see the North Koreans coming and we were out of ammo. This friend of mine got hit really badly. He was really out of it and running around with his head half torn off.

We were on an outpost and all of a sudden we were just getting run right over. There were hundreds of them coming at you and only ten or twelve of us left at that time. So finally we just said, "Well, they must have forgotten about us." We jumped on the truck and went back into town not knowing that the town was surrounded already. We drove right into them. They started shooting at us from the sides, from the roadsides. The driver and the guys who were sitting with him, they both got hit right away. There were four of us left in the back of the truck that were alive and we jumped out. We ran into this big ditch. It was toward evening already. We crawled away and into the heavy grass. It seemed to be pretty quiet then. We could hear them talking and hollering and screaming, but they never found us then.

The next morning they came down into our big ditch. This one kid, just a young North Korean kid, he spotted us. He went back up over the bank and we knew they were coming back. We had nowhere to go. We were out of ammo by this time, almost — I had a few rounds; the other guy had a

Darrell Krenz, left, was taken prisoner at Taejon in July 1950 and held until Operation Big Switch in August 1953. *Darrell Krenz*

couple rounds. This one friend of mine, he got hit really bad, tore half his head off. The side of his head...He went out of it and he was just running around like a, like a chicken when you cut its head off or something. I was on the sniperscope rifle at that time and I didn't have maybe half a dozen rounds left. So I ejected the magazine out. I knew something was going to happen, and they weren't going to get this rifle. I smashed the lenses in it and took the triggerhouse and threw it way over in the ditch one way. I ripped the scope off and threw that against a rock over there. I made sure that something was going to be wrong with it.

A friend said to me, "I don't have no ammo left; what are we going to do?" Well, we'd seen these GIs all laying around with their hands tied behind them and all that. So we put our hands up and two guards came over to us and one stuck his rifle in my face and searched us and all that. Out of thirty people in our platoon, there were three of us left. The rest of them were killed. But we survived.

They immediately took our shoes off and our shirts and then stripped our pockets and took our money. I made the mistake of having a South Korean flag in my pocket. That really ticked the North Korean guard off. He put his burp gun to my head and was ready to pull the trigger. I could almost see it. I said good-bye to my family and my little sister.

STEWART SIZEMORE When I fell back into Taejon, it was a mess. There were MPs on the bridges, hanging out of their jeeps. They were dead. I went into the division clearing where they took the wounded people. They were shot and killed. Evidently the North Koreans had gotten there with their T-34s before we got into the city. It was getting dark. Two other guys and I started up into the mountains around six that night. We walked until midnight. We got high up in the mountains and you could see down below to Taejon with flames all over the place, just burning. We walked for three days behind the enemy lines. We came out into an apple orchard and that's where what was left of our regiment was forming up. Out of 206, our company had 12 men left.

DARRELL KRENZ They marched us a ways out of town and put us in a mud shack for a couple of days. Then they took us north. We walked a little bit further and then a little further and pretty soon there were a whole bunch of people doing that. They had eight hundred of us. That's when the hell started, really. We didn't know what was going to happen. We saw GIs lying all over the place. Their hands were tied behind their backs and they were shot in the back of the head. We thought they'd do that to us too.

VALDER JOHN I started up the hill towards the mountains and I ran across another guy; he was wounded. We started up the hill anyway. I had water and he didn't have any with him. That's the only thing we had. We lost our weapons and everything else. We started up the hill and we ran across a group of six. One of them was General Dean and his staff. They were up there, too, going through the hills. We couldn't keep up with them and had to stay behind. We got up pretty high and the next morning, I could see what was happening in Taejon. They were still shooting and finding live, wounded people. They were shooting them and bayoneting them. It looked like they were throwing them all in a massive grave or something and just covering them up.

A few days later, we went into a village to get something to eat. They fed us and we started off away from that village. We saw these civilian Koreans: [North] Korean sympathizers we called them. They were going around shooting, just making noise. One of them saw us. We hid off into another mountain, but they followed us, and one of them had a grenade launcher. They shot that at us and the shrapnel hit us in the legs and my buddy in the foot. We couldn't go any further; we couldn't run. They captured us. I thought they were going to kill us right there but they didn't. They took us back into Taejon again and they put us in a jail. Those little characters would come in ten times a day. They'd threaten to kill us. They would come in there and preach to us about Communism. They'd pull back on their weapons and stick them to our heads. I was ready to give up and say, "Shoot me and stop this crap."

STEWART SIZEMORE We pulled back with what we had left. They said, "You're going to go in reserve so we can resupply everyone." But needless to say, that didn't work because the North Koreans were still crawling down the river. We ended up on the Naktong Bulge. That was a mess. The North Koreans got us in the Bulge and they were trying to shove us off into the

Stewart Sizemore re-calls how the United States underestimated North Korea's military strength: "We were saying, 'Wait until they see the Americans... we'll be back in Japan in three days.'"
Stewart Sizemore

ocean. That was the last stand for us. We either died or lived. I remember it was 130 degrees in the shade sometimes. It was just merciless. I was down to ninety pounds because I had dysentery. I can remember the North Koreans that were killed. They lay out there all day, turning black and blowing up to the size of a fifty-five-gallon drum. That smell will be with me the rest of my life. You couldn't tell a dead GI from a North Korean. They dug massive trenches with bulldozers and just put the bodies in there and covered them up. The fighting down there was so intense and bloody. It was kill or be killed the whole time. And we were down there until we started north again, back up to Taejon.

War is hell, but I felt that that was where I had to be. I was single at the time. I could say, being raised the way I was, I didn't really care one way or the other. After a while you see all these dead people and you begin to envy them. They've gotten their eternal rest and you've got to keep right on going until you get yours. You know the odds are going catch up with you.

3 Inchon

"I can almost hear the ticking of the second hand of destiny. We must act now or we will die. Inchon will succeed, and we will save one hundred thousand lives. We shall land at Inchon, and I shall crush them." — General Douglas MacArthur

American troops had entered the Korean War believing that they would make short work of the North Korean conflict and, in the words of Wisconsin veteran Stewart Sizemore, "be back in Japan in three days." The hard fighting experienced in Taejon, however, quickly showed that the war would be bloody and grueling. After only a few months, North Korean forces had pushed U.N. forces down to the tip of the Korean Peninsula, containing them in the area surrounding Pusan. With vital air support and hard fighting, U.N. forces were able to maintain their hold on the tip of the peninsula and repelled a large-scale North Korean attack on Pusan in early September 1950. It was not until the invasion of Inchon began on September 15, however, that the momentum and direction of the war truly changed.

Inchon was a port city of two hundred and fifty thousand on the western side of the Korean peninsula. Only twenty miles west of the South Korean capital of Seoul, it lay 180 miles north of the North Korean forces, who trapped the U.N. forces at Pusan. The North Korean forces had advanced so quickly down the Korean peninsula, however, that they were overextended and vulnerable. Seeing an opportunity to strike behind North Korean lines and retake Seoul, General Douglas MacArthur personally selected Inchon as the landing site for an amphibious strike against North Korean troops. By choosing Inchon, MacArthur acted against the advice of the military high command. Indeed, Inchon presented many obstacles to a large-scale, water-based operation. The tides moved rapidly and could leave vulnerable landing craft stranded in large mudflats. Moreover, the harbor itself was shielded by Wolmi-Do Island, and a high seawall protected a city that offered a large number of hiding places for enemy troops. As American

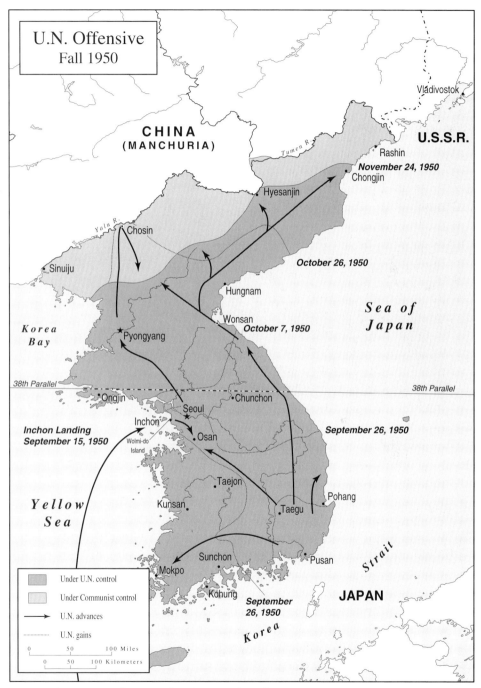

U.N. Offensive
Fall 1950

CHINA
(MANCHURIA)

Tumen R.

U.S.S.R.

Vladivostok

Rashin
November 24, 1950
Chongjin

Hyesanjin

Yalu R.

Chosin

Sinuiju

October 26, 1950

*Korea
Bay*

Hungnam

Wonsan
October 7, 1950

*Sea of
Japan*

Pyongyang

38th Parallel

38th Parallel

Ongjin

Seoul

Chunchon

**Inchon Landing
September 15, 1950**

Inchon
Wolmi-do
Island

Osan

September 26, 1950

*Yellow
Sea*

Taejon

Kunsan

Pohang

Taegu

Sunchon

Mokpo

Pusan

Strait

Kohung

JAPAN

*September
26, 1950*

	Under U.N. control
	Under Communist control
→	U.N. advances
.....	U.N. gains

0   50   100 Miles
0   50   100 Kilometers

Korea

UW–Madison, Dept. of Geography, Cartography Lab

Lieutenant Commander Arlie G. Capps stated, "We drew up a list of every natural and geographic handicap and Inchon had 'em all." Nevertheless, MacArthur insisted that the North Koreans would never expect an attack at Inchon, thus giving the U.N. forces the vital advantage of surprise. American troops spent the early weeks of September preparing for the invasion. Troops gathered on ships in Japanese harbors such as Kobe, where they weathered several hurricanes before shipping out to Korea.

At 6:33 a.m. on September 15, 1950, after two days of bombing the harbor, U.N. forces, led by U.S. Marines, attacked Wolmi-Do Island. They quickly overwhelmed the four hundred North Korean defenders and took full control of the island by noon. Meanwhile, ships gathered around the outside of the harbor, preparing to send in the rest of the American troops on small landing craft like those used at D-Day in World War II. The actual assault on Inchon beach took place around 5:00 p.m., as the Marines had to wait for high tide to avoid stranding their landing craft. Despite fears of disaster, the landing was successful and almost thirteen thousand Marines went ashore that first day, aided by air and sea cover from American ships. North Korea had not expected a landing at Inchon and American forces benefited from the harbor's weak defenses. Moving quickly inland, the Marines captured both Inchon and the Kimpo Airfield, Seoul's international airport, in the next two days. MacArthur, who had insisted on supervising the invasion from the command ship, came ashore to tour the battlefields several times.

Several days later, on September 25, a combined team of U.S. Marine and Army forces and South Korean troops attacked the city itself. Though American commanders symbolically claimed to have liberated Seoul that same day — exactly three months after the start of the war — North Korean troops still defended large areas of the city. The battle for Seoul was thus conducted building by building, street by street, destroying much of the city and trapping thousands of South Koreans in the crossfire. By September 28, U.N. forces had taken Seoul and began to move north up the Korean peninsula. Inchon turned the tide of the war for the U.N. forces, but this success was brief. As the U.N. forces crossed the 38th parallel and approached the Yalu River, the border between North Korea and China, China's decision to enter the war brought a new dimension to an increasingly bloody conflict.

LeRoy Schuff, Neenah (Marines, Fifth Regiment)
Robert Graves, Spring Green (Army, First Raider Company)

LEROY SCHUFF I joined the Marine Corps in February 1950 when I was eighteen. I actually went to the post office to join the Air Force because I had a couple of cousins that were in the Air Force during World War II and I had heard a lot of romantic stories about flying in the war. On the way past the Marine Corps recruiter, a friend of mine was in taking the test. I stuck my head in and said, "What are you doing?" The recruiter came over and said, "Be quiet." So I thought, "I might as well take the test as long as I'm here and waiting." So I took the test and the way it worked out, I joined the Marine Corps. I never regretted it. They're the best of the best. I stayed in for seventeen years.

LeRoy Shuff joined the Marines in 1950 when he was 18, shortly before the outbreak of the war. *LeRoy Schuff*

They put me on mess duty at Camp Lejeune while I was waiting for a diesel mechanics class to form. On the thirtieth day, my last day of mess duty, I went back to the barracks and everybody was packing up and I asked the corporal what was going on, and he said, "Are you all packed?" I said, "No." He used some less than flowery language to tell me to get my stuff in my sea bag because we were leaving in about thirty. We got on a bus and went to Norfolk, Virginia, to the naval air station. We relieved the detachment there that was mostly older, more experienced Marines. We were there six days and then they formed a troop train that went cross-country picking up Marine reservists. This was how I found out that there was a Korea somewhere. I had no idea where it was, what the people were like.

Robert Graves enlisted in the Army in 1948 and remembers hearing about the start of the Korean War on the radio while he was on a beach in Tokyo. Shortly after, he answered a call for volunteers for an Army Raider Company. Of the 600 men who volunteered, 120 were chosen. Graves was among them. *Robert Graves*

ROBERT GRAVES I went to boot camp down in Kentucky after enlisting in the Army back in October 1948. When boot camp was finished, we were given a choice of where we wanted to go. I chose Hawaii and Alaska but wound up in Japan and spent the two years prior to the war there. I remember hearing about Korea on a radio while I was on a beach south of Tokyo. Shortly after it all started, they asked for volunteers for this Raider Company. It was very much a cloak-and-dagger kind of thing; there were 600 of us that volunteered to go, and they chose about 120 of us. They interviewed each of us to see what our feeling was about disposing of people and things of that nature. We were trained at Camp McGill by British World War II ex-commandos and then had six weeks of training in Japan off of submarines and destroyers. We did a huge amount of swimming, demolition, hand-to-hand, a whole sequence of things that raiders and commandos are trained for.

We headed for Korea on a British frigate. We were on that for a week prior to the Inchon invasion. We didn't know that we were really decoys meant to pull the North Korean troops away from the Inchon area, down to a community called Kunsan City. When we went out in our rubber boats, we were greeted with a huge amount of fire from the North Koreans that had been pulled out of Inchon. This saved a lot of lives for the Marines and the people that went in on September 16. We discovered later as a company that it wasn't really planned that we were going to get out of there. There's normally a morning report that's done in the military, and there are no records of our company even being there until we suddenly start showing up on January 1, 1951. It was upsetting for us to feel that we'd been put in that sort of a role.

We went in at Inchon at about nine o'clock at night. The beach was the purest white sand I'd ever seen. It was almost ridiculous that we went in, because from the moment we hit the beach, the firing started from the sur-

Robert Graves' company was trained by British World War II commandos and received 6 weeks of training in Japan in swimming, demolition, and hand-to-hand combat in preparation for combat as raiders.
Robert Graves

rounding hills. We didn't spend an awful lot of time on the beach. One of our squads went in at an island just off the beach, and three of those fellows were lost. I was a sniper for my squad. They must have been of the opinion that I could see in the pitch dark. I suspect we didn't spend more than fifteen minutes on the beach before we were told by our major to pull back. We all ran for our rubber boats, which were left out in the water. We could hear the bullets hitting the boats and, of course, we were all scared spitless. We just had on "coral shoes" and black shorts and fatigue caps rowing back in. When we were onboard again after crawling up the ropes, half of us didn't have any clothes on. We kept our weapons, but that was about it. We had some burials at sea of the wounded guys we brought back. We stayed on ship until we went back to the air base and on to Kimpo airport. We spent four or five days in Ashcan [Ascom] City. By then Inchon had been a huge success for MacArthur.

LEROY SCHUFF They were getting everybody together because the Marine Corps was pretty downsized at that time. I would say about 60 percent of the troops that went aboard the ship to go to Korea were World War II veterans that were called back to active duty. So we had some pretty experienced people along with us. We sailed to Japan and docked at Kobe the day before Typhoon Jane hit. General MacArthur had a real tight time frame for the land-

The amphibious landing at Inchon on September 15, 1950, was a major early victory for U.N. forces.
LeRoy Schuff

ing at Inchon. It was impossible to send the ships to sea to weather the typhoon, so we stayed in the harbor at Kobe. The ship that I was on almost sunk. The cargo shifted from strong winds and the pitching of the ship. It was leaning at about a 40-degree angle in the morning when we got up.

We loaded our combat equipment aboard another ship and headed for Pusan. The Fifth Marine Brigade was very active in the Pusan perimeter in the early parts of the war in late June, July, and August. They were pulled back off of the lines, and most of us went as reinforcements to those companies. I joined Dog Company, Second Battalion, Fifth Marines at Pusan on the docks. I was assigned to a machine gun squad. It actually was a volunteer position because that was the work I did in the National Guard for a year back in Wisconsin. I was in a heavy machine gun squad in a weapons company. In retrospect, it probably was a foolish thing to do because machine gunners did not have longevity. It proved to be the case for machine gunners in the Korean War, too. We boarded a ship at Pusan and sailed up to Inchon for the landing. I was on the USS *Cavalier*, an attack transport. We went down the rope nets into landing craft at about five o'clock in the afternoon and headed for the beach. We landed shortly after that, probably between five thirty and six o'clock.

I remember that ride very clearly. The sea was pretty calm, so we were, too. We circled and rendezvoused and started heading toward the beach. We heard a snapping sound. One of the guys said, "Somebody's nervous and cranked off a round," and one of the old salts from World War II said, "No, that's incoming." We were cautioned that because of the tide, we might have to land on mud flats with two-by-twelve planks that we could lay out and go ashore on. You can't imagine how vulnerable we felt to the enemy. In other places, they had a stone seawall, and there was a very famous picture of some Marines going up over the seawall from a landing craft. However, the landing craft I was in was the fifth boat in the first wave, and our coxswain found a way to get into the sandy beach. He dropped the ramp in about two feet of water, and we were able to walk ashore without too much trouble.

After we got ashore, things got pretty mixed up. We had different squads in different platoons and different boats and coxswains trying to find a place into the beach and back out again. So it took forty-five minutes to get the platoon all together again and get all of our weapons together. We moved on into the city. Inchon was burning, like one big inferno. We moved through the city, but it was mostly rubble. We got fifteen hundred yards into the city and hit some pretty stiff resistance. We had a couple casualties up in the front, so they pulled us back and put us in position to hold for the night. We set a machine gun up on the road where we could field the fire out towards the enemy. As soon as first light the next morning, we headed east towards Seoul. That was our objective, to take Seoul. We hit minor resistance, mostly by the rifle platoons and squads that were out in the lead. The enemy was completely surprised. They had no idea of what kind of force they were up against.

The third day, we took positions on a hill. The road went through a cut in a large hill and there was a big high-voltage transmission line tower on each side of the road. We took positions on those hills on each side of the road. The following morning we woke up to the sound of tanks. There's no mistaking the sounds of tracked vehicles coming up the road. They were coming right straight up in front of us. We were overlooking Ascom City, which is a small city just east of Inchon. It was Russian tanks and about 250 troops led by a truck loaded with soldiers. They just came up the road in the cut between the two hills. Our fire discipline was just amazing. No one made a sound. No one appeared over the top of the hill. We just waited for them to get in between us. When the truck got around the corner, we had a tank on the road around the hill. Our signal to open fire was when the other tank opened fire on the lead vehicle. He did, and after about a thirty-minute firefight, we had no casualties and the enemy was dead. All six tanks were destroyed.

About a half hour later, General MacArthur and a bunch of his aides appeared on the scene. This was very interesting — not many people see such an impressive person in their lives. He walked up, and he had that corncob pipe. He mentioned to one of his aides, a medical officer, "Well, there's one casualty you won't have to treat in your hospital." It was an enemy. He turned away, and he actually had tears in his eyes, saying, "This does an old soldier's eyes a lot of good," seeing the results of that battle. A few minutes later when he left, one of the South Korean soldiers that were along with us jumped down in the culvert that he was over and shouted in there in Korean and took six prisoners out of the tunnel, out of the culvert. They had taken cover there. Any one of them could have reached out and thrown a hand grenade up and got himself a lot of brass. There were admirals and generals — quite a bit of brass up there. That was our first major encounter with the enemy.

ROBERT GRAVES As a result of Inchon, we'd driven most of the North Koreans up north of the border, so we got on a troop ship and headed for North Korea. We went around and up to Hamnung, and then, suddenly, we were working as antiguerrilla forces. We spent days walking because we just didn't have any real military equipment. We were attached to the 10th Corps Headquarters at that time, so we walked up into North Korea with them.

I'm not sure we ever really knew what we were doing, what "antiguerrilla" meant, and I doubt very seriously if any of us knew why we were there. A lot of us wondered. Orders would come down to the head of our company. I believe his name was Major Weir. Our company was so fragmented because we didn't have any specific leadership. I've always wondered if we burned three villages or if I was just thinking that we'd burned that many. Two of the fellows in my platoon said that we'd been ordered to burn four or five villages. I don't like to say we did that sort of stuff, but the fact of the matter is that we did burn whatever was there. We didn't know what we were accomplishing by doing it. I remember them as such small villages. Those villages we burned, we had no idea who was in them. Were there people there? Were there North Koreans? Is that why we were doing it? I have no idea how many or why. I don't even remember exactly where they were.

I took a squad up across the 38th parallel on some sort of recon to see where the Korean troops were or if the Chinese had gotten down that far yet. It was a very interesting trip because a lot of that country was really quite beautiful and reminiscent of some of our country around here. I

Following the landing at Inchon, Robert Graves led antiguerrilla forces across the 38th parallel.
Robert Graves

remember one time, and I've told my children about thinking, "Boy, if there's a place that I'm going to get it, this would be a beautiful valley to let it happen." Because it was really a lot like the valley at home, with the corn shocks we used to have.

LEROY SCHUFF A couple days later, Dog Company was given the mission of securing Kimpo [Airfield], the major international airport serving Seoul. We advanced to the airport, took cover for the night, and began the attack the next morning. We had a little resistance and some casualties, but it was a piece of cake. After Kimpo, we encountered the Han River. All of the bridges were down, so we sent an advanced party swimming across to check the enemy situation. A couple of hours later, our amphibious tractors came up and we loaded up and crossed the river on amtracs. We got formed again on the other side and continued heading south into Seoul as a spearhead force.

We hit resistance almost immediately after beginning the push to the south. This is now maybe a week after the initial landing, [so] they had an opportunity to assess the forces that they were against and to marshal some of their own forces and bring them into that area. We encountered some artillery fire, and that was a new experience for a young eighteen-year-old. We called in our Marine support aircraft with their napalms and rockets and

LeRoy Schuff, left, was awarded a Purple Heart for a serious gunshot wound through both legs.
LeRoy Schuff

eliminated that resistance in a hurry. On the day that we were to enter the city of Seoul, it was early in the morning, and the night before we'd taken up a position at the top of the high ground. Each night we dug temporary foxholes, not six-foot-deep foxholes, just scraped a little dirt together to get between the enemy and us. At about five o'clock in the morning we got up and were ready to move out. Ordinarily at night when defensive positions are set up, machine gun squads are brought forward, and the machine gun positions have a field of fire out to protect against any advance by the enemy. So we were right at the front lines, and the riflemen hadn't come up yet to continue the attack. I got up out of the foxhole and got my coat on or whatever I had to put on and reached down to pick up the machine gun, and when I stood up, I got shot through both legs. We think it was by a sniper. It knocked me down, and I think I said something real clever like, "God, I'm hit." You don't have a script to go by. I went over to the same foxhole I had spent the night in and just laid down. I was lying in this shallow hole with a pile of dirt and shale and the bullets were hitting that. I would hear the rifle fire moving on down the hill a little bit; then I'd take my helmet off and I'd pile the dirt up again.

A Marine came over to stop the blood, to see how bad it was. His name was Paul Tipton Baker. As he was kneeling in front of me, he was shot in the head, probably by the same sniper, and fell on me. Someone came and pulled him out. A corpsman came shortly after that and looked at him first and said that there was nothing he could do for him. It's so clear in my mind. I still think about it a lot. I think about that Marine that tried to help me when I was in the foxhole and got killed while doing it. I got the opportunity to visit his grave, the first time in fifty-five years that I had any contact. I met his sister and was able to talk to her. It was very unusual that this woman was Paul's older sister. She was eighty-five or eighty-six years old and senile. She'd been living alone after losing her husband many years ago. Her memory was not very sharp, so it was difficult to talk to her. I think she was comforted, a little bit, knowing the circumstances of his death. But I'm not sure that she fully comprehended what I was telling her. I thought it would bring closure to an episode but it hasn't. It just continues.

ROBERT GRAVES Intelligence was pretty iffy. After we got back down and then started back up north again, we hit a lot of problems with intelligence and recon companies and so on. We spread out a fair amount. We got in several firefights on the way back up toward the 38th parallel. They were pretty serious firefights, too. We went through nights of attacks. I remember one time being surrounded and wondering what was going to happen. There were only seventy of us. We could see the hordes of Koreans out there, and those banzai attacks went on like that for about thirty hours. And it was for fighting during that time that I was awarded the Silver Star. Three or four times during the night when you'd try to sleep in your foxhole, you'd be awakened when they approached with their weapons, beating on tin cans. Our Air Force was sent in to strafe the hills around us to try to get the Korean snipers that were constantly shooting at us. A second Raider Company was trained several months after we were. We were never affiliated with them, but they were one of the companies that came in to get us out of there. The MASH unit would fly in with their helicopters and take our wounded out.

There were times where you just knew the chances of getting out weren't all that terrific. We didn't have much for firepower except .30-caliber Browning automatic rifles, M-1s, [and] carbines. That's why we were having such a difficult time. Our saving grace was this schoolhouse that we were able to go in and get warmed up in. It was the 13th of January, so it was cold as the devil. I think it was probably an elementary school, and they were shelling it. I remember very well diving out through a window. And so it was just

1 August 1951

Sergeant Robert B. Graves, RA 16 300 739
Company "D", Staff Battalion,
Headquarters and Service Command,
General Headquarters, Far East Command,
8232d Army Unit, APO 500

Dear Sergeant Graves:

I have been informed that you are scheduled for return to the United States in the near future. Prior to your departure I want to take the opportunity of expressing my personal appreciation and the appreciation of all members of this command for the services you have rendered in furtherance of the efforts of the United Nations to restore peace in Korea.

During the early days of the Korean conflict this headquarters organized a Raider Company consisting entirely of volunteers for commando type operations in Korea. With full knowledge of the perilous nature of the duties of a commando type unit, you unhesitatingly volunteered your services and served with the unit during the period 22 August 1950 to 31 March 1951.

The accomplishments of the Raider Company during its service in Korea, particularly the diversionary attack which so materially aided in the success of the Inchon invasion, are well known to all personnel who are familiar with combat operations in Korea. You have every reason to be proud of your services with the Raider Company and you may be sure that we of Headquarters and Service Command are proud to have known and served with you.

E. W. PIBURN
Brigadier General, USA
Commanding

Robert Graves received this letter from Brigadier General E. W. Piburn after being awarded the Silver Star for gallantry in action. *Robert Graves*

back and forth from the schoolhouse out to my foxhole. We had to set up a perimeter, a relatively small one because we just didn't have that many men. A friend and I were asked to cross this riverbed that was in direct line with snipers up at the head of this ravine. I remember very well a thought that I had as this friend and I were requested to move across the riverbed to get an intelligence report from a group that had formed up across the river. There were tracers all over the place. You'd think you were ducking them, but you can't know. I remember thinking, "If we have to do this, there's just no way we are going to live." And I thought about my family and what a waste it was. I remember I felt terribly sorry for what it would do to my mother and father. When we were awarded the medals, we were up on a hill, out in a field. There were several of us who were given medals. I received the Silver Star, and there were several that received Bronze Stars. I presume somebody pinned it on me, but I don't remember it at all.

LEROY SCHUFF The corpsman put a bandage around the leg that was bleeding the worst and gave me a shot of morphine and left a couple more Syrettes with me because he had to leave for all the other action going on. I was on that hill for about eight hours. They came by to ask if I could walk, and I said I would try, but I didn't know what the bullet had gone through. I took a couple of steps and couldn't go any further. They said there were other casualties further up the hill with stomach and chest wounds that needed attention very quickly and so they would go get them first. Eventually they came back and carried me on a stretcher to the base of the hill and laid me across the hood of a jeep. We went back to where the amtracs dropped us off the day before at the Han River. They took scissors and they cut all my clothes off and laid them aside and lifted me out onto a bed. I was still filthy, all blood from my neck to my waist because I was underneath a couple of stomach and chest wounds in the ambulance and they bled through onto me. The doctor at the airport tried to treat wounds to my chest first, and I had to stop him and say, "I'm OK there." They cleaned me up, and the next morning I was put back in an ambulance, flown to Tokyo, and then taken to the naval hospital at Yokosuka, where I did most of my recovery time. They mentioned amputation. That was very disheartening to me. I had no idea how much damage was caused to both of my legs. The first couple of steps I took with the crutches were very rewarding. I spent about five months in the hospital, went through reconditioning, and went back to Korea to continue my tour until September 1951. My legs turned out to be OK and I spent another fifteen years in the Marine Corps.

ROBERT GRAVES It was a pretty special group of guys. I don't know how many we lost. We lost some due to wounds after they were evacuated to some MASH unit. It was probably the hardest part of the war as far as our organization was concerned. We were there for seven months, and we were on the front for seven months — seven months in combat. We walked miles. I remember very well that shortly after we had moved up into North Korea, we would walk thirty miles a day, carrying big backpacks. We were hungry a good deal of the time. We never had a meal, just C-rations for the entire seven months. C-rations were lousy things. The only times it wasn't pure

C-rations were when we would come into little towns and catch chickens or pigs or whatever we could and then cook them. We stole a fair amount of food. I remember I sent my mother a list of things and she sent me back a box of food. One of the things that I desperately wanted, of all things, was a can of fruit cocktail. In retrospect, I can't imagine why I would want a whole can of fruit cocktail, but I was just desperate. She sent me fruit cocktail and some Fig Newton cookies. When we would receive things like that, we didn't want to give any of it away; we were like dogs. We'd go out in the woods or to a hiding place and eat our stuff. There wasn't any way I was going to give away any of my fruit cocktail, although I haven't had a spoonful of it in the fifty years since.

It was strange, because it wasn't a war at all, you know; it was a "police action," and it was always called a police action, or "the forgotten war," whatever people wanted to call it. But we certainly lost a lot of fine people. Particularly at the very onset of the war when they almost drove us off into the ocean, and there were just a lot of people killed. Not just of us, either; we were United Nations forces really, and there were Turks and Brits and Canadians and Aussies. It was a really wonderful group of people. Coming back, I think a lot of us felt out of place because we weren't returning from a "war." I mean, who knew in 1950 and '51 and '52 when it was going on, and who cared? Nobody seemed to care that we'd gone through that, that we'd lost thousands of men. Thousands. I've often wondered why it had to happen.

4 POWs

"I used to dream over there of home...When I got home I dreamt about over there." — *Darrell Krenz*

Despite the Korean War's unofficial title as "the forgotten war," the experiences of American prisoners of war in Korea left a lasting impression on American culture. As part of the settlement that ended the war, POWs on both sides were allowed to choose the country to which they would return. This portion of the settlement was designed so that North Korean and Chinese POWs could return to South Korea or Taiwan rather than the Communist states of North Korea or China. Yet the unexpected decision of twenty-one American prisoners not to return to the United States after the war — instead staying in China and North Korea — spawned intense alarm over Communist brainwashing and the patriotism of the American soldier. Indeed, fear of brainwashing became a popular cultural obsession during the Cold War. The 1962 movie *The Manchurian Candidate* immortalized this hysteria, drawing on Cold War anxieties to tell the fictional story of a former Korean War POW who had been brainwashed by Communists to become a political assassin. Yet as the following histories make clear, this was far from the experience of the average American soldier in Korea. As in World War II and later, Vietnam, becoming a POW in Korea was a horrific experience that required strength, ingenuity, and not a little luck to survive.

When North Korean forces invaded South Korea in June 1950, they did not expect a strong military response and were thus ill-prepared to handle an influx of United Nations POWs. Yet the North Korean Army's early successes on the battlefield meant that it quickly had to deal with hundreds of prisoners. The battle lines moved so rapidly in the first months of the war that the North Korean Army found it necessary to use a central collection point to organize captured prisoners at Pyongyang, North Korea. Hoping to stay ahead of the U.N. forces, especially after the September 1950 Inchon landing, North Korea then moved the captured U.N. soldiers far behind its lines, using both trains and forced marching to push them north toward the Yalu River. These marches lasted as long as four months and were an exhausting, difficult, and often deadly experience for starving, injured soldiers. POWs who became sick or fell behind the long columns of soldiers were shot and left to die. In their hurry to stay ahead of advancing U.N. soldiers, the North Korean Army also killed prisoners outright, partially due to a lack of POW facilities and a fear of being overtaken by U.N. forces. Wisconsin POW Valder John, for example, was one of the few survivors of the Sunchon Tunnel Massacre in which, after failing to move prisoners quickly north by train, the North Korean Army shot approximately seventy POWs on October 30, 1950. Those soldiers who survived the forced march north still had to battle subzero temperatures in quickly established POW camps where accommodations, rations, and medical care were sparse. Diseases such as dysentery and pneumonia were common, and maltreatment, physical abuse, and interrogation, combined with a lack of food and water, wore on the prisoners' physical and mental states.

Like the first North Korean offensive, China's entry into the war in October 1950 also led to the capture of thousands of American POWs. These POWs were also held in camps close to China's border. Though conditions improved as the Chinese established permanent camps in 1951, POWs were subjected to political indoctrination. The Chinese Army conducted extensive lectures in its camps to encourage prisoners to convert to Communism. These lectures caused the fear of brainwashing that was so prevalent after the war.

By the time the armistice was signed in July 1953, approximately 7,200 American soldiers had been taken prisoner by North Korea and China. An estimated 40 percent of these POWs died in captivity, a number approximately ten times as high as those who died in German POW camps during World War II. Historians contest this death rate, however, arguing that it should be even higher because it does not include men who died from untreated wounds during atrocities such as the Sunchon Tunnel Massacre, or during the deadly marches north to the camps. The highest percentage of prisoners died during the time described by Darrell Krenz below, the first bitterly cold winter of 1950–1951. Indeed, after being captured by China and North Korea, POWs had little hope but to try to survive until the end of the war. Escape from POW camps was rare and there were only two POW exchanges during the war, both in 1953. This meant that men captured in the first year of the war, the majority of American POWs, were held for several years before their release. The men who survived to return home were thus extremely fortunate, yet today, many former POWs remain haunted by their experiences in captivity.

Dale King, Colgate (Army, Fifth Artillery)
Darrell Krenz, Madison (Army, 24th Infantry Division)
Valder John, Green Bay (Army, 24th Infantry Division)*

Dale King, in training in the United States before being sent to Korea. *Dale King*

DALE KING I enlisted in the service in November of 1948. I originally planned on going to college, but being a rather wild hare at the time and watching my brother study diligently every night, I decided I would take a way out for a while. We got ready for Korea after we got told we had to go. We were ready and on the seas in about five days. We were supposed to land in a port just west of Pusan, but because the perimeter by that time had gotten very, very small, we couldn't land at Misan, we had to go to Pusan. From there it was only about forty or fifty miles to the front in any direction. It was an extremely tight perimeter. We stabilized the location of the front after a few weeks and we started pushing out because we were only fighting North Koreans, and the American Army certainly had superior fighting ability than they did in terms of weaponry and in terms of the experience of the people. We had a lot of World War II veterans in our group. We pushed out and moved on up over the next several months to Taegu, and we got close to the 38th parallel.

I popped a hernia and I had to go back to a MASH unit, and they did a rather crude repair job, and then I was sent to Japan for approximately a month and a week for recovery. I was put on a ship, and I was supposed to land at Inchon at this time, but because the Chinese entered the fray, it was no longer safe to land in Inchon, so I once again landed in Pusan to get up to my unit. It was very difficult times because you hitched a ride whenever you could. I had the orders in my hand and I kept on showing

* The capture of Darrell Krenz and Valder John by North Korean troops at Taejon is recounted in chapter 2.

them to people, but there really was no organized way of getting back to the front. I did eventually arrive back with my unit, and it looked a little bit different because it had had a lot of hard times, and we had lost a lot of people because of mortars landing in command posts. I was happy to be back there with them just south of the 38th parallel.

Darrell Krenz was captured at Taejon in July 1950. Like many POWs captured at the beginning of the war, he wouldn't be released until after the armistice was signed in 1953. *Darrell Krenz*

DARRELL KRENZ We were sleeping in a cornfield one night in late October '50. North Korean officers came to us and said that in the morning we were going to move out, so to get prepared. I didn't know how we could be prepared to do that. "It's going to be bad," they said. The next morning, a big North Korean officer came with his interpreters. There was a lieutenant, Second Lieutenant Thornton from Texas, went up to him and saluted him. The North Korean was hollering and screaming about the American aggression. He turned Lieutenant Thornton around and shot him in the back of the head. He wanted us to know that he was going to be boss.

They lined us up and pointed way off over the horizon. The North Korean officer said we were going to go over the mountains. We started walking. We walked about nine days for a little over a hundred miles. But during that time they took us off the road at night to let the Chinese come in. There were five abreast on the road walking south. We had no way of warning anybody that they were coming, of course.

DALE KING The Chinese started to drive to the South, and one of the areas that they hit hard at was the 24th Division, which included the Fifth Regimental Combat Team at that time. They overran the forward observers, for the artillery. We were in position supporting the 24th Division and the Fifth RCT at that time. We were practically out of ammunition from firing so much to try to keep the Chinese at bay. Eventually, they said, "We're going to change our line of defense back a few miles because we are not holding here." Everybody was asked to retreat back as far as the field artillery, get on the trucks, and we were going to move out. We had a lot of field artillery trucks that were full of Army people, when we finally got a Close Station, March Order. Our battery happened to be the one that was in the front of those leaving. Unfortunately, the commanding officer said, "These guys are starving, the infantry men, because it's been a couple days; they haven't had any water or food, and so let's give them a meal and then we'll go on our way." During that time, the Chinese went around behind us, and we were virtually in a trap.

When we started driving out again, we didn't get very far down the road, perhaps a mile, when the first vehicle was knocked out by a bazooka round that they had captured somewhere along the way. We could no longer move, and we blocked up everybody. There were a lot of mortar rounds coming down from the hillsides. All of us had manned our 105s again and were aiming at the hills. If you know artillery, you know that it takes a while for the shells to arm themselves. They have to make so many rotations before they become live, and it was getting that it was so close they wouldn't explode. In my gun section, we got a mortar round that killed my gunner and severely wounded one other member of my group. It got me as well, with shrapnel in the back. The pieces kept on coming out one at a time over the next ten or fifteen years and I don't think there's any left now. I used to see them in every X-ray and somebody would say, "What have you got on your back?" They come out and look like little sharp points. That wasn't so serious. I think they went through my gunner first and then got into me. That's why I wasn't hurt as bad as he…well, he was killed.

VALDER JOHN One day they took us out [of the jail in Taejon] and said we were going to go north. They told us that we were going to Seoul first. We had bomber pilots they shot down, bomber crews, and people from the Navy. We had a bit of everybody in there. As we went down the road at night, more prisoners joined us, so by the time we got to Seoul there were about sixty of us. And then a Seventh Infantry Division and a Third Marine Regiment landed at Inchon and we started getting those guys in, too. We got into Seoul and there were a couple hundred of us. By the time we got ready to march out of Seoul, we had close to four hundred. We started to march at night and we were supposed to sleep during the daytime. They kept interrogating us, the same thing over and over and over again. This went on and on. This friend of mine, a little Filipino, he was in the World War II Bataan Death March. I didn't know it then but the Bataan Death March was twenty-seven miles long and it lasted about three or four days or something like that. Our march was four hundred and some miles and lasted four months.

One day we got caught in the open and there were some Navy planes that saw us. We just stood in the road and they came down low enough to recognize us. They did flips with their planes. The Navy planes started shooting in front of us and so the North Korean guards turned around and marched us backwards, back south again. The guards got scared at one point and they turned their weapons over to us. They were going to leave. We said, "Good, let them go. Don't hurt them. Just grab their weapons and go." There were a couple guys, I don't know what their thinking was, but they said, "No, the rear guard will find us and kill us all." They didn't want the guards to leave us. The guards stayed and they took their weapons back and turned us around and we started marching north again. I thought we were going to be free there for a second.

DALE KING I and some others that were in sort of the same condition went up to the very front of the convoy, where the first truck was hit. We went into a drainage ditch there and were firing at the Chinese crossing the road in front of us, and throwing hand grenades. This went on for quite a few hours and it was — by that time it was nightfall. At that time there were about fourteen of us in a ditch, most of us wounded to various degrees. All the trucks were burning and the ones that had ammunition left were exploding. It was like a big pyrotechnic display as all those trucks caught fire and blew up. Then about two o'clock in the morning, the Chinese formed a ring around us with automatic machine guns and started closing in on us. We all got up and were ready to fire at them, and lieutenant says, "Don't fire." That's the reason I'm here. We were taken prisoners and put on a hillside that night. And I thought that virtually the whole 555th had been wiped out, as well as those soldiers. I did not know until last year that in fact they found a way out, another road. And then I called my old company commander and found out he was living in Bend, Oregon. I was very happy about it.

DARRELL KRENZ We were taken farther north in the winter of '50, when it started to get really cold. That's when we really started losing a lot of guys. On this march, there was a line of guards and if you fell behind them, every once in a while you heard a gunshot. I was helping a kid from Edgerton. His name was Bill Pierce. He had given up completely and we were really getting more and more behind. Pretty soon we were back by the guards. One guard wanted me to put him down and I didn't want to. He turned around with his rifle and he hit me in the knee. I had to put him down or I went down too. The big Korean put the pistol in my face. I looked him in the eyes and I just stared at him. Pretty soon he took the pistol and motioned to get going. I got caught up to my guys again and I heard the gunshot go off.

VALDER JOHN We'd get fed this dish of puffed millet with a little spread of something that looked like mustard on top of it. Once in a while we'd get a piece of bone or something, and they'd boil it up in a kettle and give everybody the broth. We were on the move all the time and they didn't have time to prepare any food for us.

They started marching us day and night. We marched all the way through Pyongyang. There weren't very many left. There were a lot of sick and they'd get dysentery. If they couldn't keep up, the guards would just shoot them alongside the road and stick a bayonet in them to make sure they were dead. They wouldn't let us bury them. I don't know how many people we'd lose a day. They just couldn't keep up and they'd rather die than keep on going.

DALE KING We started our trek northward, as prisoners of war. It was very grueling because I was elected to be, by the Chinese, in charge of the wounded and sick group. We'd travel by night; they never took us out during the daytime because they didn't want the American airplanes to spot us, so it was always a night walk. We probably averaged fifteen to twenty miles a night. The problem was getting decent water. Most of us used our helmets and scooped up water from a stream running out of a rice paddy upstream. It caused a lot of dysentery. We also didn't get as many rations as the others who were able to get up there faster; the first ones in the camp seemed to get more food than the sick and the injured. There were some people who died along the way. It was hard to carry somebody who healthy was full-sized and you're injured yourself.

DARRELL KRENZ We finally got to our destination. It was a cold mud shack about ten by ten feet, for about twenty of us. The elements were pretty harsh. We lost about five or six men out of there. A little farther away they had a school, which had a lot of GIs in it, and they lost a lot of guys, too. Four or five a day, at least, would die. They moved us out of that little shack

During their captivity in Chinese POW camps, U.S. soldiers were forced to listen to anti-American propaganda. *Darrell Krenz*

into the school because there was more room there. It was a little bit better as far as sleeping because you had more people to keep you warm, but it's tough to live on one little millet ball and a sip of water once a day. The millet ball, it's just the size of a snowball, and not even a big one. It's all canary seed. They'd just boil it and that's it.

We had to take our dead once every three or four days and put them up on the hill. We couldn't dig holes for them. If you found some little hole or something, you'd just try to get them in it. An arm would stick out, and you'd just try to break it and put it in the hole, try to cover them up, but it didn't do any good.

VALDER JOHN When we ended up in Pyongyang, there were about half that many U.S. soldiers left, about half of us that started. I don't know how far out of Pyongyang it was, but we saw the airborne drop. It was a long ways from where we were. They put us on these train cars like we were wood. We had to lie sideways. They said we were going to eat and that they wanted twenty-five people. They took us along the tracks over into a wooded area. They sat us down in a little ditch. I looked around and all of a sudden, guards came up with machine guns on all sides of us and started shooting. I got hit and hit the ground. They kept shooting, and I still believe what saved my life was this guy next to me got shot in the leg. It blew flesh and blood all over my face. When they came to look at me, they pounded on my back and broke a few of my ribs. They stuck a bayonet in me on the right side. I didn't move; they just walked away and thought I was dead. They started pounding on other ones, and the ones that made noise, they'd shoot and then leave. When I could hear shooting again, I guessed they'd gone back and got other groups and took them in different places, in the field. I forget how many groups they shot. I understand the train was either set on fire or the Air Force bombed it. So much went on; we were being strafed by our own Air Force and bombed. I crawled out of there and there was another soldier still alive when I came out. We both crawled up the dried-up river-bank. We got underneath the thick hanging grass and kept warm in there.

DARRELL KRENZ They had a little shack with a big fence next door and everybody always wondered what was in that shack. I was game for anything, because you weren't going home anyway; you might as well just get shot doing something. I had a guy watch for me and I went over the fence. I found a bunch of red peppers so I stuffed my pockets full of them. He was supposed to whistle for me when it was all clear for me to come back but he never did whistle. I said, "Well, I'm freezing out here. I'm going to freeze to death." I came over the fence and obviously there was a guard. He grabbed a club and started beating me. He took me in the building, and in front of all the guys, he beat me on the back. Every time he'd smack me one, he'd make me eat some peppers. They were hot, too. He finally got done with me, and another guard came in. He learned what was going on and took the club and started hitting me hard real high on the neck. It knocked me out. They thought they killed me, so they dragged me out on the dead pile. After a while I woke up asking, "Where am I?" I crawled back in the building and all the guys just jumped on me right away and started rubbing me and trying to warm me up. They probably saved me. The North Koreans kept close guard over us. That's about all they did. They took us on work details, to maybe unload something off a truck, but that's about all. They just let us lay there and die, I guess. But in the mornings, we had a major that would get us all up, make sure we got outside and did some exercises and stuff. He just passed away not too long ago. Major Dunn. One of our guys got appendicitis and we had a doctor with us but no anesthesia to kill the pain. He operated on him with a jackknife, which very few had. He got better, but died later on in the POW camp.

I don't know how we made it. You'd wake up in the morning and the guy next to you would be dead. He starved to death or froze to death. My sergeant didn't get up one morning, just died overnight. It was cold. And one day we heard some planes and all of a sudden we saw the paratroopers dropping, and they were ours. They missed us! So we got up all of us in the morning, we got up, we got in lines, and we...walked in the snow and put "P-O-W" on the snow. Just in case another plane would come over or something and find it. Had another plane come over one time; we were in the schoolhouse with big windows in it and there was a Corsair, one of ours, and it came over [and] took a look at us. You could see the guys sitting in it, just as plain as day, just real slow. They made one more pass and they opened up. It took out three or four GIs and a couple of guards. He must have had to get rid of his ammunition or something and away he went. Didn't know we were there, of course, just seen a bunch of stuff going on, I suppose. He was in enemy territory.

At night, we'd talk especially about food. We'd talk about candy bars. We'd take turns going around with who could name a candy bar. In the morning you did your breakfast. "What are we going to have for breakfast?" Bacon, eggs, potatoes, and all that stuff. You couldn't stop thinking about food. All the time. It wasn't all bad, either; we had some good times too. We'd make playing cards out of any old things we could find. The winter of '50 finally got over and they moved us further north again. They said we were going to go home, but they put us on trucks to go north to the Manchurian border then.

During his captivity, Darrell Krenz kept an encoded list of those soldiers who had been killed rolled up in a tube in his mouth.
Darrell Krenz

DALE KING There was one attempt at escape by some people from there; although it was fairly well guarded, they managed to tunnel their way out to try and head towards the water. They didn't make it and they were brought back and given punishment for it. Another group was taken out of the camp and taken down close to the front lines and left there. They were told the Chinese would retreat so the American Army could recover them. Well, the Chinese retreated but the American Army never advanced. After two or three days, the Chinese sent some people down; they said to give them some additional food. The Americans, even though they were not in good shape, overpowered these guards who came down. Unfortunately for them they were caught again and they were brought back to camp and shot instantly, in front of us. It wasn't very pleasant.

VALDER JOHN I had passed out. I don't know if it was the next day, but I came to and heard voices, English voices hollering up in the hills. I listened and I looked and I didn't see anybody, so I crawled out of that little ditch. I saw a guy standing on top of the hill, above the tunnel. I started calling to him in English, and he came down. The other soldiers came down and followed him down the hill. One of them was General Allen, the Assistant Division Commander for the First Calvary Division. He was the one looking for us. He had his taskforce and they came. We got back to the aide station and there were twenty-two of us alive. One of them got out and never got a scratch, never got wounded. He's still alive and healthy today. There was one poor guy, the medics fed us a little bowl of chicken broth and before they could get to him, he ate that broth up too fast and got stomach cramps and died. And they told us, "Don't eat. Just take a spoonful." We hadn't eaten for such a long time. Our stomachs were shrunk up and the shock would kill us. They evacuated us to Pyongyang. Then they put us on planes and flew us back to Japan. We stayed in Japan getting our wounds healed up and looked at for about a month or so.

I didn't think I'd ever get captured; I thought I'd make it through, you know, some way. When we left for Korea from Japan, I was pretty heavy. I weighed about 227 pounds. When we were weighed in Japan, at the hospital, I was 91. I got dysentery, I guess, the day or two before I was shot. When you get dysentery, you last about three or four days, and then you die. I got it and when I got into Japan, I went into a coma. I got double pneumonia they said. I remember waking up to the volunteer wives praying over me. They'd put me in a private room. When they do that in a military hospital, you know you're about ready to expire. They won't leave you out in the ward with the rest of them. But I came to in that private room; I survived the dysentery and the double pneumonia. I was a pretty sick puppy there for a while.

I had to put on a little weight before I could fly. I went back to Brook Army Medical Center in San Antonio, Texas. They'd try to send you to the one closest to your home and I thought I was coming to Great Lakes, but I ended up in San Antonio. It was surprising when I got there. I was in casts because both of my legs were broken along with my left arm and ribs, so everything was in a cast except my right arm, and the bus dropped us off at

After his return to the United States, Valder John was named an honorary Chief Warrior of the Consolidated Tribes of North American Indians for his military service.
Valder John

the train station. We were supposed to be picked up and taken into the hospital. I was lying out there in this hot sun, and finally somebody came by and asked me if I'd been in an automobile accident or something. And I told them no. I said, "We're waiting here to be put into a ward because we're coming back from Korea." And he didn't know where Korea was.

When we got up to the ward, one of the nurses took my records out from underneath me and said, "Oh my God, these guys are coming back from the war. He's a liberated prisoner of war." They started shaking our hands and giving us attention. I just wanted to know when I could go home. One of the nurses said, "It's going to be a while." A doctor came around and saw me, and he looked at me and said, "I can take a chance and send you home." Coming back on the plane into Milwaukee, this guy said to me, "You know, you don't look well at all. You feeling all right?" And I said, "Yeah, not really." I said, "I'm a little sore." And he didn't say anything; he didn't know that I'd been through Korea and back. The public wasn't really aware of what was going on over there, but coming back, there was a reception out at the airport. The VFW and other organizations were there, with all my old school friends and relatives. It was quite a deal. The TV interviewed us. This friend of my father's, he organized a little homecoming dance with a band at the VFW hall there. That was real nice. That's where they presented me with the headdress for Chief Warrior. I was named an honorary Chief Warrior of the Consolidated Tribes of North American Indians. That was nice.

DARRELL KRENZ I used to dream over there of home — of being a kid again, of bicycles, and of old State Street. I dreamed about how when we were kids we used to ride our bikes to Madison and go to the museum in the big red building, old Science Hall. There was a museum that used to be way up on one of the top floors, and the fire escape had a big tunnel. We'd go down that thing, just float all the way down to the bottom again. It was like a water park, except with no water. We used to go look at shop windows on old State Street. When I got home I dreamt about over there. Just the reverse. I wake up sometimes at night just hitting the wall. And I know what I am doing. I am surprised my wife didn't leave me so many years ago. We've been married fifty-one years.

VALDER JOHN The war is always with you; I don't think it ever goes away. I think the Korean War was our first no-win situation. They trained you, indoctrinated you, saying, "You're going to win because you're the best." When we didn't, it was disappointing and degrading to come home to no victory. I guess people in general wanted to forget about it. What helped me through was the post-traumatic stress disorder training from the VA. You'd get together and talk as groups. PTSD training really helped the vet open up to family and the vet's family open up to him. It helped the veterans tell their stories to other veterans, to get their feelings out. There was a lot of crying and carrying on at first because it hurt. It hurt to tell openly because all that stuff was buried in you for years. It was down there deep and it's hard to get that stuff loose. I give nothing but praise to the program because that's what helped me and it still helps me today. I don't mind talking about it, especially to other veterans, and recommending that they talk to their families because people suffering from PTSD, they're just sitting at home, just hiding it, keeping it in. They say we are only as sick as the secrets we keep.

Yalu River

"The first wave didn't have weapons. They had knives and sticks. When the second wave came through, they'd have weapons. The third wave came through, and they would pick the weapons up off their people that our soldiers had already killed." — Don Kostuck

After the September 15, 1950, Inchon invasion, U.N. troops experienced their first taste of success on the Korean battlefield. Quickly pushing north, they took back the South Korean capital of Seoul and reached the 38th parallel, the dividing line between North and South Korea. With this accomplishment, U.N. troops appeared to have achieved the initial goal of the war: repelling North Korean aggression and containing Communism to North Korea. Yet the rapid success of the U.N. offensive forced the Truman administration to reconsider. Should U.N. forces cross the 38th parallel to pursue the fleeing North Korean forces into North Korea? The momentum caused by the Inchon invasion encouraged further American advances; in September, President Truman authorized General MacArthur to cross the 38th parallel into North Korea as long as there was no evidence of a planned Chinese or Soviet intervention. On October 1, 1950, the first South Korean troops crossed the 38th parallel, with American and other U.N. troops following a week later. With this decision, the central goal of the war changed from containment to rollback, from repelling North Korean aggression to reunifying North and South Korea through military force. General MacArthur, fresh from the thrilling success at Inchon, predicted quick victory, boldly asserting that U.S. troops would be home by Christmas. Indeed, it was widely believed that China and the Soviet Union would not enter the war; as *Commonweal* magazine stated, "that 'little war'…is about over as far as the United States is concerned."

Commonweal could not have been more wrong. On October 12, 1950, Chinese troops began crossing the Yalu River into North Korea. The war that was supposed to be over by Christmas would drag itself out for three more

Chinese Advance
November 1950
to January 1951

CHINA
(MANCHURIA)

Tumen R.

U.S.S.R.

Vladivostok

Rashin

Chinese Advance
November 1950

Chongjin

Hyesanjin

Yalu R.

Chosin

Iwon

Sinuiju

Hungnam

Korea
Bay

Wonsan

Sea of
Japan

Pyongyang

U.N. Evacuation
December 5–15, 1950

38th Parallel   38th Parallel

Ongjin

Chunchon

Seoul

Inchon

Osan

Chipyang-ni

Yellow
Sea

Taejon

Pohang

Kunsan

Taegu

Sunchon

Pusan

Strait

Mokpo

Kohung

JAPAN

Korea

	Under U.N. control
	Under Communist control
→	Chinese advances

0   50   100 Miles
0   50   100 Kilometers

UW–Madison, Dept. of Geography, Cartography Lab

long years. Mao Zedong had established Communist rule in China only a year before, defeating the Chinese Nationalists after a lengthy civil war. By entering the Korean War, Mao hoped not only to aid North Korea but also to gain international strength and prestige for the newly Communist Chinese state through a glorious victory against American forces. Though the Soviet Union did not formally send troops into the war, it aided China with equipment and air support. China did notify the United States before joining the war, acting through the Indian Embassy to send a clear warning to the U.S. State Department that it would enter the war if U.N. troops continued to push into North Korea.

In his confidence that the war would end quickly, however, MacArthur moved U.N. troops dangerously close to the Chinese border. Yet even after South Korean forces first clashed with Chinese troops in mid-October, the Truman administration did not halt MacArthur's advance. On November 24, as American troops enjoyed Thanksgiving dinner on the front lines, MacArthur prepared for a full offensive, designed to clear North Korea of all enemy troops. By this point, however, fully equipped Chinese soldiers were already pouring into North Korea; as Don Kostuck described his first encounter with the Chinese Army, "We looked down in the village and there were literally thousands of Chinese troops coming up that valley." U.N. troops and supply lines were overextended and the results of the Chinese advance were disastrous. In the words of DuWayne Lesperance, "It was a massacre of our troops. When the Chinese came down, it was terrible." Like the original North Korean offensive in the early weeks of the war, the Chinese troops overwhelmed U.N. troops and thousands of men were killed, wounded, or taken prisoner. As MacArthur himself noted, the U.S. faced "an entirely new war."

Don Kostuck, Schofield (Army, 25th Infantry Division)
DuWayne Lesperance, La Crosse (Army, 25th Infantry Division)
Cornelius Hill, De Pere (Army, 24th Division)
Chet Kesy, Mosinee (Army, Seventh Division)

DON KOSTUCK I joined the service when I was seventeen. I dropped out of high school and joined the Army. I took my basic and then they sent me to Fort Lee, Virginia, where I went to an administrative school and learned how to type. I was assigned to Fort Meyer, Virginia, at the Pentagon for about six or seven months. I was working in the retired officers section and the master sergeant came in one day and said, "I need three volunteers for Japan." He just happened to be standing right in front of me. I said, "Me, me, me! I want to go!" I wanted out of the Pentagon. I was assigned to the 27th Infantry Regiment of the 25th Infantry Division. Then the Korean War started.

We heard about it on the Armed Forces Radio Network. Of course the rumors started flying: "When are we going to go?" Finally our first sergeant says, "We're going to Korea." I was in Company G of the 27th Infantry, which was a rifle company at that time. Because I could type I had special duty with the Regimental Legal Office. They put us on a train and sent us down to Sasebo in southern Japan. We landed at Pusan the next day.

We got off the ship and they marched us over to an area to give us some K-rations left over from World War II. Then they put us on a train; it was like a cattle car. We started going north. We hadn't been on a train a couple hours and we heard machine gun fire. We didn't know where it was coming from. Somebody hollered out, "They're shooting at the train!" We all hit the deck as low as we could get. As far as I know nobody got injured. We got off the train later and got up to the regimental headquarters. I was assigned to the Intelligence Reconnaissance platoon. We had three or four jeeps and we'd go out every day looking for North Korean troops or enemy positions.

Don Kostuck enlisted in the Army when he was seventeen years old. While working at the Pentagon, he volunteered to go to Japan. Shortly after, the Korean War broke out. Donald Kostuck

DUWAYNE LESPERANCE I wanted to quit high school. I didn't like it. My dad and I didn't get along very good together. Six days after my seventeenth birthday, I joined the Army. If you were under eighteen, your parents had to sign for you. My dad signed right away, but my mother refused to sign, so I forged her signature. I went to Fort Knox, Kentucky, for my basic training, which was sixteen weeks. I was eventually accepted into Army Band School. I was there for sixteen weeks learning marching procedures and practicing how to do parades, how to do this and how to do that, in terms of music and in terms of doing it the "Army way."

After I finished my Band Training Unit, I was supposed to go to Texas, to the 82nd Airborne or one of those groups like that. There was a Sergeant that got orders to go to Korea, and he switched his orders with me. I didn't know that. All of a sudden I got notice that I'm not going to Texas, I'm going to Korea. Later on I found out that he had switched our orders, but it was too late for me then. I got a two-week furlough at home in Milwaukee. From there I went to Seattle and then to Vancouver. In Vancouver, we were put on Canadian Pacific Airline because they were in a hurry to get troops to Korea. We flew into Tachikawa Air Force Base in Tokyo. I was stationed at Camp Drake. That's where people who are coming and going end up usually. I think I was there for maybe about three weeks and then I got orders to Korea. They put us on a train to Sasebo, which is on the lower end of Japan. From there they put us on a ship and we got off at Inchon.

DuWayne Lesperance was accepted into the Army Band shortly after his seventeenth birthday. He is pictured left with his tuba. *DuWayne Lesperance*

Just as the Marines and Army were pushing the Koreans towards Seoul, we got to Inchon. It was really active, with major offensives and so forth. They threw this netting down and we crawled down just like you see in World War II films. They put us on LSTs [landing ship tanks], these big barges. They got us in as far as they could and then they dropped the front of the boat and we walked through the water and up to land. Just like in the John Wayne movies, although I didn't think of it that way then. We were all gathered together. There must have been a thousand of us gathered, trying to figure out what was going to happen to us. It took a whole day until they began to separate people out to where they were going to go. I was initially supposed to go to the First Cavalry to be a .30-caliber machine gunner, because I did well on machine-gunning in basic training, but I passed the audition [for the tuba in the Army band] and so I went with the 25th Infantry Division Band. I went back to where I was and the sergeant who was giving all the orders wasn't very happy about it. Sergeants normally aren't very happy anyway. I took all my stuff and went over to the

DuWayne Lesperance recalls times in Korea when it was so cold that that the band couldn't play for fear the soldiers might freeze their lips to the mouthpieces of their instruments. *DuWayne Lesperance*

tent and said, "Why the hell is the Army band in Korea?" Every division has an Army band because you have to play for ceremonies and you have to give concerts and you have to entertain the troops. One of my other duties was, I was put in charge of the .30-caliber machine gun for the Army band. We all carried M-2 rifles. It is a terrifying gun. I forget how many rounds a minute you could go through. At first I think it was fifteen-round clips and after a while we got thirty-round clips. Those are mean little critters, those carbines.

CORNELIUS HILL Well, I was raised pretty much alone because my mother died when I was two years old and my father died when I was nine. I was shifted from family to family. My guardian was a judge from Green Bay in the courthouse when I was fifteen or sixteen. I was kind of wild, so I had trouble. It was either going to a reformatory or going in the service, so I took the service. I was sixteen years old when he signed for me. On April 23, 1950, I entered the Army. I took my basic in Fort Riley, Kansas, and from there I went to school in Fort Lee, Virginia, for laundry maintenance, fixing up rigs and Stratton engines for mobile laundry units and all that. While I was in Fort Lee, the Korean War broke out. They rushed everything along and I had five days to get from Fort Lee to San Francisco. There were over five thousand troops on there when we left.

I was assigned to a Hawaiian outfit, Fifth RCT — that's the Fifth Regimental Combat Team from Hawaii. There was only head[quarters] and two battalions — the 19th and 21st Battalions. I was in what they called the A&P Platoon, Ammunition and Pioneer. I hauled ammunition and all the supplies that were supposed to go up to the troops: gas and dynamite. I also learned demolition real fast there, too.

CHET KESY When the Korean War started, they took a lot of our guys out of the Seventh Division and sent them to the 24th Division and the 25th Division. We weren't at full strength, so they used a lot of our guys to fill in. I was one of the guys that they kept; most of the guys that went to the 24th and 25th never made it back. I heard about a lot of them and most of them

During a calmer moment, Chet Kesy, left, with brother and female friend. *Chet Kesy*

got killed at Taegu. At that time we weren't very well trained. The occupation was a pretty easy life. You didn't really do a lot of training; line outfits didn't do a lot of training. We got a rude awakening when we got to Korea.

They loaded us on ships and we were aboard for about thirty days before we made the Inchon invasion. When we made the invasion, the Marines went towards Seoul and we went towards a town called Yu-dong. It was just a small town, but we were taking an awful lot of prisoners. Then they loaded up the board ships again and we went back to Pusan. Then we made a landing way up in North Korea in a place called Iwon at the most beautiful beach I ever saw in my life. They loaded us aboard trucks and we started out way up in North Korea, and as we were going through these little towns, there were kids out there with little American flags waving at us. You would have thought there was nothing going on anymore. That night, we hit a town. There was a lieutenant and a radio sergeant, and we had two Koreans to help us carry stuff. We called them Mutt and Jeff. One of them was a real big guy and one was a real small guy. They were pretty fearless. They were pretty damn good. I admired them. We all went up to a dry riverbed and made our little camp there. At about nine o'clock that night, a lieutenant from the infantry came and said, "You guys better come back and move back to where we are." We loaded up our stuff and moved back. It's a good thing we did because at about five o'clock that morning, the Koreans came down that riverbed and really hit us. We would've been the first ones they hit; we all would've been dead. No doubt about it. Even the artillery was firing direct fire into them. I walked back into the town later on after we chased the Koreans back a little bit, and they had a schoolhouse where they were making a hospital for the guys that got wounded.

I came out of the little town and I saw something piled up. I thought it was rice straw and I walked over to it. The North Koreans had killed the whole town. They had them piled up like a straw stack. I would say there were from three to five hundred people — men, women, and children — all stacked up, all dead. All the bodies were already frozen. That night, the infantry sent out some patrols and the guys never came back. Twelve guys. The next day we made a push and we found all of them with their hands tied behind their backs with barbed wire and they were all shot behind the ear. The Koreans had caught them that night. We moved maybe ten miles farther, and we came to the biggest valley I['d] ever seen. We stayed there for about two days and nothing seemed to be happening. Across this valley, there was a real swift running river. It was getting cold already, but it wasn't frozen over. There was a big hill on the other side of this valley. We went across this valley and we started taking that hill, and the Koreans popped out of the ground like ants. We fought all that day and we took the hill that night. The company commander I was with got the Congressional Medal of Honor. It really got cold that night: very, very cold. We tried digging a foxhole, but there was nothing but rock. It was lucky that the planes went over that day and bombed because it made a lot of rocks come out of the ground. Me, the radio sergeant, and the lieutenant — we made foxholes out of rocks. We just piled rocks around us. That night we were hit by banzai attacks. It's really demoralizing because they start yelling and hollering and blowing whistles and bugles. There was a lot of hand-to-hand fighting that night. By morning, there were probably five or six hundred laying dead on the hill. A lot of Americans, a lot of GIs. The next morning, we went diagonally off the hill. The North Koreans just melted away; there was nobody shooting at us then.

We moved on another five miles and got hit again. The North Koreans reorganized but they weren't so well organized that time. We pushed through them pretty easily. We were going through some hills and we ran into part of the Second Infantry Division. We fought about two weeks more and then made our way to the Chinese border on the Yalu River. We

On Thanksgiving Day, 1950, soldiers were given a warm dinner complete with all the stuffing they could eat. *Chet Kesy*

thought the war was going to be over. Around Thanksgiving, they were telling us, "Hey, the war is over. You're going to be home by Christmas," and there was all the turkey you could eat and stuffing. It was great, after eating C-rations all the way up there. I never figured it was going to be the last good meal we were going to have for a long time. Then the general started getting calls that the Chinese were in the war. He decided we better get back out of there. We were real vulnerable because we were only one division sitting up there all by themselves. A lieutenant came back and said to me, "Hey, we're going to load up and go back. The Chinese are in the war," and so we loaded up our stuff and started back. Those roads over in North Korea, they were just dug out in the sides of mountains. There wasn't room for our big trucks. It was getting cold and it was snowy and slippery. Some of the trucks went over these roads and down. Some of the drops were two or three hundred feet straight down; there was nothing to stop you. The only stop you got was when you hit the bottom of it. We had a few guys lost that way.

DON KOSTUCK I was assistant squad leader, a rifle man. We had a nine-man squad. We'd go out on patrols every day. They'd told us, "We're going north; we're going to the Yalu River." We walked almost twenty-four hours a day. One night we walked for ten or twelve hours and they told us to take a break, that we had some trucks coming up. We'd actually out marched our supply lines. I lay down on the side of the road and almost got run over by a truck. I'd fallen asleep as soon as I hit that ground. We got on some of the North Korean trucks we had confiscated and were using to haul supplies and troops. We were going up the road and we stopped and were going to stay there for the rest of the night. My buddy, Clark, and I went up into this cotton field and lay down. All of sudden there was firing down on the road. There were tracers all over the place. We didn't know what was going on. Then we found out that there was a truck behind us with North Korean soldiers on it. They had hooked onto our convoy. They must have thought we were part of the North Korean unit because we had those Korean trucks.

Wisconsin native and Ho-Chunk tribe member Mitchell Red Cloud received the military's highest distinction, the Congressional Medal of Honor, for singlehandedly holding off enemy fire while his entire company escaped ambush. *Courtesy U.S. Army*

CORNELIUS HILL There was an Indian named Mitchell Red Cloud there with us. He was from Friendship, Wisconsin. He helped us out when we were being overrun. He got killed. He was there; I was there with him. He backed himself up against a tree. He had a Browning automatic rifle and was holding them off while we retreated. It was the last time I saw him. We just kept on moving. A couple days later, we pushed the Chinese back there again. We found his body and got him out of there, took it back. Sent him back home. That guy saved a whole company from getting run over. He just backed himself up against a tree with a BAR and kept firing until he couldn't go anymore.

It happened all of a sudden. We just stopped to rest, and then we got orders to move out; they were coming on us and they didn't say how many or which direction or anything like that. All of a sudden they were right on us and we got orders to get out of there and pick up what we had. We kept moving and moving, and more of them would come in and all hell broke loose. We tried to fight them off, but we couldn't. I seen him when he grabbed a BAR from one of the guys and told them to get the hell out of there and he'd hold them back for us. He actually hollered, "Get the hell out of here!" He ended up by a big tree. There was just a stump of a tree there and then he just braced himself against it and that's the last I seen of him. I heard on the news what he had done and I knew right away that was him. I said, "That was him." He was still standing yet when I left him.

DUWAYNE LESPERANCE It was just before Christmas and they said, "Oh, don't worry about it. You'll be back home in a month or two; it'll all be over. …There won't be any problem, so don't sweat it." Along comes General MacArthur. We'd pushed the Koreans way, way up, and the Chinese says, "Don't you come up to the Yalu River because if you come up to the Yalu River, we're coming in." General MacArthur was ordered by Truman not to go any further than Pyongyang, the capital of North Korea, but he did it anyway. He said, "I think we have to go up there and take that Yalu River and push them into China and then we'll be done." But what happened is the Chinese came down and just like that, within two or three days, everybody was almost all the way down to South Korea. It was a massacre of our troops. When the Chinese came down, it was terrible.

DON KOSTUCK We kept going north and were almost to the Yalu River. There was a rumor going around that the Chinese were going to enter the war, that they were stockpiling supplies on the other side of the Yalu River, so they pulled our regiment back. I don't know how many miles, maybe fifty, a hundred miles south of the Yalu River, and we dug in. We were in a horseshoe perimeter. In the opening of the horseshoe, down below, there was a Korean village. My buddy and I were in forward positions called listening positions. The rest of our platoon was in back of us higher up the hill. Just before midnight, one of our mortar units started sending up star shells. They were really bright magnesium that came down in parachutes. We were one of the first units to be hit by the Chinese. We looked down in the village and there were literally thousands of Chinese troops coming up that valley. We had the whole Chinese Army hit our battalion. It was foggy, drizzling, and rainy. We couldn't get any air support. We didn't have any artillery support. We started shooting and they just kept coming and coming and finally overran our positions. I must have shot a couple thousand rounds of ammunition. There were no single shots. You fired until the clip bangs out and you load another one in; you just keep shooting. You couldn't find enough targets. You didn't have to look hard. The first wave didn't have weapons. They had knives and sticks. When the second wave came through, they'd have weapons. The third wave came through, and they would pick the weapons up off their people that our soldiers had already killed.

Digging our foxhole, there was a lot of rock and shale, so it took us quite a while to dig that thing. And the fact is, we dug for quite a while, then we sat down and our heads were still above the ground. And I said, "Clark, I don't think this thing is deep enough." So we dug some more. We were taking the rocks and piling them around the edges of our foxhole. We went down another couple of feet. Good thing we did, too, because they threw more than one grenade at us, I'm sure, because the next morning, those rocks were gone. We were probably the first, at least in our unit, the first people that the Chinese were in contact with. I saw a figure run across in front of me. He wasn't more that twenty-five or thirty feet away. And I fired twice and he went down. That's when the shooting started. That's when all hell broke loose.

I called for ammo. Next thing I know, I got three Chinese troops standing in front of me, and one of them shot my buddy in the head. Clark had a couple rounds of ammunition left yet and an antitank grenade. He was always complaining he had to carry this antitank grenade around. And I said to him, "It would be a good time to get rid of that sucker. Why don't you load it up?" I think he was in the process of putting the blank cartridge in his rifle and putting that grenade on the end of his rifle when he was shot. I think that's why they shot him. I think if I'd had a weapon in my hand, they probably would've shot me in the head too. I don't know if they would have taken me prisoner, but I wouldn't have lived. I would've died. He [the Chinese soldier] was reloading and I was out of ammo and I didn't know what to do. There was an entrenching tool lying behind me. I picked it up and I smacked him in the head with it and he went down. Then one of his buddies got me in the thigh. Earlier that night, Clark and I were firing down the hill and a grenade went off right in front of our foxhole. I was hit with it, but I didn't realize it, my adrenaline was flowing so high. Another one of these little Chinese guys grabbed me and we were wrestling. I had him in front of me, and another Chinese soldier came up and he pointed a rifle right at my head. He wasn't more than three feet away from me and he fired. That's the last thing I remember. Lucky for me I guess I had a helmet on and he must've hit my helmet. I had blood trickling down my forehead, but it was just a graze.

DUWAYNE LESPERANCE I was probably up and down that country, back and forth and side to side, at least a hundred times. We'd push up and they'd push us down. We'd push up and they'd push us down. It was just terrible. I was in Pusan, Masan, Taejon, Taegu, Suan, Seoul, Uijongbu, Inchon, and a couple other places. We were constantly moving, coming and going and coming and going, because we'd push up and they'd push us back, we'd push up and they'd push us back. It was just a constant changing of back and forth and back. When the Chinese came down after we went up to the Yalu River, all hell broke loose. That's when that whole group of Marines, and I think it was part of the 24th Infantry Division, was corralled into the Chosin Reservoir area where they just massacred all kinds. I was in Yung Dong Po at that time, which is just short of the 38th parallel. It was pretty gruesome, especially dealing with all the Chinese dead. One of our jobs was to check the Chinese dead out whenever we could. They would just leave their dead there; we always took our dead away if possible, except for the Chosin thing. Sometimes they'd booby-trap their dead and we had to try and see if they blew up or not. We also had to take their weapons off of them and turn them into our Supply Coordinate to do what they wanted with them. It was pathetic because I'd be looking at these guys and they were younger than me, and I was seventeen, and sometimes, even though it was winter, they didn't even have shoes. They would bandage their feet up. They didn't have decent equipment. I can't even think of a word — it was just really bad. Really bad. They were all over the place. When we were close to Seoul, right across the Han River, after one of our offensives, there were Chinese and Korean dead just floating all over and swept up on the beaches. The first time I had to deal with that, I didn't eat for a week. I got so sick looking at all those dead Chinese and Koreans. I was very, very upset. It was very devastating, especially in the way we were of the same age.

CORNELIUS HILL The Chinese were on all sides of us. We had to go on the roads because we had all the vehicles and everything like that. We'd dig in at night and then wait for the other troops to go through, and then they'd do the same for us and we'd go jump back, and back and forth, but we lost a lot of vehicles, night driving. You had to drive without lights on the side of mountains.

We were doing a lot of our riding at night and not in the day to just sleep. The fighting was going on and pushing us back. All of a sudden we're north all the way to the Yalu River, and the Chinese came down and we were overrun. We were on the go, backing up all the way. We lost a lot of guys over there. It was all messed up; we lost all our food, our ammunition, C-rations, everything we had. As a matter of fact, we were on rice for about four or five weeks. Whatever we could pick up on the way, that's what we ate. We even killed their oxen, using the meat with the rice. I don't eat rice anymore.

It was bad for a while. Our aircrafts weren't hitting us. They'd miss us and we'd never get the C-rations. We had to steal C-rations off of the tanks that were going by us just to get something to eat. There was one holiday when we got dinner. It was either Christmas dinner or New Year's dinner. It was cold. It was at about one o'clock in the morning they managed to get some hot chow to us somehow. And we were sitting there, eating turkey and whatever we could. It was dark out there and you had to just feel your way around, and that was the only hot meal we got for a long time after that.

It was really cold, especially when you were on top of the mountains. The wind was hell. You only had what you had on you: two shirts, two sweaters, whatever. A lot of guys were putting too many socks on and their feet would sweat and then when they'd stop moving, their feet would freeze. A lot of them lost their toes and part of their foot. They'd take their socks off and meat would just come off with it, black and everything. I just had frostbite; that's the worst that I had with the cold. Of course I was used to it, being from Wisconsin. A lot of them were from Florida or California or something like that and they weren't used to it. They just put on a lot of clothes and hoped they'd keep warm that way.

During the retreat, we'd always have more or less one group staying back, covering for us, and then we'd hold up and do the same for them to let them come through. I guess, I forgot who it was, but they asked this general, "Hey, you guys retreating?" and he said, "Retreat, hell! We're just fighting in a different direction!" Which was true. We were fighting to get back to the coast again.

DON KOSTUCK I didn't realize how bad I'd been hit. I didn't realize I was the only survivor out of my squad. My squad leader, Sergeant Harrington, he was a tough old dude. He was a veteran of World War II and he had seen a lot of combat. I was talking to these guys down in Fort Benning, and they said when they went back up after they had driven the Chinese back, there were about a dozen Chinese guys lying around his foxhole, but that he had been killed. I was the only guy that got out alive. I remember when I woke up, it was real quiet; at least at that moment anyway. I was kind of afraid to open my eyes because I didn't know if there were any Chinese soldiers around. If they had seen me still alive, they probably would've shot me again and I wanted to avoid that. So after a few minutes I kind of moved my head and looked and my feet were lying on top of this guy that I'd been wrestling with. My bayonet was lying right there, so I grabbed it and I was going to hit him with it but I realized he was dead. All the other Chinese soldiers — there must have been half a dozen of them — were all laying around, all dead. The guys on top of the hill had shot them. That's when they came down and pulled me up off the hill.

I started crawling up the hill and some of the guys up on the hill were shooting over my head. They said, "Are you hit?" And I said, "Yeah." So they came down and they pulled me up. They got me on top of the hill, they cut my pants off my legs, and I realized I had about a ten-inch gash in my right leg. They found a grenade wound, which I was completely surprised about. It was about two inches in diameter, like somebody had taken an ice-cream scoop and just scooped the meat out of my hip. They took me to a battalion aid station where they cleaned up my wound, put a bandage on it. From there, they sent us down to the division aid station, which was farther back. We were in this old Korean schoolhouse, and I'm lying in the corner on a stretcher. Guys started running down these steps, hollering. There was an airplane shooting at us. You could hear the bullets ricocheting off the tile roof on this building. I couldn't move, and finally it went away and never came back. After they dressed my wounds, they put me in an ambulance and took me out to this airfield. It was warm inside and I hadn't been warm in weeks. I fell asleep and I remember this guy pushing on me, and he says, "Hey, this guy's dead." And I was trying to say, "No, I'm not," but I couldn't, so I opened my eyes and he says, "Oh, no, he's not."

CHET KESY My job, forward observer, was kind of a thrilling job really because you saw everything that was going on. You were the head guy up there; it was a very dangerous job. It was probably the most dangerous job, especially in the Korean War because you'd take a hill and you'd get kicked off of it. They'd counterattack; they'd kick you off of it and you had to be the last one up there because when the infantry retreated, you had to be there to cover the retreat with artillery shells, but you better start running. We lost most of the forward observers from the 49 Field Artillery that I was in; they were taken prisoner. I was one of the few not taken prisoner. I had lots of close calls. One time up in North Korea, I was checking my communications wire back to the fire direction center and I walked into a North Korean. He opened up on me with a burp gun. I don't know how he didn't hit me. I jumped into the brush and he was maybe fifty feet from me. He never hit me. An infantry guy saw him when he shot at me and he killed him. Another time an artillery shell, a 120-mm mortar, landed maybe five feet from our foxhole, but it was a dud. It never went off. Real lucky.

The other time, they'd given us warm food for a change. We'd kind of pulled back off the main lines. I laid out my sleeping bag. I was talking to the Korean we had with us when some guerrilla came through and threw a hand grenade. It landed right by my sleeping bag and blew the Korean's jaw off and I was standing right by him and I never got hit with even a piece of scrap. The truck in back of me was full of holes. It threw a lot of sand and I was bare from the waist up because I'd just got done taking a sponge bath. A lot of that sand hit me and it stung like a hundred bees stinging me, but not a piece of shrapnel hit me. I had a lot of close calls in combat. I was shot at a lot because they always try to knock off the forward observer because you carry a big radio and they know what the radio is for — to call in artillery. So they were always shooting at us.

DUWAYNE LESPERANCE We tried to help the Korean children and even the adults as much as we possibly could. We were always giving them food and hiring them. We had the women, if we were in a place where there was water, wash our clothes. We would give the kids jobs to do, too. They'd get to be our tent pal: help make our bed and take care of the area and stuff like that. They'd go around and get chicken eggs for us. We'd keep them in money and in clothes and food. Overall the attitude of the Korean people toward the GIs was really wonderful. No problems at all. The little children were very, very, very friendly. They even had names for us. We liked having them around; it was really healthy for us, too, to be around kids and their enthusiasm. Even in the devastation, they were still kids. When we were moving forward up toward North Korea, that's when we would see the civilians walking. They'd sometimes have to walk a hundred miles with every possession they could possibly carry, with their kids and their animals. It was just so sad. Anytime we stopped, we would give them food and stuff if we could. I don't know if they liked it either because it was canned C-rations. It wasn't very good at all. That's why anytime we were in a place where there was a little town where there were civilians, we would try to get food from them. That worked out pretty good, for the most part.

We were always part of the front line. In my discharge, it shows I was in a forward command post. We guarded the area. We had all kinds of little assignments here and there to do that were not music related. We got a Meritorious Unit Citation because of all the duties we did in a combat zone; that

DuWayne Lesperance and his army buddies befriended several civilian Korean children during the war, some of whom became "unofficial" members of their company. Lesperance pictured middle.
DuWayne Lesperance

we went above and beyond our military specialty. There's a picture of us playing for a medal ceremony, and two blocks up, there's a battle going. I have a picture of us all standing there and it was thirty-five below zero. The generals got all the troops lined up that were going to receive medals and the band was supposed to play. When we started playing, none of the brass instruments could play. So the general stopped everything and he came over and he said, "Why aren't you playing?" The commanding officer says, "They can't play, sir." The general says, "I want you to make those guys play or I'll send you all to the stockade. I'll demote you." And the commanding officer of the band said, "Sir, if they play, their mouths are going to freeze to their mouthpieces and they'll all be in the hospital tomorrow and you won't have any band." The general wasn't very happy about that and he turned away and said, "Well, play whatever you can play." So the clarinets and saxes and drums played. I have a picture in a book of us doing that. I also

As a member of the Army band, DuWayne Lesperance often had to play in extremely cold conditions close to the battle zone.
DuWayne Lesperance

have some pictures of us playing once when there was napalm bombs dropped just a short distance from us.

Sometimes we'd have to all of a sudden pack up and start running to get the heck out of there during a battle. We were always very close. We lost one guy from the band and a couple were wounded. We had a whole range of ages from me at seventeen; I was the youngest. I was the youngest corporal in Korea at one point. I was almost the youngest sergeant. We had this guy; he had to be in his sixties. He was a lifer. He was quite a guy. Most of us were either peacetime soldiers or were brought in from the reserves and the National Guard.

CORNELIUS HILL Minefields were something else we had to worry about, too. The Chinese had mines they called shoebox mines. One night we went down to wash in the riverbed. The next morning, we looked down and there were shoebox mines all over the place and they were frozen. They wouldn't detonate because the triggers were frozen on them. I don't know how many people would've been killed if they would've went off. I think we picked up about 180 of them. Just dug them out. God was with us that night, I guess.

There were a lot of nights where it was just chaos. We'd take turns sleeping. Quite a few buddies next to me would wake up stabbed. That's the way the Chinese fought; they crawled up on you when you didn't know it. It wasn't a good idea to make friends because you lost them too fast. The Chinese were pretty quiet. There were six of us on top of this mountain one night and we knew the Chinese were out there, but didn't know where. It was dark. There was no moon. It was just pitch black out there and you'd just try and listen and listen. You're hearing noises but you're not sure what they are. You're alert. But when you're sleeping you don't know what's going on. You're so damn tired a bomb could drop fifty feet away from you and it wouldn't wake you up. That's how tired you were. When a buddy got killed, it was five o'clock, five thirty when I got up. I shook him and he didn't move. I shook him again and he didn't move. Then I took the cover off and looked at him. His eyes were open but he was dead. I didn't realize then that he was stabbed. There was no noise or nothing. How they missed me I don't know. I was maybe ten feet away.

I often wondered what the rest of the guys were thinking, too. Did it affect them? You think about those things. We were under a point system for how long we had to be there in combat. I think you got one point every two months and we needed six points before we were rotated out. I think in November of '51, my turn came along, and there were twelve of us coming off the mountain, and three of them never made it off on account of the fact that snipers got them in the back of the line. I was the third from the front. We were all happy because we were going home — that was it. We didn't even have our rifles with us because we left them back there with the rest, because they needed them. The Chinese picked off three of them, and they never made it off the mountain.

We got back into Seoul at night. We thought they had it easy back there but they didn't, because of what we called Bed Check Charlie. He'd come around in a little piper cub airplane, dropping mortars, aggravating everybody. He didn't know where the troops were; he just dropped them. He'd do that every night at midnight. We'd be shooting at him and never hit him because he had no lights on.

DUWAYNE LESPERANCE I can remember nights laying on the ground in my tent, hearing a whistle of their shells coming over us. Fortunately, we were in a situation where they were shooting over us. If the sound got louder and then all of a sudden got softer, you got the hell out of there because that was what they called a short round. It was a round that wasn't going to go as far as it should have. When that whistle started to slow down, you had to get out of there. Just run wherever you could go. You would lay there night after night with that artillery plus the sound, and of course we were shooting back. In fact, I just found a letter that I had written to my mother and father describing that whole situation with the artillery. My brother wrote me and said, "Don't send any mail like that. You're scaring the hell out of everybody." We were always considered on the front lines. In fact, in my discharge, I got a bronze medal with four campaign stars. They used to be called battle stars. We were in the band that whole time during different, major battles.

When I came back home, I think my first month or two, I slept on the floor. I couldn't sleep on the bed. It was too soft. One of my sisters was just talking to me about this recently. She said, "You know, you never talked." My former wife recently mentioned that to me. She said, "You never talked about Korea when you came home." I said, "No." I'm only beginning to talk about this recently, getting my stuff together, looking at it all. I tried to put as much of that stuff away and get on with a regular life. Mark it out of my mind. For a while, a door would slam or a muffler would bang and I'd jump up. That's what my family tells me. I remember sleeping on the floor, but I don't remember the jumping up and reacting. I did have sleepless nights at times. That morning when the World Trade Center was hit, I said, "Jesus Christ, this is just like Seoul." I just went right back again to that. Everything was just almost flattened. It almost looked like, almost looked like what happened to Hiroshima and Nagasaki because between us, our artillery and bombers and theirs, the city was flattened. When the World Trade Center got hit, it started all over again. I started to have flashbacks. I tried to be real busy and concentrate on other things and eventually it kind of died out. I'm not having any trouble with that anymore.

CHET KESY You never left your radio. That was your lifeline. The two things you would never leave were your radio and your sleeping bag because it was awful cold there. A lot of guys would wish for what they called "a million-dollar wound," to get hit so they'd pull you back and you wouldn't have to fight anymore. I didn't want to get hit. I was always in real fantastic shape. I could go up and down the hills carrying that radio and stuff. There weren't many guys that could keep up with me. I always kept myself in good shape with boxing and martial arts. The guy that carried the radio got shot at the most. Going up and down them hills I was probably in the best shape, so I was probably carrying it the most, so I was shot at the most. I never thought I'd make it out, never, never. I thought that was it for me. I was very lucky.

CORNELIUS HILL When we got back in the spring from the Yalu, we reorganized. We were starting to get fresh backup troops. Everybody was starting to get back with their own outfits. After I left my unit, the Fifth RCT, they were annihilated. I didn't know it. We were attached to the 24th Division, but you didn't really know what company you were with, or who was who. We had the 21st, the 22nd, the Seventh Division. All the units were just mixed up in there, trying to find their outfits. It was chaos.

I came back on the same boat. We went over to Japan and were separated in where we got all cleaned up with new uniforms. I came back on the same boat I went over on, the *General Miggs*. That was a little bit rougher, though, because three days out of Japan, we hit a typhoon. Five thousand troops were on that boat, and talk about sick. There were a lot of days on the water when it was just as calm as could be, when we got to see the dolphins riding alongside the boat with you, and flying fish, and it was beautiful.

I was an old guy at seventeen. I'll never forget that when I got home, the bed was there. One morning my aunt got up and looked at me, and I was sleeping on the floor. She said, "What the heck you doing sleeping on the floor?" and I said, "I can't sleep on the bed. I got used to sleeping on rocks." It took me a while to get used to sleeping on a bed. I'd been sleeping on the ground all night long, with just a blanket or a canvas tent, dug in the ground with it.

DON KOSTUCK They flew us down to Seoul and we went to this Eighth Army field hospital. This nurse took my boots off, and I said, "Hey, those are new boots." And she said, "Don't worry; you won't be needing them anymore." To make a long story short, I was in three hospitals in Japan, and I wound up in the island of Hokkaido and Sapporo. They opened that hospital just for us. They treated us like royalty. We sat around all day playing cards.

There was a telegram to my parents that said, "Your son was slightly wounded." My dad was deer hunting at that time. When she [my mom] got my first letter, I told her, "I hope this gets to you before the War Department does." But it didn't and I told her that I was fine and I was in the hospital.

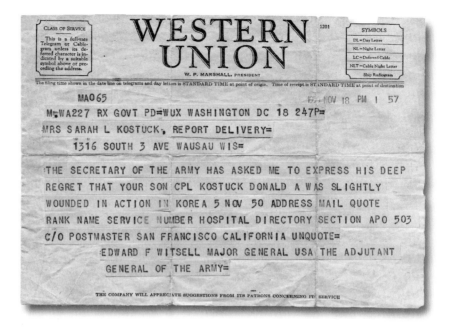

The telegram Don Kostuck's mother received informing her that her son had been wounded in action. *Donald Kostuck*

She didn't open that telegram for a week until my dad came back from deer hunting. I just can't imagine what she went through waiting to open that telegram. It must've been pretty traumatic for her.

I had been in the hospital six months and they were getting ready to discharge me. This warrant officer says, "You don't want to go back to Korea?" I said, "Not really." This was '51 and things were getting pretty hot over there at that time. He asked, "How'd you like to be assigned to the hospital here?" And I said, "Yeah, I'd like that." They assigned me to the hospital, where I worked in personnel. In February of '52, we got a new hospital commander. He was a full colonel. I was walking down the hallway one day, and he says, "Good morning, Sergeant Kostuck." I greeted him in Japanese for "good morning." Maybe I shouldn't have bowed, but he asked the captain, "How long's that son of a gun been over here? I think it's time he went home." So he sent me down to Camp Drake in Tokyo. They asked me, "Where do you want to be assigned?" I said, "I want to stay in Japan." And they said, "You can't, you have to go home." They put us on planes and sent us over. We debarked in Seattle at the Army base there. They asked me, "Where do you want to be assigned in the States?" and I said, "I don't want to be assigned in the States. I want to go back to Japan." And they said I couldn't, so I didn't pick any place. I went home on a thirty-day furlough to Wausau and then I got orders for Fort Ord, California.

DUWAYNE LESPERANCE People are always saying, "You have an incredible memory. It's almost scary." Even my former wife that lives out in Seattle — we're very good friends — will call me and I'll bring up something and she'll say, "I can't believe that you remember that." A friend recently said to me, "You know what you have? You have a photographic memory." It's not always pleasant. It has brought me down a little bit, going through some of this stuff. But fortunately it's over now.

DON KOSTUCK I remember it just like it happened yesterday. I dream about it almost every night, some phase of it. I don't have stress syndrome, or I don't think I do. It doesn't bother me that much. I never really thought about it. I never talked to anybody about it.

MacArthur wanted to bomb the Chinese staging areas. Truman wouldn't let him because he was afraid that it would start World War III. At that time the Chinese didn't have the atomic weapons, though. I think it was a big mistake, because if the Chinese hadn't entered the war, Korea would be a free country today. It'd be unified. So I blame Truman for that. I also blame him for killing half the people in my company. We had a three-hundred-man company and over half of the company was wounded or killed. I still blame Truman for that.

6 Chosin

"We were surrounded all the way. It didn't make any difference where we were ... We had three regiments down there, the First, the Fifth, the Seventh, and we were all surrounded. You could look any place you wanted to look, and all you could see on the occupying hills were Chinese." — Bob Kachel

With China's sudden entry into the war, the winter of 1950 was a grim season for U.N. forces. Chinese soldiers flooded North Korea, cutting through U.N. lines; thousands of men were killed, wounded, or taken prisoner. Completely overwhelming the U.N. troops, the Chinese Army trapped the First Marine Division, along with part of the Army's Seventh Infantry Division and the British Royal Marines, at Chosin Reservoir in North Korea. A difficult and costly battle ensued as thirty thousand U.N. forces sought to hold off seventy thousand Chinese troops while retreating from the reservoir. For the U.N. troops at Chosin, weather was as much an enemy as the Chinese forces; fighting in a bitterly cold winter, simply not freezing to death was a major challenge. The fighting at Chosin lasted approximately three weeks; of the fifteen thousand U.N. casualties, seventy-five hundred were due to cold weather-related injuries. As Donne Harned described it, "Our weapons froze. They didn't operate...I think everybody there came back with some kind of frostbite or frozen feet or ears or noses or hands." The horrific weather earned Chosin the name "Frozen Chosin," with the men who survived identified as the "Chosin Few."

Seeking to break out of the area surrounding the reservoir, the U.N. forces, mostly the First Marine Division and Army Seventh Infantry, began to fight their way south on November 26, 1950. Their final destination was the port city of Hungnam, where they would be evacuated from North Korea. At the start of the battle, the U.N. forces were trapped on opposite sides of the reservoir. As high mountains and the Chinese military surrounded the reservoir, retreat was nearly impossible. Indeed, the three thousand men trapped on the eastern side of Chosin Reservoir — part of the Army's Seventh Infantry Division — were almost destroyed by the Chinese military. As the first phase of action, U.N. troops moved south from sites such as Yudam-ni to meet up at Hagaru, located at the southernmost tip of the reservoir. From Hagaru, the troops prepared for a further retreat, aiming first for Koto-ri and eventually Hungnam, approximately seventy miles to the south. After gathering their strength at Hagaru, the Marines, joined by the remaining members of the Army, began an aggressive push south in early December. It was this action, led by Major General O. P. Smith, that led to Smith's famous, often misquoted exclamation: "Retreat? Hell, we're attacking in a different direction!" Task Force Drysdale, made up of Army, Marine, and British Royal Marine forces, also moved north from Koto-ri to help pull U.N. troops out of Hagaru, yet about half of these men were killed or captured. Indeed, the furious fighting at Chosin left little time to rest as the U.N. troops alternated between attacking Chinese positions — breaking through roadblocks, clearing hilltops — and defending themselves from a continuous Chinese assault that took place both day and night. Though U.N. forces suffered heavy casualties, the Marines still consider the breakout at Chosin to be one of their finest moments, as they successfully fought through the seven Chinese divisions trapping them at Chosin to reach Hungnam. The U.N. troops received cover from repeated and closely coordinated U.S. air strikes against the Chinese military, including the use of napalm, while cargo planes dropped needed supplies. Though Chosin resulted in retreat by the U.N. forces, it underscored the determination and grit of American men fighting in Korea.

Ray Hendrikse, Monona (Marines, First Division)
Jim McConnell, Superior (Army, 32nd Infantry Division)
Donne Harned, Blue Mounds (Air Force, 35th Fighter-
**   Interceptor Wing)**
Bob Kachel, La Crosse (Marines, First Regiment)

RAY HENDRIKSE I came out of high school in 1946 at a time when the military was a high item on the news. A friend of mine and I intended to go into the Marine Corps. I came home with papers to enlist and brought them to my father who said, "I won't sign for that if it's a day before your eighteenth birthday," so that eliminated me. Then right before my eighteenth birthday I had a sister come down sick, and my mother said, "Whatever you do, don't go now until she's out of bed." So I waited. I went in 1948, after she came up out of bed. They had a group that was going over to the Mediterranean because they had given Palestine back to the Jews. They were sending five thousand Marines over there just to be available. I wanted to go badly but couldn't get in. Somebody got sick or something before they were leaving and they said, "Well, if you still want that, you can go now as a substitute," and I did. I went over to the Mediterranean and had a nice time. I came back from that and they had a group that was going over to Labrador for training in cold-weather activities. It taught how to take care of yourself, how to take care of your feet. Movement is very important, dry feet, dry clothing, et cetera. It was very helpful to me. I came back and was a little leery about going into the kitchen on mess duty. I sure didn't want that. So I thought

Ray Hendrikse joined the Marines in 1948. He was part of a tank brigade during the Korean War. *Ray Hendrikse*

the only way I could get out of it is, if I can go out for baseball and get on that team, I'll be all set. I did. I played ball until Korea started.

JIM MCCONNELL I enlisted in '42 and then after basic, I went over to North Africa as part of the replacements. They pulled about six or seven of us out and put us in this recon unit. They called it the 117th and we made three or four beach landings over there during the war. I got out in '45. I reenlisted again and was in for two years until '48. Then I reenlisted again and I went back to Korea in '50.

Donne Harned in uniform. *Donne Harned*

DONNE HARNED It started in the fall of 1947. I had always wanted to be in the pilot training program, to become an aviation cadet. I was walking down the street in Denver — I was going to the University of Denver at the time — and here was this young man in pinks and greens, the uniform the United States Army Air Forces wore in World War II. It was a nice-looking uniform. So I stopped him and said, "Has the program started again?" He said "Yes, it has." And I said, "Well, what should I do to get in the program?" He said, "I suggest that you go to Lowry Air Force Base, outside of Denver, and make an application." And I did and was accepted. I reported to San Angelo, Texas, in June of 1948 to pilot training at Goodfellow Air Force Base. I graduated in July from advanced training in Las Vegas and was assigned to the 31st Fighter Group at Turner Air Force Base, Georgia, as a fighter pilot. When you're in training, after you finish basic, you are recommended by your instructor for fighter pilot training. I made my wishes known. Fifty-five of us where in the first graduating class from Las Vegas Air Force Base. We continued on with our training at Turner Air Force Base in the 84th. 1950 rolled around and in April of 1950 I was sent to the Naval Close Air Support School at Little Creek, Virginia, in very early April. It was a very good experience. The Navy is just a tremendous, tremendous organization to teach the close air support techniques. We continued our training in aerial gunnery and air to ground.

June 25, 1950. The start. The word came around. There were several of us that were current in the F-51 and we used that aircraft, as I mentioned, to tow for aerial gunnery. The word came down immediately that they needed F-51 drivers and ten of us volunteered to go to Korea. We had to tell everybody where we were and leave our telephone numbers with the ops office and so forth because we never knew when we were going to get the word. I was at a cocktail party in Atlanta and I had left the telephone number of the people we were at the party with. Telephone rang and someone said, "Harned, you better get down here quick. You're leaving." Atlanta was three hours away and this was about one o'clock in the morning, so I had a long drive to Turner Air Force Base.

BOB KACHEL I got out of high school and didn't know what I wanted to do, so I joined the Marine Corps. It was in 1948. It was an eye-opening experience to go into the Marine Corps. I stayed in and I liked it. In 1950, I transferred from the Second Range Division over to the Second Marines, who were going to take a Mediterranean cruise. Then we got orders to report to Camp Pendleton in July. We were shipping out. We went across country on a train to Camp Pendleton and we joined the First Marine Division. We shipped off for Korea and I landed at Inchon. We got down to Kojo where we took over for part of the ROK [Republic of Korea] Army. I was an intelligence man. I was there to gather intelligence on patrols. We also did spotting and informing on what we saw, what we found, et cetera. If we had any prisoners we'd be there to interrogate the prisoners and to watch over them. We were down there for a couple of days, and we got hit pretty bad because

Bob Kachel with fellow Marines before heading up to the Chosin Resevoir. Kachel is pictured top row, third from left. *Bob Kachel*

we couldn't get our sleeping bags off. The sleeping bags were supposed to come apart if they had to after you had zipped them, but they never did. We had quite a few people get bayoneted in their sleeping bags on that one. After that, we went up to the Chosin Reservoir. When the Chinese hit us we were formed up in another group because Yudam-ni was there. They were surrounding us there and we were trying to break through to get some more people up to Hagaru to hold them up, to hold it out.

RAY HENDRIKSE We went in at Inchon. Things were not all that serious until we got to the Han River. They knocked everything out for crossing the Han. They had to hesitate for a little while until they could get some kind of bridges built, to get the tanks across. We got the tanks across and then they knocked out a bridge in another area. So we found a railroad track going over this valley. We could straddle the tracks. I was on a Sherman tank at that time and the majority of the tanks in the company were the Pershing tanks, which was a little larger tank. We said, "Yeah, if we get a Sherman across first and that works then we can try the Pershings," and so that's basically what we did. The only thing was if you looked down, it scared the daylights out of you. We only agreed to do it if we could have three or four engineers go ahead of us to check for land mines on the bridge. And that worked out nicely.

Our next goal was the Kimpo Airfield. We got to Kimpo and then it was Seoul. After Seoul, it was kind of a yo-yo for a little while. It gave me a new experience because in tanks, each company carries about three or four napalm-type flamethrowers, and in close areas like within Seoul, we used flame tanks and got a chance to see what that would do. Then we went up to the 38th parallel and there was the big decision about whether to cross it or stay there for a few days. General MacArthur came up and cut the ribbon and away we went across it. Afterward, they changed another tactic and instead of continuing north, we all went back to Inchon. The Marine Corps went back to Inchon and combat loaded again, and combat loading means you put all water-fording gear on the tank — that's all added on to it — and then we went into Wonsan. It was the early part of fall 1950. There was a scare because everybody talked about, "Oh, the bay in Wonsan is going to be loaded with mines and everything; you're not going to get a ship in there." It was interesting; we went to Inchon, we loaded on ship, and the interesting part then was we loaded onto American ships which the United States had evidently given to Japan, and they were manned by Japanese.

Ray Hendrikse with his tank company.
Ray Hendrikse

And the manning of those ships as we came out of the harbor at Inchon, we were bouncing all over the place. They weren't well trained in handling the LSTs [landing ship tanks], but we got out of there. We went into Wonsan, landed there, and went north.

DONNE HARNED Flying out of Pohang, South Korea, one of our flights went way up north during the first week in October, and we observed an enormous number of trucks coming across the Yalu through the valleys and into North Korea. This was duly reported during the intel debrief. Shortly thereafter, the CCF, Chinese Congress Forces, streamed over the mountains and the Yalu and headed south. This is when we went to Yonpo airfield in North Korea. The First Marine Division and the Seventh Army Division proceeded towards the Yalu, north, and were met with a hundred thousand or so Chinese troops. As General O. P. Smith said, "We're not retreating. We're attacking in a different direction." The Chosin Reservoir is in a bowl and it's surrounded. On one side there are higher mountains and they were, I recall, seven or eight thousand feet and on the other side they sloped down. Then as you went east, it took you to Hungnam, which was the port on the east coast.

JIM MCCONNELL We had an early Thanksgiving and started off for what we were told was the China border. As we were going up there, the closer we got to it, the tank commander, Haskell out of Massachusetts, kept talking about

Soldiers march in the cold around the Chosin Reservoir. Jim McConnell remembers, "It was more than thirty below. I froze my feet and my legs. They still bother me." *Jim McConnell*

how these weren't Koreans who were going by us. We were all camped a hundred yards off of the Yalu River and then, all of the sudden, they just came across the goddamn creek in droves. You couldn't do anything but run, because they'd just run right over you. I don't know how many hundreds upon hundreds were killed, but it didn't make a difference. There were just so damn many of them.

They had gotten us all into position where they could knock out the lead tank, stop the whole convoy, and open fire. When they did that, of course, a lot of the people who were on trucks and jeeps headed for the ditches on either side. They had .50-caliber machine guns on each end of those ditches and it was slaughter. We later exercised that same tactic against them and we called it Operation Mousetrap where you trap somebody, cut them off, and then go to it. It was everybody for himself, and I don't even know where that was but the struggle was to get to Hagaru. We did get to Hagaru where we had opportunity to treat the wounded, stack the dead, and organize to head out and reload at Hamnung.

BOB KACHEL We got nailed before we even got up there. We got nailed right after we got out of the perimeter of Koto-ri. We got hit by the Chinese around late November, the twenty-ninth or thirtieth. Where we were situated, we could see the Chinese over on the hill. They didn't believe that the Chinese would come in, and the Chinese were there and they came in — a large amount of them. You'd throw your rifle and pull the trigger and fire eight-round clips and another eight rounds and so on because there was a mass of people coming in. It was a human wave is what it was. You could fire at them but it wasn't that effective. Our fighters would come in and they would strafe them and then they would drop napalm on them. We always remarked the Chinese didn't get out of their hole until the napalm was just about on them, then they'd jump out of their holes and run down the hill. The napalm would come in and spread out on their trenches and that so that when it was over with, the Chinese would be back in their trenches and we'd say, "Look at them, we're sitting out here freezing and those people are getting a warm place to hide." A bunch of our buddies came in from the Fifth and the Seventh Marines. I saw a few of them that I had boot camp with. We lost a couple of them up there at the reservoir.

DONNE HARNED We were proceeding up the peninsula very, very rapidly. We were transferred to the Yonpo airfield in North Korea. We were told not to rocket certain buildings because we would be staying there. It was extremely cold, getting into late November and December. The Marines and the Seventh Division had their retreat cut off. At Yonpo, we had our number 77 Squadron, Royal Australian Air Force — a great bunch of guys — Marine S7F Tiger Cats, and F4U5 Corsairs. There may have been other squadrons there. One memorable mission that I remember was one where it was snowing at Yonpo airfield. Marines were calling for air support. They were quite desperate. This illustrates the dedication of the men that fought in World War II and now were fighting in this war. We took off in the snowstorm to get to the reservoir. A flight lead had to find a pass. We climbed up through the weather, and we topped out at eleven or twelve thousand feet. And the flight lead started his letdown, trying to find this pass. He would let down until he saw the pine trees going by and then he'd pull the flights up. We were in figure four. He tried three times and I was number two, and I see the pine trees coming up, and I'd say, "Well, I'll see you later." He found that pass, and we went down in the bowl and flew close air support for the Marines.

Donne Harned on his way to Chosin, where he flew air support missions.
Donne Harned

I was assigned a Marine forward air controller, a crazy guy. There was another Marine FAC at the other end. They split the fight up. So here we are and they're directing us. This one Marine said, "I want you to hit that line of bushes over there." I asked, "Is it clear of the troops?" "Aw," he said, "yeah, they're a hundred feet away." That's how close we were operating. We made pass after pass at the enemy and these FACs, they knew where we were all the time in that bowl with that snow flying. We'd make passes until we ran out of ammunition. As far as the machine guns were concerned on the F-51, they fired six hundred rounds per minute. You had three hundred rounds per gun, so you could just use short bursts. You did not ever, ever, ever hold down the trigger. Your bursts were two and three seconds; otherwise you'd burn out the barrels, it'd get so hot. When you were flying close air support like that, we were very low. We would cut grass, particularly when we were dropping napalm. In a troop situation, when we were that close to the troops, we had to be very, very careful; we had to know what we were shooting at. And the Marine FAC at the Chosin was well aware of our concern there. But he was so sure of what we should strafe that we just strafed where he told us to strafe and it was effective. The Marines were very thankful for the close air support they received. I had some Marines tell me they wouldn't have made it out of there if it hadn't been for the close air support, Air Force, Navy, and Marines.

BOB KACHEL We had Marines, and we had our own fighter pilots. The Air Force used to drop us supplies, but when they would, half of the supplies they would drop would miss us. A lot of the time you just let the stuff go. Then one time they flattened three tents we'd set up for warming with the stuff they dropped.

JIM MCCONNELL I hardly remember anything about Chosin. I just remember getting shot at. I lost a lot of good buddies. I was just fortunate. The worst part of it was the cold. When we went up into Chosin, to dig those troops out, it was more than thirty below. I think it was around thirty-two or thirty-three below. You only get so many clothes. I froze my feet and my legs, and they still bother me. My feet, I could hardly walk on them. They hurt just to walk. I froze them in the Second World War. When I went to Korea, I don't know if I froze one or if they just got cold again. You jump up and down to keep from freezing. You keep moving because you can't build fires. The snipers are hunting for you, and with fires, all you're doing is telling them where you're at. Firing a rifle is tough because you have to keep your gloves on. Your fingers will stick to the trigger at thirty below zero because when you have those heavy gloves on and your hands sweat, you take them off and put them on a cold trigger, they're going to freeze there. That's some tough fighting that way.

I think it was one of the First Battalion or the 32nd that went up to the Chosin Reservoir to dig the Marines out, and of course, they encircled them too. They were all pushed up against that reservoir, and we went up there, and we were killing off all the goddamned Chinese. Fast as you could see. When you were surrounded and they couldn't get in to feed you, we'd call for an air drop. They'd just throw it down where they think you are from where you've told them you are, but you aren't there anymore because they just ran you off from there. When you called for air support, you got it. They were pretty good. We didn't have airstrips like they do now, where they have airstrips built at every place they stop.

BOB KACHEL It was cold. You couldn't go indoors. You were outdoors twenty-four hours a day, unless you could get back down the hill into one of the warming tents, but you could only get down there once every other day or something like that. Your canteens and everything were freezing with you. We used to carry a little block of C-4 with us. We'd shave off a few pieces of that, put it down, and light a match to it. We'd put our canteen cup over the top of it and it would boil our water, so we could make coffee. By the time you'd get it out of there to drink, you'd get about two sips of coffee before it was getting back to frozen again. The only rations you could eat would be your dry rations because your wet rations, your ham or lima beans or pork or spaghetti and meatballs, were all frozen solid. That's what you lived on for two weeks. There was a time we were up there for around two weeks; we had crackers and Tootsie Rolls, we had candy bars, but outside of that, there was no food. Tootsie Rolls helped you out; they got you through on a lot of things. The same with Charms, the little hard candies. You'd put that in your mouth and suck on it, just like you did with the Tootsie Roll. There was food, but it was frozen.

RAY HENDRIKSE There were three places up there; Yudam-ni was the one that was the farthest north, and then Hagaru, and then Koto-ri. People talk about Hill 1472 and 1921 and I didn't know one from another except that Hagaru was a plateau and you could pretty much defend yourself from up there. When we eventually got to the China border and stopped, the U.S. was starting to bring supplies into Hagaru, one of which was cases and cases of Tootsie Rolls. Going from Hagaru back to Koto-ri back to Hamnung, we had no food, but they were flying over and dropping cases of Tootsie Rolls, and that's what we lived on for the ten to fifteen days coming out of Hagaru toward the coast. There's a lot of energy in Tootsie Rolls. As the column was going out, they would drop them through to us. I received a letter from a friend of mine in Madison and there was an article in the *Wall Street Journal* about the food in the military, and one little paragraph mentioned something about Tootsie Rolls. He highlighted it and said, "Ray, you can probably relate to this." I wrote him back: "Yeah," I said, "I sure can."

I was invited to a dedication of a monument on the Capitol grounds, and after it was all over, they had muffins and sweet rolls and juices and coffee. I told my wife, "I'm going to take a walk and look at some of these other monuments." I came across the Korean monument and sitting on a bench was a person who looked like he'd just come off the streets. On the back of his jacket, he had handwritten "Chosin Few." He was just sitting there hunched over and I went and sat down next to him. He didn't even look up. I said, "Chosin Few, huh?" and he just kind of grunted. I said, "Hey, I'm one of you," and he kind of looked at me. I pulled my "Chosin Few" card out and he looked at it. We didn't talk much at all, but about two minutes later I said, "Well, I got to get up and go now." He said to me, "Oh, by the way, when you get to the parking lot," he said, "you'll find an old rusted-out Chrysler out there," and he said, "If you open up the back door, on the backseat there's a case of Tootsie Rolls. Help yourself." I wrote that to the president of the Tootsie Roll company and two weeks later I had a case of them on my front doorstep. I still have some left. My grandkids have all left town now so I don't have anyone to give them to.

I've heard that there were times that we had about roughly fifteen thousand Marines up in that area. There were about a hundred and fifty thousand Chinese. The disadvantage was so overwhelming mentally, but they didn't have that many weapons. So if I had a tank and you had a club, keep coming. That isn't to say we didn't lose people. We lost a lot of people up there. It was twenty-five below and you throw a wind chill on that up in those mountains and it was cold. There were a lot of enemies. The enemy could be people, or it could be temperature, or it could be lack of food. To this day, I look at tank pictures and I think I'm the only one on that tank that didn't freeze my feet off. It was so cold that when we got to Hagaru and started bringing people up, there was a corpsman up there. His name was Pete Hammond. He was in our company and he got shot right through the jaw. Of course, when you're shot through the jaw and you're bleeding, he had a red icicle right hanging down on his jaw. It was pretty ugly to look at, but he knew he was going to get evacuated out of that place. He was telling us, "I'm flying out of here, and you guys are staying." When I see icicles today I still think of it.

DONNE HARNED Before we moved to Yonpo airfield — it was K27; they had a K designation for all the airfields — we were told not to rocket certain buildings because that was where we would be staying, that was where our quarters would be. These were Russian, Soviet-built facilities and we slept in a large room with a samovar. It was fired by coal. That room was warm in twenty and thirty degrees below zero. We really felt guilty because the maintenance people, the crew chiefs, worked on the aircraft in the bombed-out hangars. They had sides but there weren't any roofs and they put their tents inside the hangar. We felt rather guilty about that, that we were so warm. We felt even worse when we followed the Marines at the reservoir. On a mission, of course, we would hit the sack early, and at two o'clock in the morning we'd hear the engines crank up, and of course they had to do it because of the extreme cold. Our takeoff times would be in the area of 0500, 0530 [hours]. So two o'clock in the morning we hear the rumble of the Rolls

Royces and the Wrights and the R-2800s out there and then we'd get up an hour, hour and a half later and…well, you couldn't sleep anyway with all of that noise. We'd brief and off we'd go. Crew chiefs were very ingenious. The F-51 cockpit inlet ducts were, I believe, near the wing roots, and they would put beer cans in the ducts to give us a little heat in the cockpit. Nice guys. They were all good guys.

It was very, very disturbing to me to see the way the Marines were dressed. I saw a young Marine who was evacuated in Yonpo. We're talking thirty or forty degrees below zero here, and he had on a field jacket, but his inner clothing was khakis and his face was completely black with frostbite. I recall many, many casualties were that. That was the enemy, frostbite. The Marines and the Seventh Division made it to Hungnam. The Navy did a great job. They were ready for the evacuation. They evacuated the First Marines and the Army and they also took onboard ninety thousand North Koreans who wanted to escape the regime and took them to Japan, which I thought was just a marvelous thing. It was beautifully executed by the Navy. Not only that, they blew up the port of Hungnam. I didn't get to witness that, but the pictures are quite impressive. They destroyed any useable equipment and so forth.

JIM MCCONNELL I was a master sergeant most of the time and then also a corporal. I don't know how many men I had at any one given time. If I had a platoon, you've got around thirty or forty GIs you've got to take care of. A good sergeant knows his job, knows what he's capable of doing and of what other people around him can do. There comes a time when you got to know what everybody is able to do or you're going to come up short sometime. You have to know that stuff ahead of time. A sergeant has to make sure that his men don't freeze. Some didn't have sense enough to keep warm. They didn't want to carry extra clothes; they'd want to throw them away. Then when they wanted them they were not there. If you're not in infantry, you're in an outfit where you got jeeps and trucks and you can always throw your gear on them. Infantry don't have that privilege. If you want it, you better carry it with you or you ain't going to have it.

Guard duty at night is an awful lonely job for a private. Most of the time I was in Korea, I had rank, so I didn't have to stand on a post. I used to go out, when I had my platoon on guard; I'd go out at night in between each tour. If it was one of the young guys, I'd need to make a couple of trips out, or I'd have one of the NCOs make a trip or two in between, so that this kid

Bitter cold was the number one enemy at Chosin; U.N. forces suffered heavy casualties in the 30-below weather despite heavy winter gear. *Julius Ptaszynski*

could see he wasn't there by himself. You had to make sure they got enough clothing, that they had warm stuff on them. I'd wake them at night by myself. If I had to wake a guy up any more than once, the next time, I moved them up behind one of the guns. I was platoon sergeant and a machine gunner, too, in Korea. I moved over behind one of the guns. And I could hear the minute that guy started to snore and I'd just take my M-1 and aim right by his ear. I'd put one on to him. It was one guy I just nicked. I didn't mean to hit him, I just nicked him. But I made a believer out of that son of a bitch. Every time the replacements would come in, I used to get a kick out of them. They'd say, "What's the platoon sergeant doing? Never go to sleep on that son of a bitch because he'll blow your head off." I never shot nobody for sleeping, but, except that one that I nicked. It worked, though, because that guy never went to sleep again.

Night fighting is the worst kind. You can't see anybody. If you fire your rifle, the guy over there and the guy over here, they all fire back where they figure that flash is at. You didn't shoot unless you had to, unless you had a good target. You got attacked every night practically. We called them banzai attacks. They'd come tooting their horns and beating on their drums, thinking they were scaring you. They'd bang cymbals and pound on their helmet with a stick to scare you, so you'd jump in your hole and hide. It didn't work with me. They were good fighters, though. You'd goof up and they'd get you. Every night, they'd come out. The worst time to fight was at night; you couldn't see anybody. I'd rather sit in a hole and let them come to me; then I could see two positions one way and two positions the other way. I'd watch both ways plus in front of me and each guy to your left and right would do the same thing. That was if he was awake. That's why I used to get out and make sure the squad leader is doing the same thing because the guy is no good if he's sleeping. He might as well be dead.

RAY HENDRIKSE Hagaru was a gathering place, an assembly for all the units that were caught in that trap. We stayed there and the decision was made, "OK, now we have to start heading for Koto-ri," where we had another group of people that were cut off between Hamnung and Hagaru. We had to fight our way through to them and, of course, in a tank you are not exposed to where the critical points are. All you are trying to do is to get from one to the other, and we were pretty much unfamiliar with where we were, so we stayed as close as we could to the roads. The Chinese knew where the cutoffs were and where to put their people to stop us from getting through. We depended an awful lot on what the infantry could do to keep those passes open. We'd support them as much as we could, but we couldn't get the equipment in there. We got to Koto-ri, picked up the people that were in that area that never got to Hagaru, and from there we had another opening up to get to Hungnam to get out. Once we got to Hungnam, we loaded ship, and of the twenty-two tanks we started with, we had three left. I was fortunate that one of those was the tank I was on.

When you hit an antitank mine or two or three of them, it's serious. There's such a ruckus within, everything is so disrupted that by the time it settles down and you get your bearings on who's where and what's what, then you better have a cool mind because now you have to get out of there. What we would normally do in situations like that was if you were with a platoon of tanks, one tank would come alongside and you would take the personnel from one tank and put them in the tank that was not injured and you could get them out that way. The problem is you had to do that real quickly because as soon as you're knocked down and you're not mobile, then the mortars start coming in real quick. You better be cool; you can go through two packs of cigarettes in an afternoon.

You never looked down the side of the mountain because, you know, that's straight down. They pick a spot where it's hairpin, and so the first thing to do is, whatever stopped the column, you have to get it out of the way so you can maneuver. I was on both ends of it: I was caught in the trap and I was the offensive on the trap, and that's ugly too. It's not nice to drag all those bodies out the next day. Ugly.

BOB KACHEL They'd usually attack at night. During the day, they were gone, you didn't see them. At night is when they came out. That's why I always prayed for daylight. That's what I wanted. You could at least get up out of your hole and walk around and try to keep warm. At nighttime, you couldn't do that because somebody would be there to shoot you. Whether it was your own man, or whether it was a Chinese, you'd be moving around and then, "Hey, there's somebody moving over there, shoot and don't ask questions." That was more or less the order of the day.

There were more Chinese soldiers than they had weapons. At the reservoir they'd take our weapons off of our dead before we got back to them.

They'd try to take their parkas because they were all cold too. They had tennis shoes is what they were wearing up there, and their feet were all blistered up from the cold. That's the one thing of the experience you don't forget.

We were surrounded all the way. It didn't make any difference where we were, I mean, we were all surrounded. We had three regiments down there, the First, the Fifth, and the Seventh, and we were all surrounded. You could look any place you wanted to look, and all you could see on the occupying hills were Chinese. Our weapons froze. They didn't operate. The carbines would freeze up. They wouldn't fire, period. I think everybody there came back with some kind of frostbite or frozen feet or ears or noses or hands.

DONNE HARNED There wasn't any limit to the number of missions the Air Force flew through January of 1951 before you could rotate out. We weren't concerned with that. We were very busy. Finally the mission number became one hundred missions and you could rotate either back to Japan or back to the United States. The war continued and stalemated at the 38th and was just kind of stuck there. The Army fought innumerable battles for Hill 902. A good friend of mine was in a number of those battles.

BOB KACHEL The Army and Marine Corps were all in it together. I think the Marine Corps always prides itself on being better, and I think we had better training and better discipline. I would just say that the Army they had down there were peacetime troops, is what they were. They had no advanced infantry training or anything else. We never left anybody if possible. We never left a dead or wounded Marine there. We'd always bring them out. They came with us. They were buddies and they deserved that.

JIM MCCONNELL I was standing right next to my platoon sergeant when he got hit. I was supposed to go back with him to get field commissions. I told him, "I don't want to go. I'm not going to go back because I don't want to be a second lieutenant. That's just like, to me, like being a private all over again." I couldn't see it. Sergeant Templeton was a lot older than I was. Maybe not a lot, maybe five years or something like that. He was a good friend of mine. He was my platoon sergeant at the time. We were standing on the side of the hill and he just came back from the front line again, and he was standing there and I told him, I said, "Ted, don't walk up there." But he…ah…I don't like to talk about him.…

DONNE HARNED It was very, very, very brave men that assaulted those hills, and the Air Force continued to provide close air support for those assaults. I finished up my one hundred missions and was rotated to the States in April of 1951. And so that's the end of the story of the Korean War for me.

RAY HENDRIKSE When I was in high school, there was Iwo Jima and all of those events and it sold me on the Marine Corps. I'm happy for it. Marines don't leave anybody. Didn't care if they were dead, whatever, you never left them. I always had that feeling, "OK, so I have to go in after you," and I felt the same thing: "They're going to come in after me." I took a lot of comfort in that, nobody was going to leave me be. Coming out of Chosin, we had some Army personnel with us that came out, and they were very thankful that we took them with us because with all the disruption, they lost their leadership, and we didn't. I met some great people. There's camaraderie. I still talk to my buddy, Frank Weir, periodically. He was a steam-fitter in Chicago, but he had to move to Tucson, Arizona, because his wife has arthritis and things got very bad for her, so he moved down there. He called me one time and he said, "Hey, Charlie is down here." I asked, "Well, where is he? Give me his address." And he said, "He's living under a bridge." You're never, never, never quite as close to people as you are to people that you fight and die with. I just drove all the way from Madison to Richmond, Virginia. A guy by the name of Charles Raimer died. Charles was at Hagaru with me. I sat with him one night, in our foxhole, with his feet in my armpits and mine in his so we wouldn't freeze our feet. Great guy. You get real close.

7 Hungnam

"With that amount of manpower, you can't stop it. You have nothing to stop it with. It was a solid wall. You'd kill one and there were ten more coming, kill ten there'd be a hundred. There was no end to them. We took bad casualties up there. Horrendous casualties." — Stewart Sizemore

The retreat at Chosin was part of what became one of the largest military retreats in American history. The battle of Chosin itself was only the beginning of the U.N. withdrawal. U.N. forces had fought south from Chosin to the northeast Korean port city of Hungnam; between December 10 and 24, 1950, the U.S. Navy embarked on a massive evacuation mission to remove the entire Army X Corps and American Marines to safety in Pusan, South Korea. This was an immense and impressive operation; commanded by Vice Admiral C. Turner Joy, Naval Task Force 90 removed 105,000 soldiers, 17,500 vehicles, and 350,000 tons of cargo from Hungnam, along with more than 90,000 Korean refugees, though many more had gathered at the port in hopes of leaving North Korea. In describing the operation, *Life* magazine likened it to other famous military evacuations: "For the first time in its military experience, the U.S. faced a problem such as Britain faced in the historical withdrawal from Gallipoli, Dunkirk, and Greece." Similar evacuations were also taking place on Korea's western coast; in a reverse of the previous success at Inchon, 69,000 military personnel and more than 60,000 refugees were evacuated from the port at Inchon in December 1950 and January 1951.

Upon reaching Hungnam in early December, U.N. troops had formed a perimeter around the city, behind which they sought to remove their forces to safety. The First Marine Corps, which had just arrived from Chosin, were the first to leave, followed by South Korean troops and other American troops, including several Army divisions. The Chinese military, however, was not willing to let American and U.N. forces go without a fight. On December 14, 1950, the Chinese Army forced the U.N. to abandon Yonpo airfield on the outskirts of Hungnam. In a situation similar to Chosin, air support and heavy artillery became crucial to holding back further assaults. While the Chinese Army ultimately chose not to attack the rest of the evacuation, naval ships anchored offshore — including the massive USS *Missouri* — continuously fired shells to protect U.N. forces, while carrier-born American planes bombed and strafed the Chinese forces. The last U.N. troops left Hungnam on the morning of Christmas Eve, December 24, 1950. To make sure that Chinese and North Korean forces would not be able to use the port, Army engineers and Navy underwater demolition teams destroyed the harbor as the last American ships steamed away. As Chet Kesy described it, "When we were about a mile out to sea, evacuated, the engineers blew up the harbor. It was a fantastic sight to see. They just blew up the whole harbor to smithereens." Though American forces soon reached the relative comfort of Pusan, within weeks, many of them were back on the front lines, facing Chinese and North Korean troops. Ultimately, the Korean War entered a new phase after the Hungnam evacuation. No longer would the war be marked by rapid troop movement up and down the Korean peninsula. Instead, the war settled into a long and frustrating stalemate close to the original border between North and South Korea, one marked by bloody, fierce, and difficult battles for small hills and outposts, and long hours spent dug in on the front lines.

Eui Tak Lee, Madison (Army, 25th Division)
W. O. Wood, Racine (Army, Seventh Division)
Stewart Sizemore, Lake Geneva (Army, 24th Infantry Division)
Chet Kesy, Mosinee (Army, Seventh Division)

EUI TAK LEE My father worked before the war for the railroad, but after, we had to move away from Seoul into countryside, near Inchon. They started rounding up government employees and professors and pastors. They rounded up young people and put them into North Korean Army. So to flee from the oppression, we went to a relative's living in the countryside near Inchon.

Our family came back to Seoul and I joined the Korean Combat Police, and we get trained to fight against the remnants of North Korean guerrillas.

And at that time, the United Nations forces were advancing towards the north. They reached Chosin and Hyesanjin, which is right at the border of Korea and Manchuria. I thought, "Finally we got the unification." But it was short-lived. The Chinese Communist troops intervened, so United Nations forces, the American forces, and ROK forces had to retreat [from] North Korea. At that time, the Hungnam evacuation was an event that Korean people will never forget because tens of thousands of North Korean refugees [were] evacuated to the safety [of] the South by the help of American ships. We are very grateful for that.

Keeping clean during combat. *W. O. Wood*

W. O. WOOD I was in Japan and these friends of mine that I had met were going back to the States. I said, "That's great." I said, "Phelps, I'll see you. I got six more months and I'm done with." So they left and then the Korean War broke out. We waited and waited and then all of a sudden we were the next division to go. I never knew what it was all about. I'd never been in a war. I didn't understand what was going on. It was just a bunch of kids standing and looking around at everybody. Fortunately, I had a couple of buddies I hung around with that were from World War II. One said, "What do you make of it? You'll be all right." I said, "I don't know."

I saw my first death in Seoul. I didn't know what to do. I just sat there. I just sat and looked, and they said, "This is war." I was fortunate. This sergeant buddy of mine, he came over and grabbed me and said, "Woody, you'll get over it. I did in World War II; you can do it now." So we stuck close by that night, but nobody got any sleep. The next morning we got up and got back to our units, and then everything settled in. I met a lot of guys. Soon we had a fire mission and a lieutenant said, "Woody, I want you to be my liaison with fire missions doing radio communications and adjustment radios." I said, "Well, that's why they had me aboard ship." He said, "Well, they needed somebody to carry the radio." His name was Lieutenant Flunkie. "Yeah," he said, "I'll have you." We went up on the hill a couple of times together. He'd give me the coordinates. Everybody up there liked him. A Company, B Company, G Company. We always called for a fire mission. We'd find out who was down there first from the Fire Direction Center. This went on for maybe two or three months, up the hill, off the hill, and so on and so forth. Then we made a push to go all the way up Korea. The Marines were already up near

W. O. Wood on a fifty-caliber rifle. *W. O. Wood*

the airport in Pyongyang. The 31st was right behind them, and we were off to the right. We were going north, and they were going to the Chosin Reservoir. Captain McGinn said, "They're going to be coming at us tonight. We just got it on the wire. They're sending a division." We're sitting out there and it's getting darker. The next thing you know, bugles blew, there was screaming and yelling. Over the hill, there was a bunch of them coming. We knew right away that, just forget it.

They came over the top of the hill and we cut loose. We were firing our weapons point-blank. I was between the jeep and a trailer, and it felt like something was hitting it. One of their burp guns went off. "Whoa," I said, "we're in trouble." I went back to my basic training, trying to do this and do that, because you don't know what to do. I jumped up on top of that three-quarter-ton truck and I saw them coming up over the ridge, and I just let a couple bursts up and right over the top of Sergeant Jones's gun section. He says, "Woody, can you get it off to the far right?" I swung around to the right with a couple bursts. So I'm shooting out and the gun jammed. I didn't know what to do. I took the barrel and I lay down on the seat of the jeep and I reached up to grab the barrel. I took it off. We always had a theory: if you've got the gun, you put the other barrel at the tailgate. I reached down and sure, there was one, so I put it on, and I said, "I don't have a gauge," and I remembered, "All the way in, screw it all the way in and four clicks back."

Why it came to me, I have no idea. Whatever happened, you know. While I was shooting, I saw puffs of smoke coming up over the one flank, and we were getting mortared. It was coming in. I saw A Company behind us, firing at a high angle. Some of the high angles were a little too close.

I was shooting on up over the ridge and the next thing I know, Jones yells, "Woody! Cease fire! Cease fire!" So I cease fire and I looked around and it was dead — like someone snapped their fingers. I looked up and around, and there were holes in everything. When I got done, Captain Kidd said, "I'll put you in for a medal." I asked, "For what?" He said, "What you did." I said, "What did I do?" I went off and I shook and shook and shook. I took a canteen of water and drank the whole thing. The first thing that came to my mind is, "I have to go up the street and see if Simpson's there." I went up there and he just lay there, bleeding. And I talked to him. I said the Lord's Prayer. I think I got it all wrong, but the Lord knew what I was talking about. And so I lost one of my buddies there.

STEWART SIZEMORE For all intents and purposes, the war was over. We'd beat the North Koreans. The war was won. We were sitting on the Yalu. Then the Chinese crossed with their million men. I can remember watching the Chinese cross the Yalu River, wearing just tennis shoes and it was below

Stewart Sizemore, left, recalls of his fellow soldiers, "The people that I went to war with are more like my brothers than my brothers."
Stewart Sizemore

zero. When they hit us, they just went right through us. Even with our weapons. The North Koreans had some better weapons than we had, but when the Chinese came in, a lot of them didn't even have weapons. Some of them just had rocks. They attacked in waves. When they crossed with their million men, it was just Chinese, Chinese, Chinese. When we fought the Chinese, they'd get around you, you'd fight them again, they'd get around you and you'd just keep falling back. Then they'd set up an ambush. They ambushed the Second Division up there. Just slaughtered those people. They got them in a valley and got around them. That's how many there were. They were just a mass. We lost a lot of men there coming back from the Chinese. It being so cold, the snow hampered your movements. Our units were disorganized; we didn't know where our company was, where our platoon was, where our squad is. You don't even know if you had one. You end up joining the first friendly unit that you encounter until you get back and get some stabilization of the line, because the line sure isn't stable — it's flexible. It's moving. You're fighting a retrograde movement. You're fighting and falling back, fighting and falling back until you find a defensive position, a line that you can hold.

W. O. WOOD We went up and we hit the Yalu River. We were the first Americans that went through there. We were there for about five days and had had no counterattacks, which was unusual. The snow was up to our knees. Then we went to the left toward China. We went maybe about half a mile. And we saw tracks that you wouldn't believe. You've never seen so many tracks. It just looked like a herd of buffalo ran through. They came across the river. We got back up to the communication outpost and used the telephone. A major made the recommendation that we all pull back. We got back there and heard the 31st and 32nd were really getting clobbered. We heard the reports that the Chinese came in. They estimated two hundred and fifty thousand troops behind us and to our flank. The Marines were really catching heck. So as we were coming back, we had stragglers from all over.

We got up to a bridge, and one of the tanks was across the bridge, and for some reason they hit the lead jeep. Flares went up and it started a gas-tank fire. They passed the word down, "Everybody out except the drivers." Everyone put their bayonets on and made sure they had ammo. I thought, "Well, if they're going to take us, take us now." We couldn't see anything and we crossed the river. It was cold. The big stuff couldn't cross the river;

they had no pontoon bridges. Captain Flunkie said to me, "Woody, you want to go on advanced patrol with me?" I never volunteered for anything. I was told that when I went in by my four brothers. "Don't volunteer, don't volunteer for nothing." But I said, "I'll go!" It was up and down the hills and stuff. I was strong and they always made me do stuff. A lot of people could get me to do things for them; I didn't know what I'd done until it was over with. I think that's what happened when I was on the gun.

CHET KESY On our way back from the Yalu we went through a place called Hungnam. That's where they were going to evacuate us out of there. We were pretty lucky we didn't get hit by a bunch of Chinese. The Seventh Division was up at the Chosin Reservoir and they lost pretty near every man in the whole regiment. They lost over three thousand men. That's where the Marines and the Seventh Division fought, at Chosin Reservoir. I wasn't at Chosin Reservoir. We were lucky we got out.

We got into Hungnam, but we left the Turks up there; they said they wouldn't retreat. Three days later the Turks came back into the Hungnam carrying every one of their dead. I don't know how they did it. I think they were fantastic fighters because they were fighting the whole Chinese Army up there and they carried every one of their dead out. They sent landing-ship tanks to haul us out of Hungnam. The Battleship *Wisconsin*, and a whole bunch of other battleships, kept the Chinese off until we got organized and loaded up on these LSTs [landing ship tanks]. The Army engineers wired up the whole harbor there with TNT and when we were about a mile out to sea, evacuated, the engineers blew up the harbor. It was a fantastic sight to see. They just blew up that whole harbor to smithereens. We ended up back in Pusan.

W. O. WOOD We ran into a lot of problems, but we finally got into Hungnam. It was about four thirty, just about dusk, and we were coming in. I look up in the sky and there's a big roar. Big, big roar. "What the devil?" When it hit, the ground shook. I said, "Holy mackerel, we must be getting near the guns and the shore." It was the USS *Wisconsin*. Really, that ground shook. I'll tell you, I wouldn't be on the other end of it. I looked out and thousands, thousands of refugees were on these LSTs — the ones that the Marines had. They were just jam-packed. You couldn't put a sardine between the two of them, there were so many of them.

So we were out there and pretty soon some fool colonel comes through,

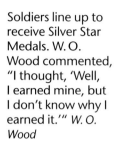

Soldiers line up to receive Silver Star Medals. W. O. Wood commented, "I thought, 'Well, I earned mine, but I don't know why I earned it.'" *W. O. Wood*

I don't know what his name was. There were a bunch of guys lined up and I was on the right-hand side, second one in. I asked, "What's going on here?" Captain Flunkie said, "Best stay there, Woody," he says, "I've seen this before in World War II." The guy came toward us with a pin. He pinned something on. He walked down to the next guy, put a pin on, and walked down to the next guy and the next guy and the next guy. When it was all done, he saluted us all, and we saluted back. I looked down, and it was a Silver Star. "I'll be damned!" I said to this one lieutenant. He took his and heaved it as far as he could throw it. He didn't want it. He said, "I didn't earn it." I thought, "Well, I earned mine, but I don't know why I earned it."

STEWART SIZEMORE I got hit up there. I got wounded and they just ran right through me. They threw a concussion grenade in the machine gun emplacement that blew me and my buddy out of it. We were bleeding from the ears and the nose and the eyes from the concussion. Then I got hit in the face with a Chinese rifle butt. They left us. They just went right on, didn't even stop. We came to after probably a couple hours. Had it not been as cold as it was and had the blood not congealed, I probably wouldn't be here today. We made it back to our lines and down to our own units. They were all on the move back. With that amount of manpower, you can't stop it. You

Stewart Sizemore, looking fatigued. He says "A lot of people that went to Korea have different views of the war than I do. They didn't walk 700 miles up to the Yalu and 700 miles back."
Stewart Sizemore

have nothing to stop it with. It was a solid wall. You'd kill one and there were ten more coming, kill ten there'd be a hundred. There was no end to them. We took bad casualties up there. Horrendous casualties.

CHET KESY They sent me back to Japan because I had frozen feet. When your feet are first getting cold, it feels really bad. Once they're frozen, it's almost like you're walking on sticks. There's hardly any feeling. My feet weren't like that for too long. When we got back from Hungnam and went back to Pusan, they put me on a ship and sent an airplane. I went to a big hospital there in Japan. They did a good job on me. I spent about three months there and about six to eight hours a day sitting in whirlpool baths. I'm walking today. My feet bothered me for quite sometime after I got out of the service. I'd take a shower and I'd wipe between my toes and I could pretty near wipe the meat right off, down to the bone. It was cold. We had very, very poor equipment in the Korean War. We shouldn't ever have been in that war with the equipment we had. We had a lot of guys who froze. We had eight guys freeze to death at one time. We found them in a foxhole dead. It was hard to keep warm. There was no place to go when you were out there twenty-four hours a day; there was no place to go to get warm.

My feet came out pretty good. They were going to cut them off so that I could come back to the States. I said, "No, I want to go back to where the guys are." So I went back to my outfit back in Korea, but they didn't send me up on as a forward observer anymore. I stayed with the guns as chief of fire and battery.

STEWART SIZEMORE I went to the MASH unit and was there for about three weeks. I remember laying in a bombed-out church and there was no roof on it. I kept seeing this guy come out with a basket. I got to wondering what this guy was carrying in that basket. It was parts that they were amputating: legs, arms, et cetera. I said, "I have to get out of here." That's when I went AWOL, back to my unit. I got up and found that there were a pile of weapons in the courtyard — any weapon you wanted — so I found my weapon and headed back to the front. My eyes were swelled up and I couldn't see. Everything was abscessed in my mouth. Anything was better than laying there to have them cut my arm off or something by mistake. I was up there I think two days and the MPs came up and got me and took me back. They gave me penicillin to bring down the swelling and then they had to cut all that stuff out from the rifle butts and concussion. Then I went back to my unit again.

The people that I went to war with are more like my brothers than my brothers. They were more brothers to me for what they'd been through than my brothers were. I had a twin brother in the Army. I had another brother in the Army and another in the Navy. But none of them saw what I saw. They weren't in Korea. You don't want to let your buddy down because he's your right-hand man. He's your left-hand man. He's there with you all the time. He depends on you, and you depend on him. That's what makes a team. That's how you live. You keep each other alive. You help each other out. You're there for each other. The camaraderie even to this day; you never find camaraderie like that. I loved the guys I was with more than I do my own brothers. That's hard to say. It may be callous but that's the way it is. You lived and died by these people. When I look at pictures of myself at nineteen or twenty, I think to myself, "How did you live that long?" Everybody says that. How do you live that long? You must have done something right that you're still here.

CHET KESY You don't hear much about the Korean War. Very little. And there are still eight thousand prisoners that are unaccounted for. Fifty-six

Chet Kesy receiving
the Bronze Star.
Chet Kesy

thousand dead. The Vietnam War, it lasted ten years and there was fifty-eight thousand dead. A lot of people don't realize how bad the Korean War was. It was a terrible war. I planned on staying in the military, but Korea changed my mind. It definitely changed my mind. I had been in about a year. I thought about reenlisting, but I probably would have ended up in Vietnam too. My brother went through the Second World War, right from the beginning; he had forty-three months overseas in the Second World War. He went through Korea and he went through Vietnam. He retired from the service. He went to Korea after I came back. He was in the later part of it.

Chet Kesy, second from left, with fellow soldiers, returning from Korea. *Chet Kesy*

That was really a tough part of the war. There were a lot of people getting killed then, too, because each side wanted to have a little bit more ground.

W. O. WOOD After we were evacuated from Hungnam, we went back into garrison. I think we went up a couple more hills, the Punch Bowl, for one. I think that we had them all licked and then the Chinese came in, and [we] had to fight a lot of that back over again. The Lord was with me throughout. My buddies that are gone…I would say the heroes are up there. We might ask why. Why did he die? For what reason?

STEWART SIZEMORE In my outlook on the war, the offensive war only lasted, I think, about nine months. After that, we started going into bunkers in 1951. We never got any further, maybe a few hundred yards one way or the other, but we didn't get up north or anything again. So I think the people in the first nine months really fought the war. We went all the way up to the Yalu River and the Chosin Reservoir, to Hungnam and all the way back. A lot of people that went to Korea have different views of the war than I do. They didn't walk seven hundred miles up to the Yalu and seven hundred miles back, so their concept of what happened or how the war went is a little different than mine. We went north; we fought over some of the same ground coming back we fought over going up. Same hill. You say to yourself, "There's been a heck of a price paid for this. Already." What do you do? You live with it. That's part of life.

Heartbreak

"He was quiet for a while and then pretty soon he says, 'Smitty,' he says, 'I don't know if I'm that scared or that cold,' and I couldn't help but laugh, because I felt exactly the same way." — Stan Smith

China's entry into the war resulted in the widespread retreat of U.N. troops from North Korea. The war was not over, however, and U.N. troops fought their way back up toward the 38th parallel in the spring of 1951. Determined to regain a strong position in Korea, they retook Seoul in March and managed to stop several strong Chinese assaults on U.N. lines. Cease-fire discussions began at Kaesong in July 1951, but the negotiators agreed that fighting would continue during the talks. The war itself dragged on for two more years. As the cease-fire discussions began, however, the war settled around the 38th parallel; historians often describe this phase of the war as a stalemate between U.N. and Communist troops. The two sides often fought over small amounts of ground — one hilltop, for example — that were constantly changing hands back and forth. Yet as battles like Heartbreak Ridge make clear, the war continued to be bloody, intense, and grueling.

Heartbreak Ridge was located in an area known as the Punch Bowl, a valley surrounded by mountains near Chorwon, North Korea. U.N. command had determined that the Chinese and North Korean armies used the high ground of the Punch Bowl both as a staging area and to call in artillery fire against U.N. supply routes. In late July 1951, U.N. troops began limited offensive operations against the area. In the battle of Bloody Ridge, which took place from August 18 to September 5, 1951, American and South Korean troops succeeded in pushing the Chinese and North Korean armies off one key ridge. The name Bloody Ridge derived from the intense and deadly nature of the battle; over the course of three weeks, the high ground constantly passed back and forth between the two sides. The steep and slippery hills made attacking difficult and often resulted in fierce hand-to-hand

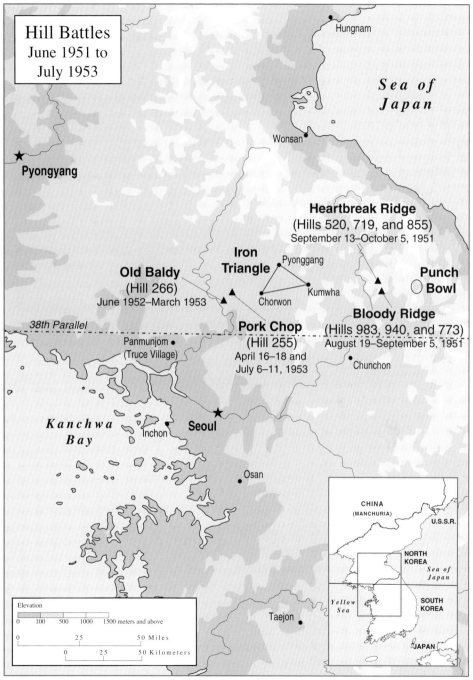

Hill Battles
June 1951 to
July 1953

Hungnam

Sea of Japan

Wonsan

★ **Pyongyang**

Heartbreak Ridge
(Hills 520, 719, and 855)
September 13–October 5, 1951

Iron Triangle Pyonggang

Old Baldy
(Hill 266)
June 1952–March 1953

Chorwon   Kumwha

Punch Bowl

38th Parallel

Pork Chop
(Hill 255)
April 16–18 and
July 6–11, 1953

Bloody Ridge
(Hills 983, 940, and 773)
August 19–September 5, 1951

Panmunjom
(Truce Village)

Chunchon

Kanchwa Bay   Inchon   ★ **Seoul**

Osan

Elevation

0   100   500   1000   1500 meters and above

0   25   50 Miles

0   25   50 Kilometers

CHINA (MANCHURIA)

U.S.S.R.

NORTH KOREA

Sea of Japan

Yellow Sea   SOUTH KOREA

JAPAN

Taejon

UW–Madison, Dept. of Geography, Cartography Lab

combat where the death rate was high; neither side took many prisoners. After U.N. troops pushed them off Bloody Ridge, the North Korean and Chinese Armies retreated to another ridgeline about 1500 yards away. Like Bloody Ridge, the intense and gory nature of the fighting would soon earn this ridge the name Heartbreak.

The battle of Heartbreak Ridge began on September 13, 1951. By the time it ended on October 15, one month later, more than 3,500 U.N. troops had died, while North Korean and Chinese casualties were estimated at 17,000. In the first phase of the battle, U.N. troops — composed largely of American and French forces — conducted a series of limited attacks against North Korean forces. Unfortunately, U.S. commanders underestimated the North Korean Army's strength; these initial attacks took the form of direct and often deadly assaults up the steep and slippery sides of the ridge by a small number of men. Supported by heavy artillery and air power, U.N. troops would destroy enemy bunkers as they climbed. For these exhausted men, reaching the top of the ridge did not end the battle. Inevitably, the North Korean Army would counterattack, often at night; as with Bloody Ridge, hand-to-hand combat was common. The first two weeks of the battle were marked by this cycle of attack and counterattack, yet even with intense artillery and air strikes, U.N. troops failed to push North Korea off the top of the ridge. Realizing the complete failure of this strategy, U.N. troops began a larger-scale offensive that focused not just on the ridge itself but also on the hills and valleys surrounding it to prevent the North Korean Army from resupplying itself with fresh troops and materials. Using armored tanks, U.N. troops were finally able to turn the tide of the battle, preventing a Chinese division from joining the North Korean troops defending the ridge and destroying North Korean troops, bunkers, and supply lines. U.N. forces were able to secure the ridge, but at heavy cost and through savage fighting. This victory hardly seemed worth the sacrifice it had required and Heartbreak Ridge was one of the last major offensives of the war. Though the U.N. victory at Heartbreak Ridge persuaded the Communists to reopen negotiations (they had broken from the talks in mid-August because they did not think they could get favorable terms from the U.N.), once again these negotiations quickly stalemated. Troops on both sides dug into an intense network of fortifications — trenches, bunkers, foxholes — that stabilized the movement of the war, yet there was no end in sight; the war continued as one of intense, bloody, and bitter struggles over small goals.

Stan Smith, Superior (Army, Fifth Division)
Elroy Roeder, Rothschild (Army, Second Infantry Division)
Roger Lewison, Sparta (Army, 24th Infantry Division)

Left: Stan Smith fought with the 5th Regimental Combat Team, which specialized in nighttime ambush patrols. *Stan Smith*

Right: Elroy Roeder was married in 1950 when he was 21 years old. He was drafted into the army the next year. *Elroy Roeder*

STAN SMITH Well, when the Korean War started, that was June. You felt an obligation. My father was in World War I, my brother was in World War II, and I felt that I should do my share. I didn't know if I wanted to go in or enlist or not. Mornings I thought "No" and by night I thought, "Yeah, I will." This went on for a while. Finally, I enlisted in September of 1950 when I was twenty-one.

ELROY ROEDER I was drafted, like everybody else was at that time. I got married in October 1950 and in January '51 I got drafted. I did my basic in Fort Leonard Wood, Missouri, and took engineering training. I laid mines, did demolition, built bridges. I got overseas and they didn't need any of it. They needed infantrymen and that's where they put me in as soon as I got off the boat. The first line I was on, they called it the Punch Bowl. They said, "We're going up to the Punch Bowl; don't ask." It sounded exciting. It was just like a punch bowl, mountains all around, in the middle was valley.

STAN SMITH I figured the Communists were going to overrun the whole country. I still think maybe they would have if we hadn't intervened. I like to think we did it for a reason, anyway. I enlisted in Rice Lake, Wisconsin, and was inducted in Minneapolis, Minnesota. From there I went to Fort Riley, Kansas, and took my basic training in the 10th Infantry Division. I got shipped to Aberdeen, Maryland. I was in ordnance supply in my advance training. When we finished our training there, they cut our company in two. Half of them went overseas and half stayed stateside. We became cadre, giving basic infantry training to the new recruits coming in. That gave us the stripes of acting corporals but no pay. We were all still buck privates. I did that until September '51 when I went overseas.

At Pearl Harbor, they took some of our gear away from us, which I never could understand. We all had trench coats — they took them away from us. Butts of our rifles, cleaning equipment — they took that away from us, too. We boarded the *Joe P. Martinez* and went up to Inchon, unloaded there, and were assigned to our units. That's when I joined the Fifth Regimental Combat Team. There were kids — eighteen and nineteen year olds — several of them, they wanted to be in the Fifth. I knew nothing about the Fifth when I joined it.

Soldiers march the seven mile-long Heartbreak Ridge.
Elroy Roeder

ELROY ROEDER I was in the 23rd Infantry Regiment of the Second Division, Easy Company. There were three of us on sixty mortars. I was a bearer, a gunner, and a forward observer. I saw a lot of North Koreans' bodies lying around. That was the first time I'd seen a dead body. I was surprised that it didn't bother me. They were all bloated, laying there for a while. The battle was cleaning up when I got there. From there we came down to reinforce and went back to the next hill. I don't think there were too many to come home with me. We lost over three-quarters of the guys that were in the Heartbreak Ridge. That was the biggest battle I was in. We'd take the hill and then they'd chase us off, but we'd take it again. Every time you came down, you'd reorganize and then you'd start back up again. It was all uphill. That was the worst part of it. You'd carry your ammunition and all the grenades you could and climb up those damn hills. A lot of places they'd tie ropes on a tree, and you'd hang on and pull yourself up. I call them mountains because they weren't hills. Every time you took a hill, tomorrow there'd be the next one, higher yet. Up and down, up and down, up and down, that's all you did. My legs were sore every time.

I know the first time I was up there, I was scared. When I first went into combat, I didn't know what to do. I didn't know how to dig a hole because we never dug foxholes in basic training. They gave you a shovel to carry with you and that's it. You learn in a hurry. That's your life. Holes are your life. If you don't get in the hole, you're dead. That's how I looked at it. There's somebody shooting at you all the time and you never know in what direction. I never got over being scared. I was worried about booby traps because there were a lot of them around at the time. Grenades tied on trees. I was worried about stepping on one of those things.

STAN SMITH They took us as far as they could by trucks, unloaded us, and we marched the rest of the way to get into position. It was on the 38th parallel pretty much. We were, most of the time, in what they called the Iron Triangle. I'm not even sure what other cities or towns were around there. If you look at a map of the 38th parallel, which goes across Korea, in the middle, the 38th goes up to a point and down again. The Punch Bowl was in that area. We spent quite a bit of time in the Punch Bowl. The area itself we called the Iron Triangle. The Fifth Regiment was what they called a bastard outfit. We didn't belong to any one division. We were attached to the 24th for a while and we were with the 25th for a while. I am not sure if we were with any others or not. We had an artillery unit that was our support, the Triple Nickel, the 555, that whenever we went on a patrol or anything, they gave us supporting fire. They were good.

Our outfit was basically a night combat unit. We specialized in ambush patrols. We would go out at night, set up an ambush, hoping the enemy would walk into it. During the days sometimes we would go out on probing attacks or recon patrols. The probing didn't make much sense. We'd go out and engage the enemy to see how strong they were. We might try and take a hill, push them off and get the hill, then pull back off and leave it. Then the Chinese and North Koreans would move back in again. In a few days or a week, somebody would go out and push them off again. I suppose just to harass them, I don't know what else. They were harassing us at the same time, of course. The ambushes were really our main objective. We'd move out, generally just after dark, in what they called a machine gunner's prayer. We walked single file on ridgelines. Korea was nothing but hill upon hill upon hill, with what we called fingers going off from these big hills. You couldn't walk in a frontal position at all, so you'd walk out single file, to where you were supposed to set up. Your squad leader would assign you positions, get you set up, and you'd sit until you were told, usually until two or three o'clock in the morning. Then you would pull out if nothing had happened.

One night, we were told to go out, to go where we were supposed to go. Well, this was our squad leader's problem. He was a veteran; he'd been over there quite a while. I suppose he didn't want to go very far if he could avoid it. He'd be going home, he hoped, shortly. We got set up and got another

Members of Stan Smith's squad, which ran patrols at Heartbreak Ridge and the Punch Bowl.
Stan Smith

[Chinese] patrol come into us, and I hate to say it, but they more or less ambushed us. We were already set up, and a fellow by the name of McConnell was two or three yards from me. We were sitting up behind bushes was about all; there wasn't really all that much for cover and it was cold. We were sitting there for several hours. Poor old Johnny McConnell would double his legs up and then he'd straighten them out and there were rustling noises coming from that. A couple times I thought I heard something, but McConnell was making so much noise I wasn't sure. I had just whispered over to McConnell, "For cripes' sake, sit still." I turned back and I saw an enemy soldier. He had straightened up, looking, and he started shooting, and then everybody started shooting. I heard burp guns going off and next thing I knew I thought my rifle had blown up. I don't know. I assume I was unconscious for a while but I don't really know.

I was a rifleman. I was a squad leader. When I first joined the unit they tried to put me in heavy weapons. I was not trained in heavy weapons. I had fired them for familiarity but had never trained on them. I requested a rifle squad. The platoon sergeant of the heavy weapons said to me, "You're crazy to ask for this." But they let me go. After I was wounded and came back to the unit, the first guy I met was this sergeant and he said, "I told you you were crazy."

ELROY ROEDER When we took the hill, the first time we tried it was at night. We got chased out right away. The second time, we went up a ridge. There were so many times I went up there, but that one I won't forget. We looked to our right and our left, and we saw guys running up at the top there, and we knew they were Chinese. We told our company commander to pass the word down, that there were people running up on top of the hill and that they would shoot us sooner or later. We kept on walking and walking and walking and finally came to a dead end and then all hell let loose. They really poured into us guys. I remember that I was lying behind and I jumped behind a big oak tree. I lost my trench shovel. It was lying on the side and every time I tried to grab it, a guy would be shooting at me. You could see that they were laying mortars down on us, and the grenades killed and wounded a lot of guys. We got back off the hill again, but most of the guys all got hit one way or the other. I never got a scratch.

We went up into another ridge and took it. It was kind of an opening, so we all dug in around there. There was a French battalion attached with us. We all dug in and then they started giving it. You could see the mortars coming in. You could hear the incoming on your walkie-talkies, the static. You looked up and you could see the mortars coming, and were they coming! You knew you weren't going to make it. Two of my buddies were right next to me. I was digging a hole like a chipmunk. There was a direct hit. I could see the shell go right in there. My buddies were laughing and then after that I didn't hear anything and I knew they were dead. Another buddy of mine was dug in; he got hit, but he was just wounded. He says to me, "I'm wounded!" I said, "Well, just lay there. Don't move!" After it was all over, the medics came and took care of everybody. We got everything reorganized and then we got another round. I went to a different spot, and I thought that this spot was not good for digging holes. I went to a different hole and I was going to jump in there, but I thought, "I'd better not; I'll dig my own." Good thing I did because the two guys in there got hit. I was just lucky all the way through Korea. I did a lot of praying.

STAN SMITH I guess it was a hallucination, but I had the feeling I could see myself laying on the ground. It was like I was in the air floating over it. I could see me, my body laying there. When I came to enough to realize where I was and that I was hurt, I tried to holler, but I couldn't. You're not supposed to holler but I tried. I couldn't make any noise, so I dragged my rifle back with me and got to McConnell and told him I was hit. He relayed

Stan Smith with his fellow soldiers from the 5th RCT. Smith is pictured bottom row, second from left.
Stan Smith

the messages back and they sent the radioman down to help me. It turned out he was a North Korean boy, about sixteen years old, that hated the Chinese. He and a couple of other guys helped me back to an aid station. They had a medic meet me. He dressed my wounds and put me on a stretcher. They carried me to a company-size outpost. I had to spend the night there because there were enemies all around us. Come morning I was able to walk out to the aid station. It was just a tent set up that had a couple of medics in it. They gave me a shot of morphine, I suppose it was, and put me in an ambulance and shipped me back to a MASH. It was a tent hospital all set up. I spent Thanksgiving there. From there they loaded us in the ambulances and took us to a hospital train that took us down to Pusan, to the 22nd Evacuation Hospital. I spent most of a month there.

I got hit at the base of the neck with a burp gun, on the left, and it came out the middle of my right shoulder blade. It was only one round. I always figured maybe I got him when he got me. That's what I always figured because he had to be right in front of me. I was lying in a prone position for

On the lookout at Bloody Ridge. Elroy Roeder remembers, "Every time you took a hill, tomorrow there'd be the next one, higher yet. Up and down, up and down, up and down, that's all you did."
Elroy Roeder

firing. At the hospital then they did X-rays. They cut my shoulder blade and made a very minute opening and took out a couple of bone chips. The doctor said that had the bullet been a fraction of an inch to the front or the rear, the front would have got the jugular and the back would have got the spine. He said it wouldn't have made any difference to me. He said I was one lucky guy to have a bullet pass through and not do any damage.

When I went back, I didn't get back into the same squad. My squad leader then was a fellow by the name of Paul Hart. When he rotated, I took over his squad. That was kind of unusual because there were a couple of veteran men in the squad yet, but Paul Hart picked me as his replacement. When they called me and asked if I wanted to take over the squad I was kind of reluctant because I didn't have all that much combat experience — some of these fellows had more. I asked Paul, "What happens if I get scared and bug out?" He said, "You will be too busy to get scared and bug out." I took over the squad then.

ELROY ROEDER The only time you slept was during the daytime. Daytime was just like a picnic. You could lie on your side, on the ground, and take in the sun. I never thought about getting hurt or killed. You just had to do it. Just go up there. You knew it was going to be rough every time you went. Same with Bloody Ridge; that was a bad one too. That was almost as bad as Heartbreak. After we got up there, the Chinese counterattacked. We held her, though. We spent three nights up there without blankets. Oh, it was cold, trying to keep warm. Two guys huddling together in a foxhole. It was two guys to a hole. You could get a little sleep, then guard while the next guy slept. Maybe every two hours, you'd wake the guy up and say, "Hey, it's your turn to watch." That's how it worked. But at nighttime I couldn't sleep. I didn't trust it. You never knew. Those guys could sneak through and cut your throat or something. You couldn't dig holes up there, so you had to make your foxhole out of rocks so you had a little protection. One night they let loose. You could see flares coming in and when they started in with us, shooting red flares up, you knew they were going to counterattack. They were coming, hollering and screaming like crazy. But we held. We had good fire power.

STAN SMITH I remember one time, we had relieved an outfit on outpost. They had a two-man listening post set up with sound power and headphones. They hadn't manned theirs that night 'cause they knew they were being relieved. I was to take two men out and man it, to set them up on that listening post. We followed the wires out, basically to know where we were going. It's funny now but it wasn't then; but I spotted what I thought was a silhouette of a soldier. It had to be an enemy because it was in no-man's-land. I'm sneaking up on this guy and got close enough. It turned out to be a fir tree. You're scared, you're shaking and yet, here it is nothing. We laughed about it afterwards. I got them set up and had to go back to my squad. We were always on hills. I was trying to get back up this one hill and it was coated with packed snow and ice. I'd get almost to the top and then slip and slide all the way back to the bottom. It took me about three or four tries before I finally got back up there, but every enemy in the country knew I was there because you could hear me. Those are just things you remember afterwards.

ELROY ROEDER I'll never forget it, on Christmas Eve, I was there. All night long, the enemy had loudspeakers up, and they were playing Christmas carols for us guys. Every once in a while they'd yell to tell us we should surrender and be home for the New Year's. But it was nice that they played that. We really got a kick out of it, sitting out there and listening to those Christmas carols. All night long they'd play those things, those old loudspeakers blaring away. We never tried to silence them either. It was cold. We didn't have clothes like you have nowadays. You were lucky if you had underwear.

We only got a change of clothes maybe once a month if we were lucky. If you went back for reinforcement, if they had any clothes there, they'd give them to you, but if they didn't fit, you throw them back on a pile. We'd take a bath in a river or a creek. They didn't have showers. Sometimes we'd wash ourselves in snow and shave a little bit. The main thing was the meal. Christmas Day they brought turkey back, a nice hot turkey meal for us, and ice cream. Boy, was that a treat. We were eating and all of a sudden, here come the shells. It was good, too. It tasted like regular, homemade ice cream from the big buckets. It was really good.

STAN SMITH The enemy knew more about us than we knew about them, I think. I think it was mostly Chinese. At Christmastime, the Chinese played Christmas carols on loudspeakers. They were our Christmas carols, and between carols they would have a supposed American POW talk. He'd tell us how good he had it and that we should surrender and come over, that we'd get good food and good treatment. They'd drop airbursts from artillery rounds with leaflets in them saying how good it was. They dropped Christmas cards to us that were nicer Christmas cards than we were given to send home. They would sneak up at night by our barbed-wire fences in front of us, and they had cloth handkerchiefs that were tied with little bundles with candy in them. We'd find them in the mornings. You wouldn't hear them; you didn't know they were there at night or you would have been shooting at them. Supposedly, they were very poor night fighters, but I don't believe it. They were very good.

They had work battalions, as I understand it, that dug their trenches, built their bunkers. The soldiers themselves didn't do it. I think they were civilians. We'd find trenches were eight or ten feet deep, and this was tough digging. We were lucky if we had a trench that was deep enough to hide in, but they had bunkers built out of logs. You didn't find that many trees over there. I don't know where they were getting them. I mean, there were trees but they weren't that big. They had bunkers that were just immaculate. They'd line them with small saplings and heat them with charcoal. That was an advantage to us because you could smell them. You know, they say you can smell your enemy. We weren't supposed to use colognes or anything because it might smell. Several times we were in positions where we could use their bunkers. They faced the right direction and we could actually use their bunker, and they were much nicer than anything we ever had. You know, what bunkers we had were sandbags, and a lot of times, all you did was stretch a poncho over the top, just to keep the rain out. You had nothing there to stop mortar rounds or anything like that.

Christmas in Korea

He crouches in his foxhole cold,
and stares at mountains bleak and old,
around the snow lies thick and white,
it is the soldiers' Christmas night.

For angels' songs a whistling shell,
for peace on earth the hellish yell
of killers drugged with assigned hate.
Dear God, did Christmas come too late?

Oh little town the thought is blurred,
his childish memories are stirred,
while well-taught hands the death march
    play,
against the foe this Christmas day.

The dead ask why at Christmastide
some strangers fought and some have died.
For peace on earth, good will toward men,
a home-sick boy cries, "Where, oh when?"

ROGER LEWISON I wrote this poem just before Christmas in 1950. We had just had Christmas dinner. The weather was very cold. The food was very cold. Coffee froze before you could drink it. I was sitting about a hundred yards from my tank in a brushy area. I don't remember what I wrote it on. I think it was an ammo box. I said, "I think I'll sit down and see if I can write this." So I wrote it and I sent it to my girlfriend in Ames, Iowa, and she had it put in the Des Moines newspaper. I also sent a copy to the *Stars and Stripes*. I could never remember the entire poem. All I could remember was the first part. I used to tell my kids about it: "This is a poem your daddy wrote." My youngest daughter said, "Daddy, where did you say that poem was published?" I said, "The *Stars and Stripes*." I don't know how she did it but she found it and didn't tell me that she'd done it. So for my birthday last year, she hands it to me. That's just how to make an old guy cry.

ELROY ROEDER Most of the time, we were on the move with patrols. I was on patrol one night with the French battalion. I volunteered, which I don't think I should have done, but I did anyway. Nobody else would go so I just volunteered, because of buddy-buddy stuff. I was on one side of the radio operator, and there was a guy who was a forward observer with a .50-caliber machine gun. We were on patrol and I was up on a ridge. We were going along, walking and walking and walking. I said to my partner, "You smell something? It's garlic." He said, "Chinese eat a lot of garlic. You smell garlic, you're getting pretty close." All of a sudden, everything let loose. Those Frenchmen, you couldn't understand them. I didn't know what was going on. Finally, the commander there — he could talk a little English — he says, "You're on your own." I said to myself, "Holy cow, now I can get out of here." I came to a ridge, so I said to my partner, "Let's jump. It's the only way we can get out of here." And we did. We hit some sand down below and didn't get hurt. Then we found our way back to the lines after that.

Elroy Roeder writes a letter home. *Elroy Roeder*

Nighttime finding your way through the minefields…They're all marked when you're on patrol, but you go back on your own and try to find them markers.

I thought I would be captured that night. It was either be captured or killed or take a chance at getting back and going through the minefield. We took the chance going back, and we made it. I could see there were no rocks below the cliff. It looked like sand, which it was. It wasn't too high of a jump, maybe ten, fifteen feet. When I got up there and I told that guy, I said, "That's our only chance out of here, so we got to jump. Either that or get captured. You can fight, but the Chinese are all around us." They were talking, jabbering like crazy. So we jumped and we made it. It seemed like we were in the air forever, but it didn't last that long. I said to my partner, "Now we got to go through a minefield. If we can find that path, it'll be all right." We found it without flashlights. The worst part of it was I was going to go home in a couple more days. I had my time in. I just volunteered because I thought it was going to be a piece of cake. I liked to go with the Frenchmen because every time you went on patrol, they always had a big meal with French bread and wine. They shaved and really spruced themselves up when they went. The French put perfume on. The Chinese could smell them, too, I guess. They really screwed themselves. They looked like they were going to a wedding or something. I had a good buddy, he was a Frenchman. His name was Luc. I wonder what happened to that guy after I left there. He and I were always chumming around together, 'cause we were in the same outfit. We had a lot of fun. I don't know if he ever lived through Korea. He was quite a guy.

STAN SMITH One time when we were in a fixed position, we had a bunker that was set up with a .30-caliber machine gun in it, so we were manning that. We had a boy by the name of Matthew Walls. He was African American and he was manning the machine gun one night. I used to try and go stay with each man for a while, at night, when we'd be on alert, because you hate to be alone. Everybody's afraid and if there are two of you, you feel better. I would try to go from position to position. I went down and was in with Walls in this bunker. He was quiet for a while and then pretty soon he says, "Smitty," he says, "I don't know if I'm that scared or that cold," and I couldn't help but laugh, because I felt exactly the same way.

You're sitting there, you're shaking, you're cold and you're scared. You would kind of relax, but then you go back to shaking again, and I felt exactly the same way he did. I didn't know if I was that cold or that scared.

ELROY ROEDER There was one hill we were going to one time. We were heading back for the line again on trucks and we got a flat tire. We waited and waited and waited and the convoy went by us. Finally, a wrecker came and put a tire on. It was getting late already, and the driver really didn't know where he was going. We were driving and driving and driving, and we knew he was going north and north all the time. He was going to hit some pretty soon. We were all sitting in the back of the truck and we didn't know what he was doing. Finally, we came to a spot that must've been a little encampment. We asked if we could stay overnight there and the guys said yes. "You can stay a couple hours, but we're moving out." So we stayed there a couple hours in that truck and then took off again before daylight. We were driving along and all of a sudden, we're on the front lines. Funny we never got shot at. It was daylight already. The driver finally found our outfit and we never got shot at. We must have driven a couple of miles on that road and you could see where the enemy was. The guys were all dug in there. Oh man, I was glad to get off that truck. If you follow the convoy, you won't get lost, but you get a flat tire and you sit there. The driver was lost. Everybody got ahead of us and he didn't know where he was going. The guys were all laughing when we came in.

The object was to take the highest hills, I guess. There was always a valley below the hill. There were roads down there and you could observe the enemy troop movements down below. When we took hills, you could look down at night and see the trucks driving, the Chinese and Korean trucks hauling supplies or taking them out along the roads. You couldn't call in fire power because the airplanes didn't fly at night. Nowadays, they do. You could call in artillery, but sometimes artillery couldn't reach them. When we took this one hill, that's when we had the Chinese really on the go. It was above the 38th parallel already. We would have kept on going and we would have won that war so fast. We had them on the go. They left their supplies behind or their clothes or guns because they were running. That's how fast we were out taking the hills. All of a sudden they stopped us. It was the end of the war. I'd say that's when the armistice was being talked about, I guess. When they stopped us, we had to come back again to where the 38th was.

A typical Korean War bunker, reinforced with sandbags and logs. *Art Braatz*

STAN SMITH You never questioned. If they said, "You're taking out a patrol tonight," and it's thirty below zero, you never questioned it. You just did it. I don't know if that's the way you're trained or what, but you know, when you're in the Army, you do what you're told. "Ours is not to question why, ours is but to do or die." That was your choice.

ELROY ROEDER I came back home to get my job back and my boss, when I left, didn't know I was in the service. He never missed me. When I got off that ship, I took my uniform off already because people looked down at you, they really did. It was like Vietnam. I come home and we never had a big celebration, like they do now. You came home on a troop ship into Oakland, California. I remember I went underneath the Golden Gate Bridge; I seen that. I went to get my job back and the guy wouldn't hire me. I had to go through channels. I got the name of a service officer who took care of veterans. His first name was Casey. I'll never forget that; he was a heck of a nice guy. He got on the telephone and he chewed that guy up. Man, oh man. I couldn't believe it. He says, "You go over there and if you don't get your job back, you come right back." He said, "We'll get that guy." I went over there and talked to him. He gave me the old, "OK, I'll hire you, but I'll have to lay the other guy off." I told him, "I quit." I said if I had to work under those conditions, he'd probably fire me anyway. So I quit.

People are funny. I came home on a train on leave once, after basic. I was sitting on the train with my uniform on and people moved away from me, as if I was dirt. That got me. Everybody I talked to overseas had the same problem. I didn't talk to anybody about it. The first time I talked was to you guys [the interviewers]. I never talked to my wife or my mother or dad or anybody else about it. They questioned me a couple of times, but you talk about it and they don't believe you anyway. That's the whole problem. Veterans don't like to talk about the war experience because the stories aren't believable. They think that you're making it up. It bothered me the first couple of months I was home. If I'd talked about it more maybe it would've bothered me more because then the memories would've come back, with all the buddies I lost.

STAN SMITH I never felt that anybody was looking down on me, like they plainly did at the Vietnam boys. While I was in the hospital, two businessmen in Cumberland started writing to me. The only way they knew me was I had played basketball and football in high school and I had worked in a hardware store there when I enlisted in the service. One of them worked in the post office. He would write to me periodically and send me cartoons out of magazines and newspapers. He'd cut them out and put them in with the letter. The other fellow was part owner of a lumber yard. Cumberland is a small town, less than two thousand. He would walk uptown Saturday night on one street, cross over, and walk down the other side and go into all the stores. When he'd write to me, it was just like you were walking with him. He'd tell you who he met, what they talked about. It was kind of fun, you know, to get letters like that. They were my people and they apparently didn't look down on us. I never felt that. People still thought maybe we were doing the right thing. I still think we were. Vietnam, I'm not sure. I feel for those boys and I feel for the boys today in Iraq. I'm not sure that we should be where we are and they should be doing what they're doing. I feel sorry for them. You got to support them since they are there.

9 ★ Jets

"You'd be talking to someone the night before they went out on a flight and the next morning you'd see their name on the board, missing in action, or didn't return home, so it took a toll on your emotions, but you had to go on. You had to try to put a smile on your face and keep going." — *Valedda Wilson*

Most of the combat seen by soldiers in Korea took the form of an intense, bloody, and grueling ground war like the ongoing battle at Heartbreak Ridge. Yet the action in Korea included a vigorous air war as well, as U.N. jets confronted North Korean, Chinese, and Soviet planes throughout the three-year conflict. Indeed, the appearance of the impressive MiG fighter in November 1950 — flown by both Chinese and Soviet pilots — shocked U.N. troops, sparking a struggle for air supremacy over North Korea. Nevertheless, through the use of planes such as the F-84 Thunderjet and the F-86 Sabre Jet and extensive training programs, U.S. pilots were able to hold their own in Korea.

The air war in Korea was not just about air combat. Planes served a variety of functions in the war, from close support for ground fighting to reconnaissance photography before and after battles to large-scale bombings of roads and bridges to prevent movement of Communist troops and supplies. The central role given to air support and air war in Korea reflected the experiences of World War II, where many believed that wide-scale bombing of cities and industrial areas in Germany and Japan — including the atomic bomb — had been key to the Allied victory. Reflecting this belief that the future of combat was in the air, the Air Force was elevated into a separate service branch in 1947. The Korean War, therefore, represented the first test of the Air Force as its own branch of military service, though it continued to work closely with the Army to offer air support to ground operations (the Navy and the Marines had their own air branches).

Although this widespread belief in the importance of air power reflected the experiences of World War II, the Korean War saw fundamental changes to both air combat and air-based support operations. First among these changes was the development of the jet engine: Korea was the first war to involve extensive combat between jet aircraft, which also included the widespread use of aircraft carriers. Jets flew more smoothly, powerfully, and comfortably than World War II–era planes and were less likely to have technical problems; as Wisconsin veteran John Hotvedt explained his first experience with a jet, "I taxied out to the end of the runway...I ran it up and down and checked it all out, 100 percent power. It was pretty exhilarating." Most air missions took off from Kimpo Airfield, outside Seoul, where the pilots stayed in small Quonset huts. Every night, headquarters would send orders listing the number of aircraft and missions required for the next day, ranging from close cover for combat operations to routine bombing patrols. The planes would take off the next morning in a display described by Art Gale as "the most god-awful noise you'd ever heard in your life."

Korea was also the first war marked by the widespread use of helicopters. Though the helicopter is often seen as a symbol of Vietnam, it performed similar functions in Korea, particularly retrieving downed and wounded pilots. This ability to rescue downed pilots — even those stranded in North Korea — was an enormous boost to U.N. morale and improved the quality of medical care given by doctors and nurses to wounded GIs, much of which took place at nearby military hospitals in Japan. As in Vietnam, however, U.N. forces in Korea also faced the problem of fighting an extraordinary mobile and foot-based enemy. Though U.N. planes bombed North Korean roads and bridges extensively, they were never able to smother enemy supply lines, which North Korean and Chinese soldiers exploited around the clock. Still, it is clear that air support played a central role in allowing U.N. forces to stay strong in Korea. Ultimately, Korea changed the nature of air warfare, spawning major technological advances and laying the groundwork for Vietnam.

John Hotvedt, Amherst Junction (Navy, VC-61 Composite Squadron)
Art Gale, Onalaska (Air Force, 49th Fighter-Bomber Wing)
Valedda Wilson, Green Bay (Air Force Nurse Corps)

John Hotvedt in the cockpit of the F9F Panther, which he flew for pre-strike and post-strike photo reconnaissance missions. *John Hotvedt*

JOHN HOTVEDT After a couple of buddies of mine got into flying, it was the one thing I wanted to do. About three of us went at the same time and some of us stayed together right through all of World War II. I always wanted to be a fighter, not a torpedo bomber or a lighter than air or helicopter, at that time. There weren't any then; the Korean War had the first helicopters I saw. I was fortunate I got into flying Hellcats in World War II. After the war, I was in an experimental unit out in Virginia for a while. I got out in 1946 and went back in 1950 at the beginning of the Korean War. I went over there early in 1951 and came back in November '51.

ART GALE I lucked out. I got into the Air Force. I went down to the Navy, and they were full. The Marines were full. I knew the Army was on my tail and so I jumped into the Air Force, and the day that I was supposed to go down and be sworn in, I got my draft notice. I asked the guy what to do, and he said to send it back.

Basic was eight weeks. If you were kind of cocky, a good drill instructor would take care of that real quick. They humiliated you and put you down to where they could make something out of you. It was great. I think everybody, especially these young children now, eighteen or twenty years old, should spend a year in the service. We went to Oakland, California. It was great out there. Colder than the blazes in the morning, hot in the afternoon, colder than the blazes in the evening. You'd change your uniform three times a day. There were fifteen weeks of school that was pretty much all aircraft at Oakland Municipal Airport, which was very close to San Francisco. From there we went to Chanute, Illinois, and that's where I got my jet training. I loved that.

VALEDDA WILSON I really wanted to be a chemistry teacher, but nine of my high school classmates were going to that same college and my father said, "No, no, you'll only learn 'campusology,'" so I went into nursing at age seventeen at Lutheran Hospital, in Sioux City, Iowa. When I joined the Air Force I had just finished six months postgraduate work in operating-room tech-

Valedda Wilson originally wanted to teach high school chemistry, but went into nursing instead at the urging of her father. She enlisted in the Air Force in May 1951, hoping to travel. By July 1952 she was at K8 in Kunsan, South Korea.
Valedda Wilson

nique and management at Baylor University Hospital in Dallas, Texas. One of my classmates had been a Navy nurse and was going back into the Navy, and she said, "Why don't you join one of the branches of the service, because you like operating-room work and you like emergency-room work and you'll do a lot of that in the service." I applied to get a commission in the Air Force because it was the only branch of the service that let you go outside of the United States in less than two years. I was hoping to travel. I didn't care whether it was Europe, the Far East, or what, but the Korean War was going on, so obviously that was where we were going to be going. I went in May of '51. By October of '51 I was in Japan, and by July of '52 I was in Korea.

JOHN HOTVEDT One guy I deployed with — Herb Tompkins was his name and he was killed sometime later — said to me, "I think I'm going to take the next detachment out and it's going to be jets." I said, "Well, I don't want to sit around here forever, so how about I go along?" He says, "Well, I'll talk to the bossman." I reported to COMAIRPAC, Commander Pacific, and they said, "Can you fly jets?" and I said, "For one who hasn't, as well as the next guy." Howard Cruise was the XO [executive officer]. There was just the one plane and a lot of people wanted to fly it. With the old Hellcat, almost all of them were spitting oil and your windscreen would be covered. You had to stick your head out and wipe it off your goggles coming around for a landing. With the Panther you just sat up there in that bubble and could see everything. No bugs, no oil, no nothing. It was nice. The conditions in the cockpit were pretty good. You didn't need much room. Shoulder to wall. Everything was right there. The cockpit was real comfortable. So Cruise said to me, "Work out the handbook exam and meet me here tomorrow morning. We'll get you checked out." I went through all the procedures; you have to really study that handbook, for the first time. It ended up he got up on the wing and showed me how to start it and I taxied out to the end of the runway with him standing on the wing. I ran it up and checked it all out, 100 percent power. It was pretty exhilarating. Then he said, "Idle her down." Then he got off. "Go." So I did. I came back in the afternoon and did the same thing again and on Sunday, too. So by Monday, I was a pro. I had three flights in already.

While in the Air Force in Korea, Art Gale worked as a mechanic on F-84 Thunder Jets. *Art Gale*

ART GALE We flew over to Korea. We landed in the trench at night. They put us in the transit barracks and there must probably have been maybe twenty-five or thirty of us. We were the replacements for the guys that had been there and seen the worst of it. That night we all got in bed, and we were woken at around four thirty in the morning by the most god-awful noise you'd ever heard in your life. There were three squadrons in the 49th and then the Air National Guard. Now, I'm not sure which one it was; I thought it was Alabama, but I couldn't swear to it. Anyway, they had several flights there also. If it was a maximum effort, that would put it at somewhere like one hundred airplanes in the air. You get three different flights taking off, fifteen minutes apart, and anywhere from fifteen to twenty airplanes in each flight, and that can generate a lot of noise. It was a hell of a wake-up call. That was what we were going to hear every day from now on.

We were brand spanking new, green as grass, and we're going to go down and watch the airplanes take off. Well, this is fine. Here they go. We're maybe the length of a football field away from the runway. Of course I'm eager beaver; I'm right up in front. I'm the point guard. I'm up there watching everything. Something falls off this airplane as it's taking off. It bounces down the runway in front of us and I turn around. "What the heck is that?" Everybody's lying on the ground. It was a thousand-pound bomb. If it had gone off, that would have been the end of everybody. It wasn't armed, thank God.

Art Gale with fellow airplane technicians. Art is pictured third from left. *Art Gale*

The F-84 Thunder Jet was Art Gale's favorite plane. *Art Gale*

Fixing jet engines, I liked that; that was a good duty. I excelled. I don't want to brag, but I was very good at it. It was different. The gasoline engine, the reciprocating piston engine had been around a long, long time. This jet hadn't. This was new, just like everything else. It was different and it was something very few people knew how it worked. They did a great job teaching it, they really did. They had just built the B-47, which had the J-47 engine in it. The fighters had the F-84 Thunderjet that I worked on in Korea, which had the J-35 engine in it. It was a really good airplane. It was the workhorse of Korea. It would carry bombs, rockets, and napalm. It had eight machine guns that could just rip up something real bad. They did a lot of strafing with it. They did a lot of low flying and of course that was where they got caught so badly. The 49th Fighter/Bomber Wing lost a lot of airplanes, we really did.

VALEDDA WILSON It was like going from day to night: the smells, driving on the opposite side of the road. There were five of us that went. Two went to one hospital and two went to another hospital. I went by myself to FEAMCOM [Far Eastern Air Material Command] right outside of Tachikawa, Japan, where they brought in all the planes from Korea, which we triaged whenever they came in.

I started over to K-8 by way of Seoul, and we had a blackout while I was in Seoul, so I had to spend the night there. The next day I was on a plane

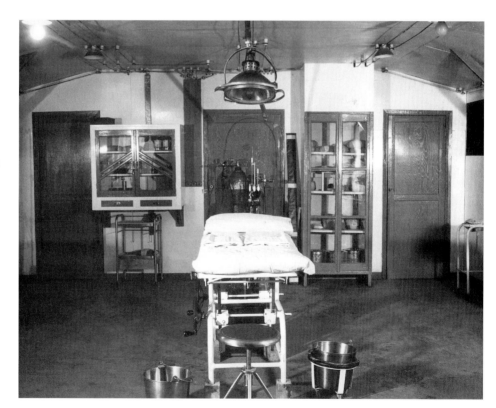

Valedda Wilson recalls the operating room as a Quonset hut with cement floors. Nurses used two-by-fours to set surgical instruments on. *Valedda Wilson*

headed into K-8. I got off the plane and they handed me a .45, and I looked at them and said, "Well, if I've got to carry this thing, someone's going to have to teach me how to use it." I said, "I can shoot a rifle, but a handgun, no." So one of the fellows said, "OK, I'll teach you how to use it because I don't think it'd do too much good throwing it at somebody." I learned to shoot that .45 quite efficiently. We didn't have red crosses on our helmets even though we were medics, because they said that, for the guerillas and stuff, that was just a bull's eye. If they could get rid of the medical people they figured that a lot of other people wouldn't survive.

K-8 is south and I would guess you'd say west of Seoul, nine miles from Red China. That's why sometimes little planes would come under that radar from Red China and shove bombs out of the cockpit filled with broken glass and rusty nails. When that happened, air-raid sirens would go off, and everybody that lived on medical row usually sat on their helmets in the middle of the street instead of the bomb shelter, which was right down from the Korean latrine, which didn't smell very good. So we didn't go in, though I imagine if they started dropping bombs we probably would have, but they didn't drop them on medical row at all. This was a base that had been set up by the Japanese after World War II, when they occupied Korea. We had Quonset huts that we lived in, and a Quonset hut for the hospital. The operating room had cement floors, and there was a medical ward on one side and an H-shaped hospital with the surgery ward on the other, and the X-ray and surgery on the line in between the two. There were no inside walls; you used two-by-fours as a table to set things on.

JOHN HOTVEDT My first mission over Korea, I had an easy one, I guess. We flew photo missions. We photographed troop movements and bridges prestrike and poststrike. Damage assessment was what it was mostly about. We didn't have any air opposition, really, at that time. The Air Force had already pretty well taken care of what they did have there. Our fighters, they were strafing; railroads were their biggest target. They were also bombing bridges to cut down on supply capabilities. I did a lot of trail mapping, too, at a little higher altitude where you could pick out gun emplacements and antiaircraft emplacements. There were a lot of them, too. It wasn't quite as severe, except for the small-arms fire, as World War II. The big thing we ran into at low altitude was that small-arms fire. We always had an armed escort with us. Most of our stuff was quite low, but we hadn't had many jets over there yet, so they were shooting behind us mostly.

John Hotvedt with photo reconnaissance pilots and crew. Hotvedt is pictured bottom row, second from left. *John Hotvedt*

Photo crews took aerial pictures of Korea to map terrain, view damage, and plan strategies. *John Hotvedt*

The camera was in the nose section. There were technicians who would load the cameras and then haul them; we called them photo mates, that did all that. They were extremely great guys. We set up our own little lab after a while on the carrier and we developed a lot of the stuff ourselves as soon as we came down. With the poststrike damage assessment, it was always interesting to see if there was anything left to go for. They were ingenious; they could rebuild a bridge overnight with something or other. We didn't have a lot of the same targets then, of course, as we had in World War II. They still were formidable with that antiaircraft and on the ground; they had hordes of people fighting. That was really tough on our troops with the losses.

ART GALE The 84 wasn't a bad airplane to work on because of the fact that the intake was quite high. You could walk under without your head being at the intake. The 86 was on the ground, it was that low. You walked in front of that thing when she's running up and you're inside it. That did happen. Not once, but several times. Walking around the backend of the airplane was a different story. You didn't get sucked up, but just knocked over. The gas coming out of it is pretty warm. If you got close to it once, that was enough. You knew what to look out for.

We had three or four flights a day. They would be anywhere from an hour and a half to two hours gone. You went early and you went late. You made sure your airplane was ready to go when it was supposed to. The pilot would come back and if he had a red "X" on that puppy, you knew you had big trouble. Something had grounded it. If it had a red diagonal line, there was a problem but it could fly. It was safe. If it had a red "X," it meant it was done.

JOHN HOTVEDT What we felt bad about most of the time, we had so many good friends in the Bitterbirch Corsair Squadron, and I think they lost ten of their twenty-four. In short order, shot down by small-arms fire on their close air support. I was thankful that I was in jets over there because we didn't have any real bad losses. But the guys flying the Old Hose Nose Corsairs, they had it rough. They were in there right close air support with the troops. We had chopper helicopters with us that always flew plane guard behind us and when somebody would go in the drink, they were right there to pick them up. We had a few we lost. I guess we lost more jets off the front end of the carrier, due to bad cat shot or something like that, that landed in the water in front of the carrier. The captain of the carrier always managed to get the thing heeled over enough and the pilot got picked up in short order. The secret to landing on a carrier at that time was a good landing signal officer. It was speed control, and you had to be lined up. You had to learn not to dive for the deck. It's supposed to be at the right speed so when they give you the cut...They don't cut now. In those days, the cut was mandatory. There had to be good coordination between the pilot and the LSO. The LSOs got to know each pilot pretty well. They had pretty savvy boys. Coming in on the deck, you had to rely on the LSO. You could see it way back when you lined up. But all his signals would tell you to come on, or when you

John Hotvedt performed carrier landings with the Panther after photo missions. *John Hotvedt*

were fast. You watched the carrier all the way around until you picked up the landing signal officer at the approach.

We'd fly any one of the four planes. I had one that I was a little partial to but whatever came up was fine. They were identical. Sometimes I'd do the poststrike on the same flight as the prestrike. I'd just go in there ahead for the prestrike and it wouldn't take long. I would just fly around while the strike happened and do the poststrike immediately after. We were flying quite a few missions there toward the last. We were running six missions every two days. So with four pilots, we averaged one and a half missions a day in the last couple of months. This wasn't much in terms of what they had done in later wars. Being a photo pilot, you didn't have to do any night work. That was kind of nice.

ART GALE We had different pilots on our planes. These guys flew a lot. If they flew once a day, that was too damn much. With three flights or four flights a day, you couldn't ask one guy to do that. Each unit had an airplane that was a pilot assigned to your airplane, but if he flew your airplane three times a month that was pretty good. Usually it was a different pilot, but you got to know these guys. You got to know them. The pilots would tell you where they were going. If they were going to the bridges maybe they'd be back in two hours, maybe they wouldn't be back. If it was strafing, that wasn't so bad. They had a little flight plan and while you're strapping them in and getting them ready, you talked with him a little bit. "Where you going today?" "A milk run." You know, "Hey, good." If he was quiet and really concerned, it wasn't a milk run. He would be worried, of course, and justifiably so.

A lot of our airplanes got shot down. We lost a lot of planes. Their wingman would come in too close and one bomb would blow up and maybe hit something big and it would blow up and they had to fly through it. My airplane, the 537, the guy got it in the cockpit and never knew what hit him. I talked to his wingman and it was just one big puff. That was the end of it. It was kind of tough. I knew the guy.

VALEDDA WILSON It was in the evening, and I had just stepped out the shower when I got the call that they needed me in the operating room. My replacement was there, but I beat her to the operating room, because I knew when they called that there'd been an explosion on the flight line. By the time I got there, there were litters on the floor in the operating room, and we had to triage them and start operating. It was a pretty hectic night and I think I was up seventy-two hours without sleep, as I had been up all that day before it happened, and we operated continuously. Surprisingly, you can do it. You were busy, and then you sort of got rubber knees when everything was finished. Course then you had the memories and you couldn't get to sleep, so it was a rough three days. There were only eight nurses stationed at the K-8, including me, so there was only seven to rotate the shifts on the floors. When you figure there were three shifts every twenty-four hours, there wasn't much time off for people. I was the only operating-room nurse, so anytime the surgery was in session, I was there, day or night.

It was emotionally difficult, especially when it was somebody that you had known before they got injured. In Korea, we had patients that I had known before they became patients. One time we had a faulty bomb explode on the flight line, and we ended up with several people, two of whom I had known prior to their injury. One was a young man who had just had a newborn son. He was a football player, and he was talking about getting home to teach his boy how to play football, and he lost both legs in this accident. Luckily, he survived, but one of the other young men that I knew did not. It could be very emotional at times. You'd be talking to someone the night before they went out on a flight and the next morning you'd see their name on the board, missing in action, or didn't return home, so it took a toll on your emotions, but you had to go on. You had to try to put a smile on your face and keep going.

As an operating-room nurse, you see a lot. We'd operate for three days, and then we'd go out to the ward and help take care of the patients we had operated on. Most of them were like your kid brother, about your age or younger. A lot of them were eighteen, nineteen, or twenty years old, and I was a few years beyond that. You got used to some horrendous wounds. I'll always remember one young man who had the craziest sense of humor. He had a wound from his ankle all the way up to his hip bone, but yet he kept the whole ward in stitches day after day, because he just was that type of person. He went from bed to bed, teasing people. I don't remember his name, but I remember his wound and his funny sense of humor. You remember mostly the good part of being there and not the bad. The bad gives you nightmares. You could have good times, but mostly it was pretty serious times.

JOHN HOTVEDT It was pretty cut and dried as far as our photo missions were concerned. We knew from day to day just what we were going to do, pretty much, except for small-arms fire and your normal difficulties on- and off-carrier. You didn't ever really look forward to any of your missions. It's never a sure thing. It's a job. You knew you were going, and you had to prepare both physically and mentally.

Korea from up high looked like all mountains. You wonder where they were getting their food, really. I didn't see too much of South Korea, just North Korea. I don't think South Korea was probably as mountainous. It was more agriculture, and more widespread hills. But further north you got up toward the border and all that, it was rough terrain. You always wondered, "Where am I going to set this thing down if I have to?" They had good ejection seats. You could get out of a troublesome airplane very quickly, but I never had to. My fighter escort never had to save me. We never had any air oppositions. Once in a while, he'd go down and strafe and I'd wait around. I made another pass or something like that if we found a good juicy target. Generally, the job was just to be along in case of any trouble. You got a different one every time you went up.

We flew altitudes anywhere from the ground up. I did some trail mapping at twenty thousand feet. Those were a piece of cake. The lowest was a couple hundred feet, oftentimes under five hundred. They always tried to set you a limit, but it didn't always work. There wasn't too much need for getting a lot lower than that.

ART GALE Not everybody that went down was lost. Some of them went down in the ocean, some of them went down in friendly territory, and some of them made it halfway back and had to bail out. We didn't lose all, all our pilots. Thank God.

VALEDDA WILSON We were the only American women in the area. It seemed anybody that got a "Dear John" letter ended up coming up to talk to one of the nurses. You'd think you were going to stay home for the evening, and take a shower and wash your hair, which never dried, and you'd walk out and the living room would be full of people wanting to talk to you. I know after I got back to the States I was stationed at Midwest City, Oklahoma, right outside of Oklahoma City. One of my sergeants was from Oklahoma City, and about four of the other corpsmen came into Oklahoma City to visit him, and they called me and said, "We're taking you out to dinner. We were lucky. We met fellows that hadn't seen an American woman to talk to the whole time they were there and we had you to talk to every day of the week."

I came home in March of 1953, just before they started exchanging wounded prisoners of war. I was at my parents' on leave when I heard it on the radio. My dear mother says, "And what are you thinking?" and I said, "I'm thinking I wish I was there setting up one of those tents." She said to me, "Don't you dare volunteer to go back." Some of them were people that I had known whose planes had gone down or something and they didn't reappear, so if they were prisoners, and were going to be returning, I would have loved to have been there to take care of them.

JOHN HOTVEDT I was back in the States in November of '51. The war continued on for a year and a half past that. I was glad to be out of it, but I think they were still getting pretty well shot at. But it was pretty discouraging a lot of times when you'd hear these discussions going on aimlessly.

VALEDDA WILSON I knew why I had gone, and I had a job to do and I tried to do it to the best of my ability. So I never felt that the almost nine years I spent working for the United States Air Force Nurse Corps was a bad thing at all. I was regular Air Force when I got married, and back then if you got married, got pregnant, they told you good-bye, whereas now, women can stay in. My daughter-in-law was one week from delivering a baby when she was promoted to lieutenant colonel, so things have changed.

10 United Nations

"They sent me sixteen South Koreans. I called myself the 'United Nations Platoon' because I had four Guamanians, four Puerto Ricans, and sixteen South Koreans." — Jim Mendyke

Though the main participants in the Korean War were the United States, North and South Korea, and China, Korea was an international war. South Korea and the United States made up 90 percent of the U.N. forces, but more than fifteen countries sent soldiers, who came from six continents, and other countries sent support missions, especially medical support. The U.N. forces included not only France, Australia, and Great Britain, but also Ethiopia, Thailand, Turkey, and the Philippines. Other nations sent money, food, and battlefield supplies as well as aircraft, ships, and ambulances. Indeed, more than half of the military casualties were not Korean and the Korean War was the first war to be fought under the guise of the United Nations. U.N. forces fought both in separate national groups and as a combined international force; all U.N. forces, however, were under the command of General Douglas MacArthur and, later, General Matthew Ridgway as commander in chief, United Nations Command.

As the experiences of Wisconsin veterans Lee Haspl and Jim Mendyke demonstrate, fighting with an international force had its fair share of difficulties, not the least of which was language and communication. As Mendyke noted, "I called myself the 'United Nations Platoon' because I had four Guamanians, four Puerto Ricans, and sixteen South Koreans...I didn't have an interpreter and that is not easy when they can't understand me or me them! But we made it." Communication difficulties sometimes did lead to frictions between American and international troops, especially South Korean troops, as they were the other largest battlefield contingent. South Korean personnel also served in KATUSA (Korean Augmentation to the United States Army) units, a program that employed Korean recruits in American units. Though the program initially struggled — the Korean recruits often received no training before joining their assigned units — Korean soldiers proved particularly helpful in patrolling and scouting, and also helped to move heavy equipment. The KATUSA program is still in place today. Korean civilians, many of whom were displaced by the war, also played a vital combat support role through the Korean Service Corps, carrying supplies, food, and ammunition to the front lines and, when needed, removing wounded soldiers. Anticommunist North Koreans who left the North and wanted to support the U.N. war effort were also utilized in guerrilla units, aided and organized by the American Eighth Army.

The U.N. forces were not the only international war effort. On the North Korean side, the People's Republic of China sent thousands of soldiers, while the Soviet Union provided large-scale material assistance. Even though the Soviet Union was not formally part of the war, Soviet pilots flew combat missions around the Yalu River area. Like the U.N. forces, the North Korean and Chinese militaries suffered their own conflicts, particularly between the leadership of the two states. The Korean War thus truly was a global event and can be seen as a precursor to the international peace-keeping missions that are central to the United Nations' role in the world today.

Lee Haspl, Madison (Army, 25th Division)
Jim Mendyke, Stevens Point (Army, 45th Division)

LEE HASPL It started for me in Prague, which is now the Czech Republic. I was born in a war. I was eight years old when the war began for us in Europe. When the Germans marched into Prague, it lasted six years. Six years is long; it's a lifetime. It was a pretty scary time. My mother was also born in Europe but came to the United States when she was a little girl and spoke American English without an accent. So she spoke to me in English and my father spoke to me in Czech and I became bilingual. I do have an accent, but perhaps not as bad as some others. She always told me how she was just homesick for the United States. This was in the '30s and of course then the war started and we were stuck there.

I saw some horrible things, during those days. One memorable thing I saw during the war was a dogfight. I was on the roof of our house and I saw an American plane, and a German one was on his tail. The German shot

Top: Lee Haspl sitting on top of Howitzer shells. *Lee Haspl*

Right: Lee Haspl enjoying R&R in Japan. *Lee Haspl*

him and I saw him go down, and I went over there to see if...It made me so sad to see this poor young American fellow die. It sort of made me a little older perhaps than my cousins when I came to the United States. They seemed to me like they were about ten years younger than I was. Six years of war kind of ages you. So I said to myself, "Well, that is the end of wars for me. No more wars."

I planned on going to the United States at my earliest opportunity, which finally came about after the war in 1946. As a matter of fact, the whole family came to the United States, but then they returned, unfortunately. Two years later in '48, the Communists took over. I stayed here and they were over there. So I was on my own from age fourteen on. What really hit me for the first time was the smell of gasoline. I guess it was because of the number of cars in New York. I landed in New York and I got this smell of gasoline. That's the first thing I remember. It was awesome, to see the huge buildings. Before we could dock, we were in the harbor close to the harbor of New York, so I could see the skyline and the Statue of Liberty. I think I got up at about four o'clock in the morning and I couldn't go back to sleep because it was so awesome. I swore, "I'll never go back to Europe. I've had it."

I went to high school in New York. I had a scholarship to a rather prestigious school in Tarrytown, New York, called the Hackley School. I was the poorest student in that place. When the Iron Curtain fell in 1948, I was very fortunate. A family from Illinois, whose son was at that school, befriended me. I was broke; I didn't have any money. They paid for the rest of my education there for the next two years. That was unbelievable! After finishing high school in 1950, I applied to two universities: The University of California, which was my first choice — that's where my parents went to school — but nothing happened. The second one was University of Wisconsin. They accepted me, so off I went to Madison, Wisconsin. When I came to Madison, I had two dollars and fifty cents in my pocket. I got a job and I was going to work and go to school. Well, it didn't work too well. Then I get this letter. I was being drafted. I said to the sergeant who was interviewing us when I went down there, "Hey, look, you know, I'm not a citizen." He said, "Well, if you don't take that one step forward…" They said to us, "Now if you agree with everything, you take one step forward and now you're in the United States Army. If you don't take that first step, then it'll be very difficult for you to become an American citizen later on." Well, I just asked just to be sure. I had no intention of pulling out of this thing. So I went.

Jim Mendyke remembers hearing returning soldiers singing, "You'll be sorry! You'll be sorry!" from the deck of the landing ship tank that took him to Korea.
Jim Mendyke

JIM MENDYKE When I graduated from high school, I was approached by several schools. One of them was Ripon College and they were interested in athletes. Ripon was a Division III school, so they were not allowed to provide athletic scholarships. You could only get a scholarship if you had need. Well, one of the representatives from Ripon came to our home and visited with my mother and she was asked a question: "How much could you afford for your son's education?" So, she was getting into the five or ten dollars a month situation and the representative was the happiest guy in the world because he found an athlete who also had the need situation. I went to Ripon and they took care of everything because we had nothing. One of the conditions was that I take ROTC. The first two years of ROTC are mandatory at Ripon, and my third and fourth year, I took it because they paid $29.85 a month, which I needed to support my meager habits.

Upon graduation, I was commissioned. We went to the infantry school in the same program that all draftees are enlisted in. The only difference was they had to treat us nicer because we outranked them. I kept saying prayers every night that I'd go to Germany. My past background didn't count much in whomever I was praying to's eyes and I ended up in Korea, via Japan. I truly loved the Army and I had planned to make a career of the Army. So, I knew it was good to go to Korea to get that on your record, which might help in the future.

LEE HASPL I was in the U.S. Army. It was kind of exciting at first. I ended up at Camp Chaffee, Arkansas, for basic training, which was in 105-mm artillery. I thought maybe I could get to Europe. I have a facility for languages, so I took some language exams in the Army, and I thought, "Well, maybe I'll end up in something to do with translation or whatnot." After basic training, there was another course to take, a leadership course, which I took because that gave you another two or three weeks of not going overseas. Then they decided, "Well, you took all these language tests and one experience you don't have, that's Korea. So maybe that's what you should do, go to Korea and learn a little Korean." I sort of got a butterfly in my stomach. Fear, really fear. I knew nothing of Korea when I was drafted. I was in my first semester here of school. That's when the Korean War started and I had a roommate who one morning had a telephone call and it was his brother who was killed in Korea. So, I knew what was going on. That was about the last place on earth I wanted to go to. I thought Europe would be about where I should go with my background.

Anyhow, I got to Japan and we ended up at some old Japanese World War II Army base. The next day, we were in a big area, like a football field, and they started calling names. And they would announce the outfit and where people were going and some were ending up in Japan. I thought, "Well, gee, this would be pretty good duty." They had no occupation. I could stand that. And then my name came up. 25th Infantry Division, Korea. And that's when I got that butterfly again. I was scared. In the next day or two, we were on a boat to Inchon where we got off, and then they put us on a train and then on a jeep. I was a replacement into my outfit and actually, I felt pretty good. I got into my outfit with bag and baggage. Who comes to the jeep but a first lieutenant. Now here I was a buck private, and he welcomed me. He was so glad to see a human being coming into the outfit. He took that duffel bag; he said, "C'mon, I'll show you where to go." I thought, "My God, this is unbelievable, a lieutenant helping a private," so that made me feel really good. The spit and polish was not there, not in Korea. Not on the line. Everybody made me feel at home and I adjusted and that was it for almost a year. I went from the lowest job in that outfit to being in charge of all six units in our battery, and I left there as a sergeant first class in one year. It wasn't that I was smart, but I was in the right place at the right time. They said to me once, "If you stay one more month, we'll give you an extra stripe," and I said, "Uh-uh, that's it, I want out of this man's army."

JIM MENDYKE My first impression of Korea was very bad because we were on a landing ship tank and as were going towards Korea, ships were bringing troops back, and those troops were singing, "You'll be sorry, you'll be sorry!" I didn't appreciate that particular song. The odor was also unbelievable and somebody said, "The reason it smells like that is because they use human fertilizer." I thought, "How in the world can anybody live on that island with that odor?" It turns out, after you're there for about a day or two, you don't notice it anymore. We were not happy campers when these troopers were telling us that we were going to be sorry.

We landed and I was at the regimental headquarters my first day there. The colonel said that there were two openings. One was for the mortar platoon, 81 Mortar Platoon, and I was overjoyed because I loved gunnery and I thought this would be right up my alley. Unfortunately, that night there were attacks made by our regiment all along the line and two of the officers in one of the companies, I don't know if they couldn't handle it anymore, but they bugged out, so instead of continuing the fight, they ran back to the line. They were promptly discharged and so the colonel said, "We've got a change in plan. You will be a platoon leader in Company B." So instead of having a plush job, I ended up being a platoon leader, right on the front line with a buddy of mine. It was a coincidence we both were from Ripon. How you could go through all that stuff and end up in Korea and be in the same company is quite something.

I had to get accustomed to the men and they had to get accustomed to me and whatnot. Everything was going fine until the 45th National Guard had served as many months as they were supposed to in Korea. They withdrew the soldiers from the 45th National Guard, which left us without many soldiers. Somebody said, "We know what we can do. We will give them South Korea soldiers." My platoon should have been somewhere between twenty-five and thirty-two people. They sent me sixteen South Koreans. I called myself the "United Nations Platoon" because I had four Guamanians, four Puerto Ricans, and sixteen South Koreans. I ended up with four or five American soldiers who could speak English fluently and they gave me an interpreter. He wasn't the smartest. One night, we were in our bunker and he decided we needed a candleholder, so he took apart a grenade, put the candle in it, but wasn't smart enough to throw the firing pin someplace and later he stepped on it and lost his foot. So then I didn't have an interpreter and that is not easy when they can't understand me or me them! But we made it.

LEE HASPL I landed at the Punch Bowl. That's where I started and they moved us around and if you were being shelled or shot at, you got combat pay, which was really a lot of money. We got an extra fifty dollars a month, and I got that each month I was there. There were periods of time when for two days, nothing happened. Then all of sudden, three o'clock in the morning, all hell would break loose and there we'd go. The Chinese were pushing and we had to support our infantry and had to get out there and start shelling. So it could happen any time. You'd get a call and then everybody's alerted. We had six guns in our battery just like a company. They were alerted. They each had the same instructions about how far we were going to shoot and what we were going to be shooting at, and then we'd be firing for an hour or two just as fast as you could go, one after another. We let a lot of shells go. It's pretty noisy, but you know when you're nineteen, twenty years old, it doesn't matter. Today, I couldn't take it. It was pretty scary, being shelled.

The Korean War was the first in which American military units were integrated.
Lee Haspl

One time I had to put a gun to a guys head to dig a hole. You're calling the shots to about sixty people and there were times when some people would get unruly. We had some fights. We also had a Korean detachment with us. We were taking care of them and making sure they didn't kill each other. We had one guy come in one morning and part of his skull was gone. That was from a fight among themselves. By and large, everybody was pretty peaceful and pretty nice. We had both blacks and whites in our outfit, I think for the first time. President Truman made the Armed Forces integrated, which was very good. And we all got along. It was wonderful. Our one first lieutenant was a black soldier; he was a law student. He was a wonderful person. I hope some of those people are still alive. We were very close, very close; although perhaps not as close as our outfits that went through basic training together and then went overseas. That would've been even better, but here I was a replacement. And I joined these people for one year. I was in for two years.

JIM MENDYKE When I first got there, there were fierce battles on one hill; it was called Old Baldy. Maybe two hundred yards away, we were on a hill called Checkpoint Easy. I was on Checkpoint Easy. We were there for a couple of days and I said, "I don't know how one can survive, for nine months or however long it'll take to rotate." Filipinos and Turks went through Old Baldy on one occasion and everybody was taking a shot at trying to capture Old Baldy, which they could not do. Every time they did, they were counterattacked unmercifully and they'd end up losing it anyway. There were hundreds and hundreds of casualties on that one stupid hill, and I, as a young officer, kept saying to myself, "Why are we so adamant about taking that hill? Even if we have it, what good does it do? There's a hill right behind it that's even higher, so even if you're on it, the enemy is looking right down your throat anyway."

Fortunately, the captain said, "OK, we've got orders to move back." We were going into a reserve position; we called it a blocking position, so in case there was an attack, there would be some forces to hold them back until more forces could come and help. We were there for perhaps two weeks, and then we were called on to replace the Third Division. We made a night transfer so that the enemy wouldn't see us. When I got to the position I was in, I talked to the lieutenant who I was replacing there and he gave me a real good orientation, and he said, "Now, see that hill about three hundred or four hundred yards from here?" He said, "Its been the practice [that] we'd

While stationed at Checkpoint Easy, Jim Mendyke could see Old Baldy two hundred yards away.
Jim Mendyke

Old Baldy, seen from above.
Jim Mendyke

Lee Haspl's unit, like many others, felt compassion towards the Korean civilians they came across, particularly children who had been orphaned and abandoned. *Cliff Borden*

send a patrol out there and they stay there all day and about five o'clock they come back, and the enemy takes it and they stay there all night." I kind of smiled and I thought he was kidding me and I said, "Are you serious?" He says, "Yeah, that way nobody gets hurt." I thought, "Well, what a way to run a war."

LEE HASPL I used to keep everything that I owned in a metal fuse box. That was all my possessions. Most guys kept something like that for themselves. But that went on a two-and-a-half-ton truck. We jumped on, and of course our ammo was on the bottom. We got on top of it and off we went and never thought twice about sitting on the ammo. There were things blowing up all over. One time, out of nowhere, we saw this little girl, about eight or nine years old. Korean children are a little smaller than our kids. This little soul came out with no shoes, with just a piece of rag over her. She came out of nowhere. There she was, in the middle of our outfit. Never said a word, so we invited her up, gave her some food, which she took. It was evening.

Where did she come from? What were we going to do? We fixed up a place for her to sleep in one of our bunkers and the smallest guy in the outfit had to donate his clothing and we dressed her. We put some fatigues on her, gave her some shoes. She looked like a little GI. I tucked her in bed, thought she was going to go to sleep, but in the morning, she was gone. She vanished with all the clothing and everything that we gave her. Where she came from, we never knew. She never said a word. I thought maybe we helped her a little bit.

JIM MENDYKE While we were there, it was either Truman or the Pentagon who decided that we were going to have a hot meal for all the troops including the front liners for Thanksgiving Day. Being executive officer, I coordinated that for our company. I said, "How are we going to get the food up there?" The captain says, "You'll find a way." We had KATUSAs. These were obviously a whole bunch of very unintelligent people who didn't know anything other than how to carry ammunition and do anything that the sergeants or officers told them, and I felt sorry for them but that was their job: taking the food in big containers up those hills. While we were having our magnificent, so-called warm dinner, I had a couple of soldiers run over to me and say, "There's a problem." And I said, "What is the problem?" I ran about seventy or eighty yards and I saw a whole bunch of people walking down the hill, towards the enemy. And I said, "What's going on?" Well, it turned out that the enemy didn't bring any weapons, but there were at least twelve or thirteen of the enemy that infiltrated our lines and got in the line for eating, and they had a warm Thanksgiving dinner. I don't even know if they liked turkey. They say they liked fish heads and rice, but they came and ate and left.

For almost two months, we were in a lull situation where they'd send out patrols and we'd send out patrols, and maybe they were hoping, like we were hoping, that we wouldn't find anybody. So, nobody was interested in fighting when the peace talks were going on. You're saying, "You know they might just settle up tomorrow. I'd hate to be killed tonight." So, there was that attitude that was running through the troop's mind. I can recall on one occasion, probably the best soldier in our whole company refused to go out on a patrol, and I was executive officer then. The platoon leader and platoon sergeant called me and I went over and he said, he said, "My time is up." He said, "I cannot go on any more patrols." He says, "I know if I go out tonight, I'm going to get killed." Then I looked at the lieutenant and his sergeant and

I said, "Do you want to send him out or not?" He [the lieutenant] said, "We gave him an order and he is disobeying it. We want him court-martialed." So, I said to him, "I'm going to repeat again or have the lieutenant repeat a direct order. If you disobey this, I have no choice but to recommend a court-marshal." The soldier said, "I don't care. I don't care if I'm jailed the rest of my life, but at least I'll be alive. I won't go." And he was truly a super soldier.

They did court-marshal him. He was found innocent. They were going to reassign him to the same company and I told the captain, "We can't get him back here, because somebody is going to shoot him." He was assigned to some other division, and I felt pretty good about that because I didn't want to countermand an order by a platoon leader, but they had been using that guy because he was so good. He'd lead every patrol and eventually I think he got to the point where he was getting nervous about all that because they had some pretty good scrapes. In my opinion, that was a senseless exchange of "you patrol and we patrol." We had enough listening posts out there, so if there was some kind of an attack that was imminent, that would have been discoverable.

LEE HASPL We had a Turkish regiment right next to us. Quite often, I liked to go over there because those fellows knew how to prepare food much, much better than our cooks did. What those guys did with food, they got the same rations as we did, but, oh my goodness, with the spices from the Middle East, I mean those guys were fabulous. I didn't speak Turkish and they didn't speak a word of English, but I found out what kind of women they were interested in, and their food. Somehow with just facial expressions and hands, you can really understand people. I have done that in my professional life as well, when I would travel overseas and talk to people. It's amazing how a person can make himself understood. It's wonderful. The Turks used to complain, saying, "You know, you people don't get close enough to enemy." They did; sometimes they'd come back with a piece of an ear or something. That's how close they would get. They were wonderful people. I came home with one of their knives. It was made in the town of Bursa or somewhere like that. I just loved the Turks.

Mail call was so important. We lived for mail call. In my case, my mother and father didn't know that I was in the Army. I mean, they were living in Prague. I had to write to them through this roommate of mine, the one that fixed me up with my wife. I would send letters to him and he would take it out of the envelope, put it in a different envelope, and mail it

Many units included soldiers from several nations. Here, Turkish and American soldiers pose together.
DuWayne Lesperance

to Prague. I would write stories like, "I'm having a great time, I'm doing this and that." I mean, just creating stories for a whole year. Of course I couldn't tell them where I was. My God, they would have really suffered. They would have been arrested probably. They told me later on, it was a good thing that I kept them in the dark. My mother said to me years later she suspected something was wrong or something was different because of those letters. I really felt that my family was stuck over there because of the Communists and they couldn't get out. I couldn't go over there to see them. And I felt bitter about it, and every time I shot that thing against the North Koreans or the Chinese, I felt good about it. I felt like I was doing a little bit to a get even.

JIM MENDYKE On one occasion, I was going from my bunker to visit an officer in another bunker, and as I was nearing his bunker there was an artillery officer and three of the soldiers from one of the platoons. They had brought a daily occurrence when these helicopters would fly between the hills with two stretchers with a guy on each side going back to MASH. I always thought, "God, I hope the guy makes it," and about how lucky I was. If I was all alone, I think I'd have been scared to death. But with sixty or seventy people around and not far away from the Turks, I felt pretty secure. But we were on our toes all the time.

One time we got into a new location and we had an order that every man had to be two feet underground, so everybody had to dig a foxhole. I remember one fellow just wasn't going to do it. He said, "To hell with it, I'm not going to do it. I'm too damn tired." He was a sergeant and I got him busted to a private. He dug that hole, but he was a private the next day. By the time he left, he got his rank back. There were times when we were so damn tired that we just didn't want to do anything. That was the order; we had to dig in. First, you take care of yourself, and of course the equipment. We had to build a parapet for our gun, or start filling up sandbags if we had them. Or if there was a tank around, sometimes the tanks would come in and push up dirt for us so that we'd have a little protection in front. Then we'd string a canopy over it so that we were not seen. That was the first thing that would have to be done. Then somebody would have to dig the trench. That had to be done right away.

We often took fire. I came home with a piece that hit in my foxhole near my face. Red hot! Red hot! And I watched that thing smolder and just become red, and finally it cooled down. I thought, "I better take the sucker home with me." This was meant for me, but I beat it.

JIM MENDYKE One day, I got a call from the regimental commander, and he said, "Jim, I want to talk to you about your future. What are your plans? Do you plan to stay in the Army?" I said, "Sir, at one time I did, but I've had a change of mind." He said, "Well, you're the ranking first lieutenant in our regiment. I don't know what to do with you. I can't put you in a company, because they're all lieutenants and you outrank all of them." He said, "I've got two openings coming and if you're not planning to make a career of the Army, I'd prefer to assign two officers who are to those companies. They're both West Pointers and it'll look good on their record." I said, "That's fine with me, Colonel."

Eventually the colonel says, "Jim, I think what we're going to do is send you back to Chunchon. We have an organization called the School of Standards. You'll be training the new men coming in, and we'll be sending people from the front line, soldiers who are promotable to squad leaders and things like that. So, you'll be in training." I said, "Well, sir, I've only got one more month to go." And he says, "Well, I could put you on the line for a month." Then it dawned on me: if I go back now, I might have to stay an extra month, but it's a sure ticket home. I thought, "Thirty days in one's life isn't that bad," so I accepted the transfer to the rear. I stayed there for two months, instead of the one month I normally would have. Then I jumped on a boat going to Japan and as I was leaving Korea, there were soldiers coming in, and guess what I did? I sang the song, "You'll be sorry." I got on the ship, went to Japan for two days, and pretty soon we were on our way back to the States. That was my tour.

Lee Haspl on a blind date with his future wife. *Lee Haspl*

LEE HASPL The most memorable day was when I was told that it was my time to rotate. And that's when I left. When I got back to Wisconsin, the girl that I met on my last blind date here at the University of Wisconsin before I went overseas, she decided she was going to be my witness in front of the judge when I got my citizenship. This was in Milwaukee. I didn't even have my civilian clothes yet, and so the judge was kind of impressed with a young kid becoming a citizen, already a Korean War veteran. We got married. She was not of age, but the judge said, "Well, since you're going to be married, you'll be a good witness." So she was my witness and today, more than fifty years later, we're still together.

It was my roommate's idea to fix me up with someone special before going overseas. We went to one of the halls on Langdon Street — I can't remember the name of it anymore. I didn't know the lady that he was going with and who I was going with, but just then, there were two women coming downstairs. I saw one coming down the stairs. What did I see first? The legs, and I thought, "Gee, I hope this is the one, not bad." Sure enough, she was the one. We went out that day. There was a place on Park Street. We danced in the parking lot. We kind of hit it off. The next day, we arranged to have breakfast on the Union Terrace, my favorite place. We had a nice breakfast there, and that's when I asked her if she would write to me. She must have felt sorry for me. She certainly did write to me. In fact, she even sent me packages. That was very nice of her. When I got back it took one month and we were engaged. Three months later, we were married. My friend said, "This will never last more than six months." Well, here we are.

JIM MENDYKE There was no reason why they would want the hills we were on. The hill we were on was lower than the ones they were on, and as you proceeded north, the hills got higher and higher. So no matter where we would be, we'd always be at a disadvantage in terms of them being higher than we were. It was beautiful countryside, to go there, sit there now, as a painter for an example, you'd say, "Wow, is this gorgeous!" But then it wasn't. It was terrible! There was nothing there; no homes, no little cities, nothing. It was just like the mountainous areas in the States where there's nobody around. If you fly over those mountains, they look nice, but if you have to live in there...I think the peace talkers were trying to straighten out that 38th parallel a little different and it was getting near the end. I don't recall after I left how long it took to end the battle, to sign the cease-fire and peace agreement, but it was good that it ended.

I didn't really think of the politics of the situation much because we had been so brainwashed from the time I was fourteen to nineteen, during World War II, with all the movies we saw with John Wayne and Robert Taylor. All of the old-time movie stars were all heroes, even when they were killed in Bataan or Koji-do or whatever it was, and there was such a sense of patriotism. I was one of them. I recall prior to going to Korea, we had a week off, and we went to Chicago and my fiancée met me there. We were planning to get married as soon as I got back from Korea, and we were standing in line at one of the theaters, and I can still remember we were going to see *Death of a Salesman*, and there was a pretty good line. I'll bet it was a block long, and there was somebody tapping me and this other guy on the shoulder and they said, "Come on." I thought, "What did we do?" It was a police officer and he took us to the box office, and people moved and they let us go right in and buy our tickets, and I thought, I'd heard of that in World War II where they took care of the soldiers, but that was still prevalent in Chicago. I was of that mentality then, where I thought, "Look what the guys did for us in World War I and World War II. I have to do my duty." So I did exactly that.

Out of the nine months that I was on the line, the first few months were pretty bad. You accept the fact that death is inevitable for certain people. We lost four or five officers while I was there, every one of them married. You thought about death every day because you never knew when the shell was going to fly in.

LEE HASPL I think something like World War II was such a tremendous undertaking and it certainly demanded much more attention than what we got. But it's true they called it a police action. It was no police action. It was war. And we lost a lot of people. I went out and got my education. The military was good for me. I got my GI Bill and I used it to its full extent. I'm also the recipient of good care at the VA today for which I'm grateful.

Today, at my age, I do a lot of thinking and reminiscing, but when you're twenty years old, what do you think about? You think about girls, you think about food and getting out of this man's army. I think the values were a little different at age twenty. Youth is wasted on the young. That's so true. I always say I wish I had the body of a twenty year-old and the mind I have today. What a wonderful thing that would be.

11 Night Patrol

"You go out at night with maybe eighteen guys that you know, and come back the next morning and there might only be twelve. It can happen so fast that you tend to look at life a little differently. You appreciate every day. I still do appreciate every day." — Don Arne

One of the ironies of the Korean War is that the armistice negotiations lasted almost as long as the war itself. Though the war did not end until July 1953, the two sides began cease-fire talks in Kaesong in July 1951 that continued in the city of Panmunjom that October with few interruptions, until the end of the war. These ongoing discussions changed the nature of the fighting, as it became clear that neither side was willing to expend the manpower for an all-out offensive to retake the entire peninsula. Still, to maintain a tough stance at the negotiating table, it was vital that U.N. forces maintained a strong position in Korea. By the end of 1951, the fighting had settled into a combination of fierce, intense "hill battles" like Heartbreak Ridge and a fixed line of combat that stretched across the peninsula close to the 38th parallel, resembling World War I trench warfare. The two sides faced each other across an extensively constructed network of bunkers, fortresses, watch points, and tunnels, a stationary existence broken by occasional artillery battles and night patrols.

For the men stationed on the front lines, the main action came at night, when patrols ventured out into the no-man's-land between the two lines, an area fraught with dangerous wires, land mines, and booby traps. Historian Max Hastings described this part of the war as the "platoon commander's war," as most action resulted from small-scale unit activity. As Wisconsin veteran Robert Kimbrough described his experiences as platoon leader, "Anytime you go across no-man's-land and you're making a raid or setting up ambushes, you are in danger, and to come back, you may not have caught any provisions on that particular trip, but your blood pressure and your awareness of every sound you hear is up." Often it was up to the platoon commander to decide how much he was willing to risk his men during these dangerous nights. For the U.N. soldiers' Chinese and North Korean opponents, the U.N.'s general dominance in the air made this fixed warfare even more exhausting. While U.N. troops were able to emerge from their underground strongholds during the day, surface movement on the other side was generally followed by a barrage of bombs from U.N. planes. The Chinese, however, sought to undermine the will and determination of U.N. soldiers through the continual broadcasting of propaganda from their lines, telling U.N. soldiers that they were on the wrong side or commenting on the discomfort, tension, and strain of frontline duty. Chinese forces also occasionally launched surprise attacks, breaking the silence with a cacophony of bugles and drums as they tried to overwhelm U.N. positions before U.N. forces could mobilize a response and call in artillery support. Most units spent two or three months at a time on the front lines, a mix of intense action, tension, and tedium. Indeed, for many soldiers, the reason and logic of the war drained away as it dragged on in a seemingly never-ending stalemate.

Robert Kimbrough, Madison (Marines, First Regiment)
Don Arne, Oshkosh (Marines, Seventh Regiment)

ROBERT KIMBROUGH When World War II broke out I immediately became enamored of the Marine Corps. I followed the war in the Pacific quite closely through maps. My father was in Africa, and then Italy, so I was fully aware of the movements. I particularly kept an eye on the Marine Corps. In school I'd write "USMC" on the edge of my textbooks, along with my girl-friend's name sometimes. When the war was over, I was still in high school and I really felt gypped. I had not had my chance to go and fight for my country and defend America in the war to end all wars — all of that macho stuff. It was really compounded when I went to college, because there were a lot of battle veterans in school, taking advantage of the GI Bill or resuming their education. There were a lot of older guys. For a kid just out of high school, I thought "older" meant mid- to late twenties and it made me feel sort of bad. In my freshman year, a Marine recruiter came through trying to get people to enlist in what was called the Platoon Leaders class, which was

Robert Kimbrough in uniform. *Robert Kimbrough*

basically two summers of boot camp, during summer vacations, but nothing during the school year. On graduation you got commissioned in the Marine Corps as a second lieutenant. Once you were commissioned you went to school for the Marine Corps in a thing called Basic School.

This sounded good to me, and as I neared my senior year in college, the North Korean Army crossed the 38th parallel on June 25 and Harry Truman immediately activated the Army troops which were in South Korea. The next day happened to be my birthday. He took it to the United Nations and what we had initiated as a counterattack really became the United Nations' war. I was born in 1929 and I remember when Wendel Wilke, who lost the presidency to Roosevelt in '40, went around the world and came back saying, "It is one world." I was already interested in the idea of world federalism, and so as the war went on and the idea of the United Nations came out of it, I was very excited by that. I looked at the Korean War as the first time the United Nations was able to express itself to maintain boundaries. I took with me to Korea this double vision. I really thought it was an important thing that the United Nations express itself as a maintainer of world government and of world peace. I still carry that hope with me. When I tried to talk to my troopers about it, they'd say, "Hey, Lieutenant, that's a bunch of shit." You know, "Goddammit, I just want my flak jacket and I want my Tommy gun and I'm going back to Chicago and I'm going to rob banks." So there wasn't a whole lot of international political conversation going on on line. But those were the two major motivating things for me: get into the Marine Corps and prove myself a man by fighting for my country and for the United Nations.

DON ARNE I was living at home with my parents when I was nineteen years old. While in high school I was a solo trumpet player. So, I had been out of high school for two years. I thought it would be very interesting if I could get into the Navy band. They set up an interview for me down at Great Lakes, in Illinois. The problem was I hadn't really devoted as much attention to the trumpet as I should have. Quite frankly, I just failed the test. Having some pride, I didn't want to go back to Oshkosh as a failure, so I decided that, "What the heck, I'll just stay in the Navy anyway." So I joined the

Don Arne in flak jacket and helmet. *Don Arne*

Navy in January of '51 and went to Great Lakes Naval Recruit Training Center for eight weeks of boot camp. While you're there they give you an aptitude test to see what you might be qualified to do. For some reason my testing came out that I would be valuable to the Navy as a medical corpsman. They sent me to school in Bainbridge, Maryland, for six months and when I graduated they sent me to the Philadelphia Naval Hospital. While I was there, a lot of the Marines were coming back from Korea. As I worked there at the hospital, seeing all these guys coming back, I decided I'd feel better if I was where the action was. I asked to be transferred into the Fleet Marines, which had combat situations for corpsmen. They sent me to Camp Pendleton for combat training. We did the same thing that the Marines go through: how to take a rifle apart and put it back together, marksmanship on the shooting course. Cold-weather training was held at a place called Pickle Meadows, up near Barstow, California. In March of 1952 I left for Korea.

ROBERT KIMBROUGH Right after college, I was called up. The forces were pretty low. The Marine Corps had to leave the mountainous east coast of Korea to go over to the Panmunjom Corridor, which was already in operation as a kind of communications line between North and South, and there were armistice negotiations going on. The Army was protecting that corridor and was really getting beat up by the Chinese, so the Marine Corps came over and regained a lot of territory. The most vulnerable casualty in active war was the lieutenant platoon leader in an infantry. I was flown over to Korea in June of 1952 with a planeload of second lieutenants to be part of the replenishment for the tremendous casualties that were taken in regaining this territory that was lost by the Army. When I went up and joined the rifle company, we were pretty much in a line that was south of the 38th parallel, but we'd come from a place that was north of the 38th parallel. There was kind of a wavy line that went across Korea and it was more or less understood that no one would go territorial. They did, but the sort of uncertified agreement was that we would maintain and see if we could hammer out an armistice.

All the time I was there I could see the big search lights marking the

Don Arne and puppy in a moment of down time. *Donald F. Arne*

Panmunjom center where the treaties were going on. At the same time, I'm out on a patrol with my guys, and guns are being shot and grenades are being thrown and it was a weird situation to be in that way. The war had gone up and down the peninsula a couple times.

We would read in *Stars and Stripes* news from the States that "nothing happened on the main line of resistance last night." Well, anytime you go across into no-man's-land and you're making a raid or setting up ambushes, you are in danger, and to come back, you may not have caught any prisoners on that particular trip, but your blood pressure and your awareness of every sound you hear is up. To read in the paper that "nothing happened last night," it became a very personal kind of stress. The very first day I was on line, I was assigned to the weapons platoon, which was 60-mm mortars and light machine guns. My first day up I was taken down the line to see where my people were stationed and where their forward observers were, and someone shot at me. Someone had the nerve to shoot at Robert Kimbrough with a live bullet. I had this reaction, I said, "Wait a minute, I haven't done anything to you. Why are you shooting at me?" I suddenly realized that I was not in my backyard anymore playing "Ch-ch-choo! You're dead!" This was it. I swallowed hard on that and it wasn't too many days after that the Chinese launched an attack on our particular position. We got attacked, and I was down with the command bunker when all of this went on. It went on and on and I went up to see what was going on and they said, "Get your butt up to the Second Platoon, they need a platoon leader." So I went up with mortars coming in and firing going on. It was getting light and so I had my first chance to see blood and guts on the ground and people dead and people wounded, and it became more than just somebody shooting at me from across the line.

DON ARNE The Marine Corps had been holding the position on the east coast of Korea and in February they started to move the division to the western part of Korea. When we got there they were just finishing moving the whole division over there. When I joined the unit, our Third Battalion was in reserve. The First and the Fifth were on the line. In late May, we went on the line. It was called the Jamestown line of defense. It was an entirely different kind of warfare. They called the war in 1952 and 1953 the Outpost

War because it involved holding your position and having stabilization across Korea. It meant a lot of going out on patrols at night. Mostly it was trying to secure prisoners, which were still causing a lot of casualties, but it wasn't as extreme as what they had when they were over on the east coast.

ROBERT KIMBROUGH One particular night we were told to go very deep behind the Chinese lines with a full-moon cloudless sky. With that kind of moonlight and the fact that the Chinese really had higher ground than we did, I took them out there and we stayed about an hour and a half about a hundred yards in front of our line, fired some shots. I came back in and I reported something to battalion that was fiction, a lie.

Robert Kimbrough
leads his troops.
Robert Kimbrough

I got hit three times. I got banged on the back of my head with a concussion grenade. Up until about ten years ago, I was still pulling gravel out. I was out of it for hours. Then I was evacuated after daybreak. I was ambulatory by that time, so I was able to walk back with some other wounded people, and then we were transported to an Army MASH unit. I didn't agree that the wounds were important enough to warrant a Purple Heart. We had three Purple Hearts and you went home, and I didn't want to leave my troops. That sounds stupid now, but I was there, I was with them, and I get very emotional about it because I had — at age twenty-three — I had ninety people that I was responsible for. We had heavy machine guns and we had forward observers and antitank drivers coming up occasionally to shoot. It was an experience that I'll never get over in the sense that these kids, some who were older than me, would do anything I asked them. It was just an incredible binding kind of thing — the danger and life and death in working in a theater company where you become a unit.

When I went off line at night with my platoon, our switch was at night and by the time we got back to the convoy that was going to take us further back to where we would set up reserve positions, without my even being aware of it, I started to cry. It was just a release of the tension and the responsibility of three months of very intense times. I was off line for about five or six days with that wound. I was in a MASH hospital and then came back to my platoon.

DON ARNE We would be doing two things. We would try to, if possible, get prisoners, and otherwise it was just to probe their defenses and see where they were stronger and where they were weaker. It was kind of like a cat-and-mouse situation. They were doing the same thing to us. They were probing,

Enjoying a lighter moment with a friend. Don Arne is pictured on the left.
Don Arne

too. They knew what we were doing and we knew what they were doing. That's how they would mine a certain area. I remember one particular night we somehow stumbled into a minefield. But the people up in front that were heading the patrol realized it right away, and everybody froze where they were, and the Marines would take their bayonets and probe for the mines, and they got us back out of it. We didn't have any casualties, thankfully. The training that's given to Marines is remarkable. Here it was, pitch black, and they are on their hands and knees with their bayonets probing, and when they would find a mine, they obviously would let everybody be aware. Then we would just kind of back out of where we were. It was a hairy situation. You know there is nothing worse than saying, "We're in a minefield." But thank God nobody got hurt that night.

As a corpsman, I tried to stay somewhere in the middle when we went out on patrol. We had a new sergeant that came to our outfit and he was supposed to lead a patrol out that night and he said, "Doc, you ever been on this patrol before?" I said, "Sure, I've been on it several times." He said, "Would you mind kind of directing us in where we are supposed to be going and what we are supposed to be doing?" It was very unusual that I was the point man on the patrol. That only happened once. I look back on that: "Why did I do that?" I did, though, and we came through it fine.

ROBERT KIMBROUGH We had an attack patrol one night where we were told that there was suspicious activity going on between two points behind the rice paddies, that there were some trenches being dug. I took a patrol out, and we could hear the digging going on and we had already prepared artillery fire that I could call in on that stop. Before we did that three of us went up crawling along to see what we could see, and I said, "We'll open fire," and then at the same time I called in the artillery thing and then we pulled back where it was safer and worked our way back. My platoon sergeant had a Tommy gun but he forgot to test-fire it and his firing pin was broken. I'm up there spraying away with an M-1 carbine, which is a tiny little weapon, magazine-held, and we went back and reported the fact that there was indeed a trench there. After I made my report I found out that I had killed twenty-three people. It was all made up. I may not have killed anybody, I may have killed somebody, but the body count stuff was used to make it look big and it probably got bigger as it went up the line. That's what I mean when I say that "the enemy is your own." It's the command — the officers who aren't actually fighting. I'm very bitter that we waste our kids.

It's wrong. We covered people over with ponchos and evacuated them at night, as best we could. I just thought that war was wrong.

DON ARNE When we were in a patrol situation and something happened, you would hear the word, "Corpsman, up!" That's the call for us to go and do what we were trained to do. It's entirely different than going to the hospital for some kind of treatment or whatever because you know exactly what's going to happen then, but we never knew as corpsmen what we were going to run into. It could be not such a major wound or it could be something very, very serious. I would carry a medical kit that I would compare to the size of a twelve-pack cooler. Scalpels, needles, sutures, that type of thing. We could do a certain amount of that type of thing, but nothing to compare with what they would get when they got back. We had a lot of bandages and tape; it was a pretty compact little first-aid kit. It seemed to work pretty much in any occasion that we had. A lot of the wounds were such that they were able to be ambulatory; unless it was a leg wound or something, they could walk. We'd patch them up as much as we could and send them back. Of course, there were cases, too, where we had to use stretchers. But the majority of the wounds that we got involved in, and it could be anything like a major wound to a superficial wound, we were able to do what we were supposed to do and get them back again.

Most of the situations in combat were major first-aid situations — stomach wounds, chest wounds, legs, arms — and we would put dressings on them or give plasma if it was needed. It was more or less like emergency medical technicians going out, not pretending to be doctors or physicians, but giving the first aid that's needed before the soldier can get back into where the medical facilities are. At that time we were starting to use helicopters for evacuation, not to the extent that they had in Vietnam, but the helicopters could carry two patients, one on each side of the craft. It had a pod, with a stretcher on each side and a bubble over the top. We'd put the wounded in there and then they'd fly them back out to the hospital ship or the battalion aid station, wherever was more convenient.

ROBERT KIMBROUGH We were on the west side of the peninsula. The Chinese and the North Koreans had no Air Force. No air and we bombed the hell out of them for three years; a cruel, cruel thing. We called in air to strike artillery positions that we could spot. It was a very unbalanced kind of warfare and yet it was this frozen thing because they were trying to get to this armistice. Seoul was very close to the lines and when you were off line, in Regimental Reserve, a battalion would come off and two battalions would go up. The battalion that was off could take troops down in a truck to Seoul to spend the day. And it really gave me a chance to see the devastation of war in terms of the civilian and urban population. Seoul was just a bunch of rubble. It was incredible; you'd walk along and, of course, there were all sorts of merchants trying to sell you T-shirts and souvenirs. The pathos and devastation of it all…I've never been back to Seoul. Now, of course, you'd never know war had ever hit it. But it was absolutely leveled by us and the Chinese. The rural population was pushed around. North of Seoul, villages were abandoned, villagers displaced by fighting. When we went into Regimental Reserve, they had put barbed wire around our little encampment, because there were so many people who wanted to sell you this or that. And of course the troopers would go buy bad booze and die from it or get syphilis. Not to blame the Koreans. We created those situations. It's an ugly, ugly thing. My ire, in 2004, is still boiling. I even dream about it. I've never forgotten my experience in Korea. It was nonsense and now I see through it.

We had land mines that the Army had left behind and didn't give us any charts of where they were. A friend of mine practically lost his leg. He was a regular officer and he lost his career. A man in front of him stepped on a mine, he got killed, and then my friend got wounded very badly in the leg and they couldn't heal it enough for him. So, when you're out there, you could be stepping on a land mine. If that full moon was out, and I knew we were going to get the hell kicked out of us, I didn't do it. No purpose served, except somebody back at battalion could say, "Well, we sent a patrol there from Second Platoon of Charley Company and they went out there and they just cleaned out this many people." Then this goes up the line into and then to Division and then to Corps and then to the whole Eighth Army and then Mark Clark gets news of it over in Japan.

I remember one enlisted man who was in our basic school saying, "Boy, I'm going to Korea because that's where the line for the congressional Medal of Honor is." And that's what he was out to do. I have a Bronze Star and one Purple Heart, though I was hit three times. It got to be a joke among us second lieutenants that those were our Good Conduct Medals, because if you're doing your job as a platoon leader, you're going to get shot at and you have to make some decisions that might be interpreted as "above and beyond" or whatever that crap was all about. But, you concentrate on what you're doing, your job, and hope to hell that you can protect your troops as much as possible, and then come out whole out of the thing.

DON ARNE I had a situation when we were in Camp Pendleton. I met a Marine by the name of Don Story. He came from a small town in California, Marysville. We became pretty good friends over in California. One weekend he took me and another one of our friends to his aunt's who lived in the foothills of L.A., and we spent the weekend. It was the first time I ever had a taco, I'll never forget that, because I didn't know what a taco was. We were put onboard ship, not knowing where we were going, and lo and behold, me and Don Story were both in the same outfit. One particular night we were on a patrol and a call came up. I'd heard a loud explosion, and they said, "Corpsman!" I went up in pitch black and it turned out that it was Don Story who had stepped on a mine and it had pretty much split him open. There wasn't anything I could really do. I administered morphine, and his last words to me were, "Don, I don't want to die." I said "You'll be OK, you'll be OK." I think within twenty minutes he was deceased. I still have that memory implanted in my brain and every time there is a patriotic observance, I think of that particular night and Don Story. I would really love to go out to Marysville, California, and see if he has relatives. I'd let them know that he died doing his duty, and that he didn't have a lot of pain and that he died quickly.

We had this lieutenant, O'Brien. He was the recipient of the Medal of Honor for an action he took part in. They were pulling back from a position they had been trying to capture from the Chinese and O'Brien was giving the orders and saw this Marine on the side and said, "Take that Browning and get down the hill! Do it now!" And the Marine said, "Lieutenant, I can't. I'm hit." He said, "Well, you're hit, everybody else is getting hit. Take that BAR and get down the hill." Well, after things calmed down a little bit, it turned out that this Marine that he hollered at to get down the hill with his weapon had lost a foot. So when he said "I'm hit," it was a little more severe than probably Lieutenant O'Brien thought, but the guy hobbled down the hill with his weapon on one foot. Remarkable. I think it shows the training and the dedication that Marines have that I was proud to be a part of. When you hear things like that it makes you say, "God, how can that happen?"

ROBERT KIMBROUGH We would communicate by wire back to the company headquarters, which was maybe two hundred yards back. We started hearing some funny clicks in our phone conversations. One morning we had people leave the company headquarters and trace the wires up this little ridgeline to my place and I brought another group down, and by the time we met, we found the Chinese had infiltrated and were listening to all our conversations. Of course, they even caught on to the fact that we had caught on to them. They had a little nest right there between us and our command post. They were a hell of a lot better fighters than Americans. They had the patience. They would fire a round right behind your lines. Three days later another shell might come in somewhere else in the general area. Four days later, the shitcan, which everybody went to, would be blown up. If you're out on a patrol, they might start playing bugles and cymbals, which usually meant an attack was coming. You would turn your attention to that and then they infiltrated behind you and started shooting at you from the back.

I was on what they called Bunker Hill, which the Chinese really did try to take. It was a ridiculous piece of ground because we had higher ground over Bunker Hill and they had higher ground. That's where I got wounded and was evacuated. They wanted that piece of land and we didn't want them to have it. It cost my platoon; we came off that hill with nine people after going up with about thirty-two people, and the Marine Corps simply pulled back from Bunker Hill. It wasn't worth trying to have people there. It didn't serve any purpose. The futility of the thing was just beyond belief. You say, "My God, look at all the people I lost. I was wounded myself, and now we don't even care about it anymore." I took that a little personally. It's war. Some commander on the Chinese side says, "Go get it," and our people say, "Keep it; don't let them get in there. Defend it." After a month goes by you realize, well, it's really pretty silly to keep having people shot up out there every night, and they abandon it. You could survey it from the high ground anyway.

The first time we were attacked, when I was just brand-new there, they got by and wiped out that point and were in our lines. So, the company commander had the wise idea that the strongpoint, which we regained, had to be redesigned. So, I, he, and my platoon were given the job to actually redo that whole strongpoint, so the outpost could really protect the strongpoint. When the next attack came, we were prepared with fields of fire that actually covered the advance, and they weren't able to get to the main line. We were attacked twice, but once they got over the outpost into the line, and that's when I got my platoon, because the platoon leader was killed, and the second lieutenant. The first attack, they wanted to surprise the outpost.

They opened fire; we were ready for that. They would do the bugles and cymbals as a distraction, but that kind of onslaught that the Army particularly experienced up in the north...I'm not defending the Marine Corps as being better than the Army, but they prepare themselves a lot different. They're much more scaled down, and they're not as equipment-heavy as the Army. The Chinese would try to attack Army divisions to our right, that way. The Chinese used to try to tease us over loudspeaker about being Marines, and they'd try to get us to come and fight them. I lost a Marine on a patrol, and they got on the loudspeaker and said, "We have him. Aren't you going to come get him?"

We didn't put a political label on the Chinese and Koreans at all. They were just out there and we were on this side and they were on that side, and there was no hate. I don't know; I remember when we were on Bunker Hill, during daylight, one of my troopers really took to sniping, and he got a big kick out of that. He caught a bullet right through his forehead. I thought it was almost symbolic; he really wanted to get them, he really wanted to kill them, and he got killed. Let's face it, it's fate. I'm not a religious person, but I took that as emblematic. He was probably a better Marine than most of us if that's what you're supposed to do: "Kill, kill, kill." I don't think we had animosity. They'd play some Chinese music over the loudspeakers, and we just kind of laughed. Nobody would say, "Oh, the goddamned chinks." There's nothing to be gained from that. I like the stories about World War I when there was sort of a peace. The Germans and the English or the Germans and the French would play soccer. These are human beings. These are kids.

DON ARNE The Marine Corps has a long, long tradition of never leaving their wounded behind. I saw that firsthand. If a Marine was wounded and it took three men to go and get him and bring him back, or if it would take fifteen men to go out and get him and bring him back, they would do it. All I can say is, God bless the Marine Corps, because they really believe that it is their mission to go out and make sure that there is nobody left behind. They bring their wounded and their dead back. I saw that time and time again. Might take three guys going out after a wounded buddy of theirs and maybe two of those guys would get wounded trying to bring the first one back. But it always worked.

One particular night we did run into a situation where our lieutenant got hit pretty bad, and I mentioned to the sergeant that was taking over, I said, "Why don't you give me a radioman, two stretcher bearers, and I will try to make sure that we get our lieutenant back to the main line of resistance." That was another experience that I had that I won't forget. We did in fact get him back to the main line of resistance and it worked out very well, but I don't know if we were being observed by the Chinese and they just knew what we were doing and let us go, or if they didn't know where we were. They knew where a lot of our patrols were, and we knew a lot of their patrols, so if possible you'd go out and set up an ambush in the hopes that one of their patrols would come through. I am sure they did the same thing. They're looking to ambush our patrols. When I say "black," I'm telling you those nights seemed blacker than any I've ever seen before in my life. I guess it's maybe just the situation, it's the unknown. You don't know what might be three feet ahead of you. It became daylight and we were right out where we certainly could have been observed very easily. But it all worked out great.

ROBERT KIMBROUGH We were doing something we were ordered to do; we were there, and we did it as best we could for our protection. We didn't, you know, lie down and mess up our guns or do any sabotage. When I came back, I got so tired of hearing people say, "Oh, Bob, I'm so glad you're home. You don't know how we worried about you. Oh, we're so glad you're home, we don't have to worry anymore." And there was one veteran besides my father who was very good about these things. He said, "It's good to have you back." That meant more to me than all the, "Oh, you don't know how we worried, oh, it's so hard on us," like I was to blame for them having to think about me once a week or something like that.

We were an occupying army. It really makes me sick at heart because it was said that we were bringing "liberty and freedom" that these people needed. "They don't like freedom, but we're going to give them freedom." Our war was a phony thing but people got killed and wounded. One of my sergeants got his arm blown off when we were out on patrol one night. I had a kid whose legs got knocked off, and of course people died. War is not the way to settle anything internationally. It's a crude way of getting your own way. It makes me sick. I'm a member of Veterans for Peace and have been since it was started about seventeen years ago. I really became a pacifist in Korea, not just a theoretical pacifist, but I came back advocating unilateral disarmament.

DON ARNE It gave me a whole different outlook on my life. I don't think anybody can go through a set of combat experiences and not come back a little bit changed. I was one of those who was changed. You go out at night [with] maybe eighteen guys that you know and come back the next morning and there might only be twelve. It can happen so fast that you tend to look at life a little differently. You appreciate every day. I still do appreciate every day.

I'd be lying if I said there wasn't some fear there. I think everybody had fear. You rely on people on either side of you. We'd all been trained; we were all trained how to handle ourselves in situations. Your life might depend on the Marine next to you on either side. It's hard to explain, but you go in there feeling confident that everything is going to be fine, yet down deep inside you know there are going to be losses. So you live with that. You take advantage of spending time with guys and appreciating their capabilities. You work as a team. That's probably what makes the Marine Corps what it is. When you say "Semper Fi," it means a lot. I have some good friends that I still keep in touch with from fifty years ago, and it's like we are still close friends. I appreciate that.

12 Swift Care

"Pushes were being made, ambulances were coming in, and helicopters were coming in. We didn't have much time to think of home." — *Julius Ptaszynski*

Though portrayals of the Korean War are rare in American popular culture, the film and television series *M*A*S*H* offered both comedy and pathos in its depiction of a mobile army surgical hospital (MASH) in Korea. Though *M*A*S*H* acted as a commentary on Vietnam, the show's medical setting depicted a crucial element of combat care in Korea. Indeed, MASH units played a key role in reducing casualty rates throughout the Korean War. The concept of the mobile army surgical hospital was first developed in 1947 to solve a major problem of World War II medical care: 25 percent of men dying from wounds (that is, men who survived being removed from the battlefield) died before reaching surgery. Indeed, in World War II, only 4.5 percent of men who reached a medical installation ultimately died of their wounds; in Korea, this number declined to 2.3 percent. MASH units, which used tents and thus could move with the lines of battle, reduced the time that men waited for surgery and saved many lives. Ultimately, the survival rate in Korea surpassed any previous war.

A visit to a MASH unit was only one part of a long chain of travel and medical care that soldiers endured after being wounded in Korea. The first step involved getting wounded men off the battlefield to battalion aid stations; litter squads, using jeeps, or simply stretchers when terrain was rough, were responsible for retrieving wounded men from the front lines. In Korea's mountainous areas, it could take up to a full day for a litter squad to move a soldier from the front lines to the local aid station. Small helicopters, which could carry up to two wounded soldiers on stretchers attached to each side, also evacuated injured men from isolated areas. While the use of helicopters saved many lives, they were not yet widespread enough to take over the strenuous work of carrying patients on foot. After reaching the battalion aid station, an ambulance took the men to a collection point and then to a MASH unit. From the MASH unit, a combination of railway, bus, and air transport (both planes and helicopters) brought the injured to an evacuation hospital; located far behind the front lines, these hospitals were equipped to provide full medical care. The continuous travel required by wounded men was often agonizing, as they rode in jeeps, trucks, and buses that traveled over bumpy, rough, crowded roads, and trains that might take as long as two days to reach Pusan on the southern tip of the peninsula. Yet for the seriously wounded, this was only the beginning of the journey. In the Korean War, the evacuation policy was 30 days for Korea and 120 days for Japan; this meant that if a soldier needed more than 30 days of treatment, he would be evacuated from Korea to Japan, but if he needed more than 120 days to recover, he would be evacuated through Japan to the United States. At the evacuation hospital, seriously wounded men were loaded onto planes where nurses like Wisconsin veteran Alice Dorn would care for them on the trip to Japan. In Japan, men would transfer to several different Army hospitals, or to American air bases from which they flew home to the United States. Overall, the trip from Korean battlefield to American hospital could take as long as a month. However, as medical institutions and staff adapted to the situation in Korea, they became able to treat men in Japan and get them back on the Korean battlefield with increasing speed.

Battle wounds were only one component of the medical care required in Korea. The number of men suffering from disease and noncombat injuries (due to the frigid winters, frostbite was especially common) often exceeded the number of men being evacuated for combat wounds. In particular, medical personnel in Korea and Japan confronted several new diseases not previously seen in American troops. Wisconsin veteran Robert Strand was one of many men who suffered from an outbreak of hemorrhagic fever that began in the summer of 1951; of the 837 troops who caught the disease in 1951, almost 8 percent died after only a few days. Strand was thus lucky to survive. As in any war, medical care was vital to maintaining the strength and effectiveness of troops fighting in Korea, yet it is one of the ironies of combat medical care that survival in a war zone often meant heading back to the battlefield.

Julius Ptaszynski, Wausau (Army, Eighth Division)
Alice Dorn, Middleton (Air Force, 801st Air Evacuation Squadron)
Robert Strand, Iola (Army, First Cavalry Division)

After being drafted in 1951, Julius Ptaszynski trained as a combat medical technician.
Julius Ptaszynski

JULIUS PTASZYNSKI My name is Julius Ptaszynski; I was drafted out of Milwaukee in August of 1951. I worked for Woolworth Company and they were going to transfer me and they decided they wanted my draft status. So I checked with my local draft board and thirty days later I got a notice that I was going in the service. I didn't have to worry about the transfer with Woolworth Company at all.

I was sent to Fort Sheridan in Illinois and then I went to Fort Meade, Maryland, which was a medical replacement training center. There we had eight weeks of military infantry training and then eight weeks of combat medical training. We were training as combat medics. It was regular combat infantry training along with training in treatment of the wounded. After eight weeks of that, we went to Fort Sam Houston Medical Center. There, we took a short course in preparation of wounds and procedures for operating rooms and so forth. Then after eight weeks of that, I was sent to Madigan Army Hospital in Tacoma, Washington. And there I finished up my training. I was graduated out of there as a medical technician and after a two-week stay at home, I was sent over to Korea.

ALICE DORN I was in high school during all of World War II and I used to read the magazines and follow the Army nurses and what they did. That was wonderful for me. It sort of moved me into nursing. I was living in San Diego when the Korean War began. I was assigned to March Field in Riverside, California, and did hospital duty. At that time, we used to get all of these soldiers with frostbite — toes and fingers — and we knew they just weren't well equipped with the clothing and the boots they needed. I thought, "Gee, flight nursing is something I've never done," so I went to the school in Alabama for two months to learn about taking care of people in planes.

After my school was finished in six months, the chief nurse said there were two openings for the Far East. Another nurse and I decided we'd like to see where we would be going. And we did go. We went on C-54s. It took us

After finishing flight nursing school in Alabama, Alice Dorn was assigned to the 801st Medical Air Evacuation Squadron. Alice is pictured here, top row, second from left. *Alice Dorn*

two days to get to Tokyo. They didn't know where to put us. Were we flight nurses or were we hospital nurses? We were assigned to the 801st Medical Air Evac Squadron, which was part of the 315th Air Combat Troop Carrier Squadron. The reason we were with the troop carrier squadron was because they would take supplies to Korea and come back empty. So Chief decided that this would be a good way to bring patients from Korea back to Japan. Wherever they were going, they would usually be treated in one of several big hospitals in Japan.

In Korea, we used a smaller plane, the C-47s and the C-46s. They were not insulated, they were very noisy, and there was very little heat in those planes. We would do six or seven flights a day. We would pick up patients each time and then come back to Seoul to offload them at the hospital. They were screened and treated and the decision was made whether they would stay, recover, or go back to fight. I was there in the winter and I was there in the summer. In the winter it could be forty degrees below zero and in the summer as high as 100 degrees. We didn't have our own coats. We would trade coats, whoever worked that day would; we had two coats. We would trade coats every day. I remember writing to my mother and asking her to send me some of that Sears long underwear because we weren't equipped for this.

Despite poor vision, Robert Strand was drafted into the Korean War. *Robert Strand*

ROBERT STRAND I was drafted and I was 4-F to begin with because I had really bad eyes. My eyes are like 20/200 and I didn't pass for World War II. That's why I went in a little older than a lot of them were. As long as it was correctible with glasses, then you were OK. We had bayonet practice, and I was jabbing the bag with the bayonet and I caught my glasses on a limb of a tree that threw them off my face and I was next to blind. I was down crawling around on my hands and knees looking for my glasses. And the sergeant came up and he says, "Strand, what are you doing?" He used stronger words than that, but I told him I was looking for my glasses and he said, "My God, what they don't send us."

JULIUS PTASZYNSKI We worked in the operating room and we worked in other phases of the hospital also on medical wards, whenever needed if a push was going on. Wherever you were needed, you filled in. Sometimes we would take part in autopsies and so forth, and it all depended on what was going on at that particular time. Our duty hours were supposed to be from seven in the morning until seven o'clock at night or from seven at night until seven in the morning, but

The field hospital where Julius Ptaszynski worked as a medical technician. *Julius Ptaszynski*

Nurses from Julius
Ptaszynski's hospital.
Julius W. Ptaszynski

sometimes we went round the clock for twenty-four hours. The need made the hours. Pushes were being made, ambulances were coming in, and helicopters were coming in. We didn't have much time to think of home.

The number of wounded depended on the size of the push and what was going on. A lot of them would be fragments from grenades, mortars, and machine guns. I remember one time ninety-three or so wounded come in. They had 128 wounds on them. Some were very serious and others were a couple days' rest and medication and it would be back on line.

ALICE DORN The helicopters brought them from the front because the terrain was terrible. There were no roads in most parts. This was the beginning of the helicopters coming to get the patients and they could carry two. It would be on the outside and I don't know if that was a scary experience for those patients. Then they would land at the first aid or the MASH hospitals and we would pick them up from there after they were treated. Some good things came out of this war. Collapsible IV fluids came out of this war. They used to have bottles. Now they have these packs. There's no breakage. It was getting the patient to the specialized medical care that he really needed that I think saved a lot of limbs, and lives.

I had a nice experience one day when I went to one of the strips. Two men said, "Hey, Alice." I looked and they were my neighbors. They were two brothers who were stationed, and they said, "We've been meeting this flight line every day. When [a] plane came in, we hoped we'd see you." I thought that was just great. The next time I went, they were gone. They'd been moved to the front. I was surprised that they hadn't been separated, which they would do now. I think of those boys. I think of that loss.

ROBERT STRAND They had helicopters there. But they weren't always the foolproofest things at that time. I remember having one helicopter come in to pick up wounded up on the line right in front of us and they got hit. The small prop got hit by rifle shots, and that broke and hit the big prop, and

The Korean War marked the beginning of the use of the helicopter to evacuate the wounded. *Don Arne*

they came tumbling down right amongst us practically. It just folded into a little ravine and the one that was wounded lived the longest. He died before they got him out of there.

ALICE DORN We lost some nurses to pilot error. I think [the plane] was going to leave Seoul to come back to Japan and our nurses were staffed; we had two nurses staffed and two techs and [the pilot] was confused about the signal to take off and a fighter pilot came. The fighters used the same airstrip and they just were gone. And then we lost a nurse because the flight [took] off over the water. [It took] off over the water and I don't know what happened. The plane just dropped. We lost one of our nurses, a tech, and the crew.

There weren't cell phones you could call. You couldn't say, "My patient is doing this, I need some medical advice." You were really on your own. You hoped you made a good decision. On the C-54s coming back to Japan, there were always two nurses and two medical technicians. On the other flights, there was one nurse, one medical tech. We didn't know the patients well. We did have records and we were told about the patient as we left. But you didn't get to know him. I always liked the idea of people — getting to know them — over a long period of time. But you didn't get to know them; you didn't see them after that. That was the part that I did not like.

Alice Dorn recalls of the highly charged time, "You couldn't say, 'My patient is doing this, I need some medical advice.' You were really on your own. You hoped you made a good decision." *Alice Dorn*

ROBERT STRAND I think it would have been right around three weeks [since I arrived]. One morning I woke up and I just couldn't get out of bed. I was in pain and had a high fever and after they finally realized I was sick, they got an ambulance and took me up to Sapporo. I remember lying on the floor of the hospital there for a couple of hours waiting to get admitted. I'd never been so sick in my life. As soon as I got up on the fourth floor and into a bed, I just passed out. I was out for a week and when I woke up, I still had a fever of 105. It was pretty rough. You ache so, too, and then I could hardly move. I got eight shots a day of penicillin and finally pulled it through. I had double pneumonia and pleurisy. My lungs were practically filled with fluid. They finally tried something they'd never tried before where they went through my back with a tube and drained out my right lung. They took better than a glass of stuff out of there and that's when I started feeling better. Up until that time, I think that I was about gone. A lot of them that contracted that hemorrhagic fever didn't make it through it, because of the fever and that.

ALICE DORN Hemorrhagic fever started. I think that started because we got it at March airbase. We had patients and no one knew what it was or what was happening. It was from contact with rodents; you couldn't pass it to each other. Those men were sent straight home. They made better recoveries when they were near their families.

JULIUS PTASZYNSKI We would usually get the alert that the ambulances were coming in and we would go to the pre-op stations and receive the patients. We'd check their wounds to see which ones were the most serious ones that had to be taken care of. I did several other jobs in the hospital. As a medical technician, I worked on medical wards. I worked with hemorrhagic fever patients, which was a disease that was carried by a mite and that would get into the patient's bloodstreams and cause bad hemorrhages and very high fevers. I didn't know about hemorrhagic fever until the day they told me that I was going to help with the fever patients.

Alice Dorn confers with a flight technician in front of a C-46.
Alice Dorn

While we were there, there was nothing, no medication, that could be used to prevent it. They used DDT on the uniforms to prevent the mites from getting into the skin. A lot of those patients had medical problems afterwards. We would bathe them in alcohol and pack them up in ice chips to keep their fevers down and give them a lot of fluids and IVs.

ROBERT STRAND I'd never heard of it [hemorrhogic fever]. We tried to keep as clean as we could. All we had to wash up in was our helmet liner. We did that pretty regularly, but you didn't wash your hands every time before you ate or anything like that. I suppose I got it into me somehow or other there. I couldn't believe that I was that weak and in that much pain. They had reveille call and I couldn't get out of bed. I couldn't even begin to think about it, and the sergeant came through and told me to get my tail out of bed. He was more or less threatening me, but the warrant officer came through a little bit later and he said, "Can't you see that that man is in pain?" He said, "You get the ambulance and get him to Sapporo." I think they thought I was being lazy because I was a frontline troop. I was really in rough shape, but they got me there.

It's a really weird feeling. I remembered dreams or nightmares that I had during that week. It was like a huge abyss, like a lake or an ocean, but I could

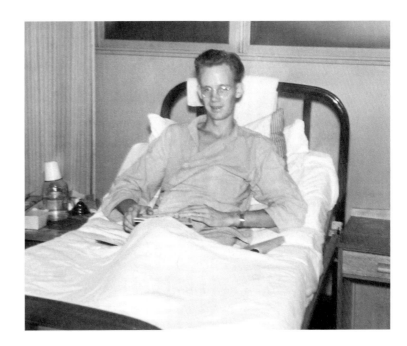

Robert Strand recuperates from hemorrhagic fever, known as the war's Silent Killer. *Robert Strand*

see across it. There was a girl across the ocean and I was trying to get to her. It was a gal that I used to know in Minneapolis when I worked there. I was trying to get to her and every time that I'd start trying to get away, they'd grab me and take me back again. It seemed to me that it was like I was a prisoner. Really what it was, was that I was at the stairwell and starting to climb over and they'd grab me and take me back to bed again. That's the only thing I remember about that whole week. When I woke up, I still had a 105-degree fever.

JULIUS PTASZYNSKI You had to hold it back sometimes, to give those people courage, and you got to care for people. The days just kind of went from one to another after a while. There would be lulls, and we would have a little bit of free time to play practical jokes on one another to keep our sanity, but there were also times, the longest time about three days in a row, where we were just going constantly.

I'd go through the wards and write letters for some of the patients who were unable to write, and I would answer some of the mail for them. I would hold little prayer services in the chapel. It was kind of rewarding work. I enjoyed it. I've always liked to help people out. I guess maybe that's why I got into the medical field. Maybe they knew I liked to help people, so they put me in the medics. I did get a few letters from parents thanking me. I had one experience where my dad wrote me a letter and he asked me if I knew of a Marine by the name of Jerry and that he had worked with Jerry's dad on the railroad. When Jerry's dad found out that I was at the 11th Evacuation Hospital, he wanted me to check up on his son. About the same time that I got that letter, I had just made arrangements for the missionary from Wanju to give Jerry the last rights. Jerry had been run on the kidney machine, but he had passed away. When I got out, about two months after I left Korea, I had gone to Jerry's parents' house and assured them that he had gotten the last rights of the church, and that meant very much to them.

ROBERT STRAND I was recovering pretty well; I was down to 130 pounds at my worst. They moved me down just out of Tokyo a ways. There was a rehabilitation camp; they'd give you physical training. We ran and did a lot of

Hospital personnel behind the quarantine line. *Robert Strand*

Alice Dorn, during a break. *Alice Dorn*

good training like that. When I left there, I weighed 190 pounds. It was a month later, so I snapped out of it pretty fast. The Eighth Cavalry had already gone back to Korea again. They regrouped and a lot of the guys that I was in with had went and rotated home, which I would have done earlier if I'd been there, but I wasn't in camp then. They moved me into the Seventh Cavalry Division and I stayed with them. Then I was shipped home. I got home on the 9th of December of '52. Discharged.

JULIUS PTASZYNSKI We were a semimobile evacuation unit, which meant that we could divide it into a stationary and a mobile unit. Later on, toward the end of the war, in 1953, our hospital took care of Operation Little Switch, which was the repatriation of the first wounded during the Korean War. It was prisoners, but they were the seriously wounded prisoners. The North Koreans did not take care of the American POWs very well. I left in July, but shortly after, our hospital helped with the Big Switch, which was the repatriation of all the prisoners.

On the Fourth of July, we left our unit and went down to Pusan, and we took a train, and it took about eighteen hours to get to Pusan from Wanju. On the way there, we stopped at Taegu and one of the four fellows I was drafted with got on that train at Tagu. Leon happened to have a little bottle with him and the four of us celebrated that we were going home. We were in Pusan for about ten days, and then we loaded up on the ship and started back to U.S. The ship we were on was the first ship to land in the U.S. the day the cease-fire was signed on July 27 of 1953. As we unloaded off the ship, we had the Can-Can girls there with the confetti and all of the serpentines and all the little fancy things going on. We were pretty proud to be the first ones to get to the U.S. the day the cease-fire was signed.

ALICE DORN It was a terrible war. I've tried talking to some of the men sometimes and they just don't want to speak about it. I met a Korean lady last summer at the Y and I asked her where she was from, and she said, "You would not know my country." And I said, "What was your country, I'm interested." And she said, "Korea." I said, "I know it very well." I told her the parts I was in and she bowed and she said, "Thank you, thank you for coming to save our country." I've never gone back. I have no desire to go back. I don't know what it is because so many people do, but I remember it the way it was. Too many sad things with patients. These guys were eighteen years old, some were even seventeen and they're lying there and missing limbs. That was a real tragedy for them, their families. I often wonder where they are now. I was ready for peace.

13 Armistice

"When you send somebody to war, you're giving them fifty years and maybe a lifetime of memories. You better have a good cause. It wasn't a good war, but it was a just war. It did the job and we paid a very high price."
— *Richard Hemlin*

When North Korea attacked South Korea in June 1950, President Truman's decision to send American troops to aid the South Koreans received wide support from the American public. Indeed, many Americans believed that North Korea was acting under the direct control of the Soviet Union and that the conflict in Korea could in fact be the beginning of World War III. Yet as the war dragged on with no victory or even an end in sight, American opinion on the war shifted. The American public as well as the men on the battlefield began to question the lengthy stalemate that Korea had become. It seemed the war would never come to a resolution. Presidential candidate Dwight D. Eisenhower sought to utilize this sentiment to his advantage, declaring on October 24, 1952, "I shall go to Korea," implying that by electing him, the American people could bring an end to the war. Though it is difficult to determine how much Eisenhower's promise actually contributed to his election, it is clear that his declaration resonated with an American public that was tired of seeing men drafted into what had seemingly become a hopeless war. Eisenhower made good on his promise, touring Korea in December 1952 as president-elect, a visit that convinced him that the static war could not drag on forever. His visit, however, had no immediate effect on negotiations. Indeed, negotiations to end the war had been taking place at Panmunjom since October 1951 (talks originally started in Kaesong in July 1951), but they had stymied, particularly over the issue of prisoner repatriation. While the United Nations wanted to allow prisoners to choose the country to which they would return (thus allowing Chinese and North Korean POWs to choose not to return to Communist China or North Korea), China and North Korea were resistant to the U.N. plan. The negotiations thus proceeded in a sporadic way, stopping and starting erratically.

Even more frustrating was that the fighting continued, and even grew in intensity. In February 1953, the negotiations stopped once again. Yet on the front lines, the two sides continued to clash. In the last months of the war, U.N. troops were not allowed to move into new territory, but U.N. command instructed them to hold the main line of resistance (MLR) at all costs. This continued to prove difficult, as the Chinese and North Korean troops were determined to demonstrate their resolve and increased the intensity of the war even as the possibility of peace drew nearer. The Chinese and the North Koreans believed that if the armistice coincided with a strong military offensive, they could claim victory in the war. They further hoped that a strong military position would also strengthen their position at the negotiating table.

In March 1953, the Chinese and the North Koreans again hit the U.N. lines at two hills known as Old Baldy and Pork Chop Hill. When Commanding General Maxwell B. Taylor decided that Old Baldy was not essential to U.N. defenses, U.N. forces retreated. But after Chinese and North Korean troops again struck Pork Chop Hill — still in U.N. hands — on April 16, a fierce fight ensued. According to the armistice line agreed upon in November 1951, Pork Chop Hill would have to be surrendered by whoever held it at the end of the war; however, as historian Burton Kaufman explains, "It was political prestige and a test of wills that was at issue over Pork Chop, not military logic." After three days of back-and-forth fighting, including hand-to-hand combat, U.N. forces managed to hold onto the hill. In June 1953, however, the Chinese launched an even larger attack on Pork Chop, overwhelming U.N. defenders. As each side poured forces into the battle, casualties mounted dramatically; after three days of fierce combat, General Taylor decided that it simply was not worth the American casualties. He reluctantly withdrew American forces.

By this second battle of Pork Chop, negotiations had resumed and the final cease-fire agreement was only a few weeks away. A decision to exchange sick and wounded POWs — Operation Little Switch — had helped push negotiations toward a conclusion as China and North Korea accepted large parts of the U.N. peace proposal. Still, in the last weeks of the war, the Chinese and the North Koreans launched their largest offensive since spring 1951, and the fighting continued without end until the cease-fire agreement went into effect on July 27, 1953. In the end, Korea remained divided between North and South, with a demilitarized zone splitting the two along a line close to the original 38th parallel. Indeed, the armistice was not a settlement and to this day, the two Koreas remain technically at war with one another. As desired by the United States, the armistice also allowed POWs to choose their country of return. Thousands of Chinese and North Korean soldiers chose not to return to China and North Korea. Though the first major conflict of the Cold War ended not in decisive American victory but in a frustrating stalemate, American forces had accomplished their stated duty of defending South Korea.

Richard Hemlin, Madison (Army, Seventh Division)
John Breske, Elderon (Marines, First Regiment)
Dick Nooe, Neenah (Marines, Fifth Regiment)

RICHARD HEMLIN I was drafted. I think that was the first time I ever swore. When I opened up that letter, I said, "SOB!" That really hit me. Hell…that was it. I remember going down to sign up. There wasn't any thought of not going. It was just that I wasn't prepared for it. This was in '52 when everybody was hoping Eisenhower would come in and it was going to be over. I thought maybe I'd sail right through, and that didn't happen.

We got into Pusan; it was all barbed wired. Pusan was awful; the whole place stunk. It was terrible. You'd walk up to the kids to buy something and they'd blind you with a mirror in the eye. They'd grab your watch. I don't think anybody really minded. They felt really bad. I don't know how long we stayed there. I think a couple weeks. Then they put us in what they called a red ball express and we went up to the front. It was very much like World War I at that time. You went up to the front lines.

JOHN BRESKE They'd had a lot of casualties in Korea. We went down to Milwaukee and we got into the Marines. They must have taken about forty guys out of that bunch that came from Marathon County here. The Marines had a lot of casualties. They just picked "this guy, this guy…" They just pointed the guys out. That's how I got in the Marines. I was assigned to Easy Com-

Richard Hemlin, center, helps rebuild the bunkers used to defend Pork Chop Hill which lay in a strategic position just in front of the main line of resistance. *Richard Hemlin*

pany and that's where I stayed the whole while I was there. Most of my time was on the front lines. Out of my year over there, probably, I'd say 80 percent of the time I was in combat.

DICK NOOE In 1950, I went to the University of Oregon and I went for the wrong reasons. I went there to play football because I was a good football player. My grades came hard, so I quit. This was right near the beginning of the Korean War, and so I decided that I was going to enlist. I enlisted in the Marine Corps and went through boot camp in San Diego. I had wanted to go into the Navy, but they weren't taking people at the time. I thought, "I'm going to go into the Marine Corps."

After boot camp, I was assigned to a naval base in San Francisco Bay called Treasure Island. I was what was referred to in the service as a "Pinkie." A Pinkie works in an office. That's what I was doing and we were reassigning Marines that were coming back on rotation from Korea. We'd reassign them to other duty stations and cut their orders and get them going. I was never real happy doing that. It just wasn't exciting enough. I kept putting pressure on the sergeant major to get me out of there. I said, "I want to go to Korea." Finally he got tired of listening to me, and I went in March 1951.

RICHARD HEMLIN A lot of the replacements were coming in. We had this guy from my town. We were given a detail to clean these field stoves. They were full of grease and we took them down to this creek and started cleaning. It was hot. We cleaned them with sand. We got them done and we were just full of grease. We stripped everything off and jumped in to clean up. As we did this, an old master sergeant from the Second Airborne, kind of crippled up, came hobbling down with his cane. He grabbed our dog tags; he figured we'd been goofing off and here we were just trying to clean up. He gave us a detail and we had to dig a 6X. I remember that we were digging this 6X and you could hear artillery taking off. I didn't know what it was. It turned out that this was the first big attack in April on Pork Chop.

Three days before the Armistice was signed, Dick Nooe received injuries to the face that blinded him for life.
Dick Nooe

DICK NOOE When we got up there, we were at what was called the MLR. At that point, the warfare was trench warfare, a little like the First World War, really. We had a trench. The thing was probably dug as deep as a couple feet over my head. There were bunkers off of the trench line. Out in front of that MLR, probably three hundred yards, the Chinese had a trench line. At that point in time, we were fighting the Chinese. When we got to the MLR, it had been raining and raining, and we were relieving an Army outfit, and when we got down in the trenches, we were just wallowing through the mud. I was young, twenty-one, and it was still kind of exciting. There was a lot of machine gun fire, a lot of artillery going off here and there and everywhere.

JOHN BRESKE There were a lot of trench lines, and the MLR, the main line of resistance, was a trench line pretty much all the way across Korea. There were bunkers so that you could take artillery and mortars. I think the biggest thing where I saw most of the combat was on the outposts. They were somewhere half a mile out in front of the main line. That's where we spent most of our time. There were a lot of them. At the end of the war there was Boulder City, Vegas, Ashcom [Ascom] City. They were named the cities from Nevada. We moved around, never in the same place. You'd stay in the area thirty days, tops. The main thing the guys would go out for were the listening posts. I would go out and find an outpost and see if I could detect anybody trying to sneak up. We did a lot of patrols. If you'd get an outpost then you'd patrol probably into no-man's-land, probably a mile. You'd see about ten or twelve guys that would sneak around to see if you could find out something.

RICHARD HEMLIN Trucks were coming in and they started taking us up on line. It was in the middle of the night. It was all the different regiments. We were in the Second. We wound up in George Company, Second Battalion. And bang, they got us in. Flak vest, the whole bit, ammo, and bandoliers, and you dropped your duffel bag and the next thing you know, we're on the trucks and we're going up. We wound up in the blocking position on the Chop, which probably saved our lives because we were on the right side of the access road blocking. The regiment had Pork Chop Hill and Hill 200 and 347. It was a very vital sector because it was the main route that the North Koreans had used when they started [the] war and ran right down to Seoul. That's where all the attention was in April and July. I think there were 214 including the cooks and administrative. They probably went up there with 160 or 170. Fifty-seven came back. That was our baptism of fire. That was it. There was no time to fool around. It was unnerving; that was every day. I mean every day. "Where do we go today?" The worst was when they said, "We're going up on the Chop." Your nerves would start to get to you a little bit.

John Breske in full gear. *John Breske*

JOHN BRESKE I can remember a lot of the stuff real plain. I remember some of the guys. You took a few casualties every day like guys getting hit with shrapnel. You'd always bring back your dead, but it didn't always happen. I had a couple of good friends that were MIAs; you didn't know what happened. So much was going on and all of a sudden this guy wasn't there. It's not that we didn't try. We worked the area again where we had casualties if we'd lost a man and we'd go back and sometimes you found him, sometimes you didn't. I tried to follow up on some of the guys that were MIAs and never did really find out what happened.

The attacks, when they came, they'd come one bunch and then another bunch; they'd come in waves. There was no strategy behind it — they just figured if they kept coming you'd run out of bullets pretty damn quick and they'd overrun you. That would happen a lot of times. In fact, in the outposts when it got bad, we had a big bunker that we could all scramble into. We had a wire. We'd call in our artillery right on our own position and just pound the hell out of them. Say five minutes of that and then you'd come out. It worked. It was actually a

President-elect Dwight Eisenhower holds a press conference in the War Room at Eighth U.S. Army Headquarters in Korea on December 5, 1952. *WHi Image ID 39901*

good feeling. When it got bad you could always get away. Boom, everybody's in there in a hell of a hurry. Didn't take very long and you're in there. Then you were controlling the artillery. It was great. It was survival. There'd be a lot of dead. They weren't really ready for that, I don't think. Especially if they threw Willy Peter they called it, white phosphorus, you'd throw that in. That's damn tough stuff. Even if you're lying in a hole, that stuff comes down and just gets on you, and you've got a problem.

DICK NOOE On the main line, the Chinese would tube mortars in every now and then. You know, we had to keep our heads down. There was some sniper fire. Between our main line and the Chinese line were outposts. Korea is a very hilly country and so you'd have a main line here and then about three hundred yards out was the Chinese line and then in a valley, periodically, there were hills and there were outposts. They were different sized outposts; most of them were named after women. Our company essentially was in charge of an outpost right out in front of us that was called Esther. Off to the right was Dagmar. Dagmar was a bigger outpost, and then Esther and Ginger were smaller ones. Howe Company had the responsibility to man

Esther, to keep troops out there. There was room for about twenty. That was about it. It was like reinforced platoon out there.

Out in the outpost, there was a lieutenant in charge. I went out there. I was assigned out there for a week, and there, you are closer to the Chinese. We had to keep our heads down more because of sniper fire and mortars coming in. I was out there for a week. I was the sergeant in charge out there. I was back on the main line, and then later on, there were some guys in my outfit that had been there a long, long time. They'd been exposed to more combat than I'd been exposed to and they were really uptight. They were due to rotate out on that outpost and some of them really didn't want to go out. I thought it was kind of exciting, so I said, "I'll go out." So I went out a second time.

RICHARD HEMLIN We lost Baldy. Old Baldy was on the west side of Pork Chop. That loss gave the Chinese an observation post so that when our troops went up in the deuce and a half, they could call in fire. The worst part of it was, when you had to get in those deuce and a halves and they'd say "OK," the lights went out, [and] they revved it up to go forty or fifty miles an hour. We just roared through there.

You'd get into the checkpoint and then they'd send up a squad at a time.

Richard Hemlin, right, standing with a friend in front of a bunker on Pork Chop. *Richard Hemlin*

Richard Hemlin's view of Porkchop Hill from his bunker. *Richard Hemlin*

You could take fifteen or sixteen people plus ammo. The thing about that was again, from the vantage point of Baldy, they would radio back to their troops. It was a cut like Pork Chop. We'd come down here and you had this little cut in, that's where we were on blocking position. When you went up this access road, you had to make a turn. You were wide open. We nicknamed it Clobber Corner. I mean that was it. The incoming would either hit you or go short or right over your head. You had no protection. When you got there, they would put in mortars on you because they knew we were coming. We'd open the doors and when you went out, you had to sprint down the road to a trench and then duck in the trench. Then you were relatively safe for a while.

Most of the casualties that were taken on Pork Chop were because the trenches were too narrow. Pork Chop had sixty-four fighting positions. We'd send company after company. It got to the point where a company would lose a third of their men trying to get in to relieve somebody. Then because the trenches were so narrow, nobody could move any place. There were wounded and the dead and it was like you're stepping over bodies. After seven days you come back, take a shower, and you go up to another hill. That's how life was every day out there, month after month. That was it.

JOHN BRESKE We had a hill that overlooked Panmunjom and with binoculars, you could watch [the armistice talks]. Our side would come there in helicopters. They'd come flying in there and then the Koreans, they'd come in some black cars. You'd see them pull in there and they'd meet and sometimes they were in there five minutes, sometimes they were in there ten minutes. In the *Stars and Stripes* they'd tell us what was going on at Panmunjom. We knew what was going on, better than they did, because we were watching it every day. At any time you could watch what had happened there, so you knew nothing was going to happen. When they met for five minutes, you knew nothing was going to come out of it. If they met for longer, you'd get your hopes up. The word was always that you were going to get relieved by some division...always. I heard that from the day I got there. It didn't ever happen — just wishful thinking. Everybody was hoping it would end.

Peace negotiations went on for two years, first in Kaesong and then in Panmunjom. Here, Korean officials leave talks at Panmunjom. *Don Arne*

RICHARD HEMLIN It's July 9, morning hours. All of a sudden, this first lieutenant yelled out, "Hemlin!" I said, "Yeah, that's me." How did he know my name? And then I realized I had this big blue patch with white H-E-M-L-I-N. He spotted me from leadership, and I still don't know his name. He called me out and he says, "Got to get somebody up on the Chop." He says, "Here's

U.N. Soldiers guard the entrance to Peace Village (Panmunjon) where armistice talks took place. *Don Arne*

what's going on." He said, "We have to get a plat, a layout of all the sixty-four positions. We have to know where we are, where Joe is." Joe Chink. "We got to get that information back and it's got to go to artillery because, whatever it is, at 1530 hours we want to hit it; we're going to saturate with VT [variable time fuse]. So your job is to go up, get this to Major Noble, get that plat filled out, and then bring it back." I'd gone up to the Chop in these APCs [Armored Personnel Carriers] but all the time with a group, see. I remember it was really nerve-racking because that thing was just loaded with all kinds of ammo and everything. We had a .50-caliber up on top. You couldn't even see a little bit to get up there if you had to. There was just enough room for me to get in the back. I got in the back and the tanker says, "OK, you let it roll." Bang. He takes off.

The imagination takes over, because we were going "up there." We were going along, you know, and then we came around Clobber Corner and — Bababoom! — I could feel it. These were as close as I've ever heard it. Then it stopped, and then it seemed like it went faster. Well, my imagination got the best of me, and I figured the tankers got it, this thing is running on autopilot, you know, we're right through the cut. I'm heading to North Korea. This thing is going to blow up in my face. Then we stopped. I could hear a couple Koreans talking and I said, "Who is he?" It was like a class B movie. They open the door and I fly out. I think about that now, and it was kind of dumb. I realized what was going on. Things got kind of back to reality. I go in and there's this African American SFC [Sergeant First Class], nice guy, and I told him, I said, "Whatever it is, I've got to get this plat filled out, sergeant. I'm up here to see Major Noble." I didn't know who the hell Major Noble was. It turned out that he was the regimental commander. He said, "Major Noble is being taken care of." OK. I thought Major Noble had some problem and he was being attended to. Then he says, "There are no more officers on the hill." Every officer was killed. He says, "So, I'm in command. I'll get this taken care of."

Safe Conduct Passes were dropped by the thousands over North Korean and Chinese troops in an effort to entice them to surrender. The currency-like note guaranteed the humane treatment of the surrenderer by U.N. forces. While thousands surrendered, many Chinese and North Korean troops were threatened with execution by their own military if they tried.
Robert Strand

My company was up on the hill. I got up there and spent the whole night in the checkpoint. It was a tough experience. I remember the sergeant coming in and he asked if I had a cigarette. I smoked and I gave him a cigarette. I remember all the smoke coming out of his lungs and his neck. He was hit with Willy Peter and it was burning holes in him. It was like a freak movie. Here's all this smoke coming out under his back. I'll never forget that poor guy.

When they set up the main line of resistance, which ran a 155 miles east to west, if you looked on the map, Pork Chop was the key thing. That was because if they broke through Pork Chop, they'd be able to run. It's only thirty-three miles to Seoul. MacArthur had been embarrassed. It was the worst embarrassment since Bull Run. His ego got the best of him and he wanted to go out with shining stars. He was a heck of a general, but that was the end, and rightly so. Matthew Ridgway came in and we got it back and got things put together. The Pork Chop for us, the April Pork Chop, was the first big attack where they tried to really break through. The last one was July 6 and lasted five days. That was the biggest one. That was the one where all the coverage was. People were at Panmunjom, and nobody was expecting that. They thought it was all going to be a truce. Then that one hit. That was a tough one. That was like the finale.

DICK NOOE The evening of July 24, 1953, one of the guys on the main line brought out to the outpost what were called chiggy-bearers. Chiggy-bearers were South Koreans; they carried our supplies out there: water, C-Rations, and all that kind of stuff. During the day, we had more incoming than I'd seen for a long, long time. Mortars, mortars, mortars. People were getting hit out in the outpost during the day. We were, of course, up at night on watch. So he came out with five, six chiggy-bearers loaded with stuff for us out there. While they were unloading, he came into my bunker. Now it's night, dark guard duty, and then during the day, we could sleep. And I was sleeping in the bunker in a kind of bunk.

There was a wall...with sandbags and dirt separating me from the trench line. A Chinese tubed a mortar right in there. It just landed right outside this dirt sandbag wall. Literally, it blew me completely out of that rack I was in. It didn't hurt me, but, boy, I'll tell you, it really jarred me. All that day, the day of the twenty-fourth, we were getting it and had to really keep our heads down. We were returning a lot of fire. Behind the MLR, there was a mortar outfit dug in. So they were returning a lot of fire that night. At that point in time there was a Marine down the trench line a bit that got hit. He was bleeding all over the place and screaming. We hauled him back to the command post which was around the other way, and there was a corpsman in there, and I really got the shock of my life when we hauled him back there because I didn't realize how many guys had gotten hit, and they were just lying in there, wounded, probably some that were dead. Then we went back to our bunker and at that point, at that point there's a mass of humanity coming down the trench line, screaming and yelling. At first, I thought somebody was having a party. I was just in complete denial. What had happened is that the Chinese had been over on Dagmar. There was a big firefight over there. We could see it going on, and they came off Dagmar and they came on our outpost. Our outpost was small, so they came over the top of the trench lines and got in the trench lines. There were hundreds of them, all over the place. There were a bunch of them coming down the trench line, and I had a machine gun and I took it out in the trench line and you keep the things half-loaded. I full loaded it; it didn't work. I full loaded it again two or three times and it didn't work, then I just swung it.

I got back in the bunker. By this time a couple of Chinese came right by the bunker. I'm sure they were all doped up because they didn't even see us. The guy that was with me dropped and killed a couple of them. We had a string of grenades that we started throwing. We just threw them, threw them, threw them, and threw them. There are explosions going on. I tell you, war is absolute chaos. This is where I think I began to realize it isn't all that exciting. In any event, I got hit in the back of the legs with some frag or something or other, I don't know. It could have been a mortar; I don't know what it was. I got hit in the back of the legs and it felt to me like my leg was cut off. I thought it was gone, but fortunately, as it turned out, they were all flesh wounds. I got out of the bunker and then I got hit in the face. I'll never know for sure with what. It could have been what's called a potato masher, slang expression for the kind of grenades that the Chinese used. It wasn't a frag grenade, because if I got hit with a frag grenade, I wouldn't be here. My face would have been just torn...

JOHN BRESKE We had replacements come in, and every once in a while they gave an announcement that anybody that was seventeen years old did not have to be on the front lines. There were a lot of kids lying about their ages at that time, and they'd be in there. We had three of them in our company. And I told them, "If I were you guys, I would get the hell out." I'd give them a job ten miles back in the supply or anything like that. We lost all three of those guys in one night. All three of them. They could have gone back.

John Breske being awarded the Silver Star for gallantry in action. *John Breske*

We knew it was going to end. We knew it that night about twelve o'clock that the armistice would be tomorrow morning at eight o'clock. Why throw all that stuff out there? That meant more guys getting hit and wounded and killed. I think it was eight o'clock in the morning when they shut it down. Everybody just went and picked up their dead. I was damn glad it was over. It was just like a baseball game or a football game or anything else. Everybody kind of shook hands and was glad it was over with. I didn't see that. I was evacuated before that.

I was hit with shrapnel in the legs and in the back about ten thirty, eleven o'clock at night. I got bandaged up and there were so many more casualties that I went back. I shouldn't have gone back. We were on the front. It was a mortar. I'm sure it was. In the legs and back, it wasn't so bad. It hurt but it was short. The second time that night, that I got hit, was with bullets; burp gun slugs. When I got hit in my right arm and right shoulder, that hurt. I mean, that hurt! That's when I went, "Woo, this really hurts, hurts me a lot." All the other ones I could handle. I got a little dizzy. I knew I was probably going to have a little problem with shock, and so I tried to talk myself out of it. It must have been more nerves or bones or whatever. I thought the arm was gone and when I picked myself up, it was still there… The last time I was hit, there were a lot of casualties. I think it was kind of stupid that everybody was getting rid of their ammunition because they knew the war was going to end. The Chinese and the Koreans, they were throwing everything out and so were the Americans. We were throwing all our stuff; it was daylight I think for three days. I don't think I saw any darkness through those last three days.

DICK NOOE I've talked to guys that I was out there with and I've got some sense of what happened. There's a very good possibility that the Chinese were running patrols between the MLR. It could be that they found me, because I remember getting these severe blows to my face. It was just horrible. Painful, just one after another. As a result of all this now, this eye is a prosthesis — that's an artificial eye. This is my own, but I've just got a little bit of light perception. I can't see anything out of it. And then I've got a fracture here, a fracture here, and fractures on top of my head. That's where I think they were hitting and knocking me with rifle butts or boots or something.

Then I remember being probably in a helicopter. I remember somebody yelling at me saying, "Keep your goddamn feet down." So I must have been waving my feet around. Then, I don't remember it but I'm sure that I was sent to a MASH unit because I got all these medical records and stuff — I don't remember any of that. By this point in time, my mother, God bless her soul, she was getting telegrams from the military. Those telegrams said something like, "Sorry to inform you, your son, Sergeant Dick C. Nooe, has gotten hit and he's wounded." That's like the first one. Then a few days later another was sent, saying, "Sorry to inform you, your son is serious and he's lost his sight." So my poor mother…It makes me feel bad to even think about that to this day.

The armistice was signed the twenty-seventh, so this was three days before the armistice. We knew all about the talks, and you know, we were waiting and waiting for the armistice, but I thought a lot about, "My God, here it is three days before and I get it." I haven't really experienced any resentment because I wanted to go over there. I wanted the excitement, so I don't have anything to be resentful about.

JOHN BRESKE I thought that the arm was gone but when I found that she was still dangling, I felt pretty good. When they got me back to that aid station, they knew the war was over, so the doctors were celebrating, too. They were having a good time about it then when they brought me. I was lying on a stretcher. The doctor came in and said, "Get him ready," and laid down right alongside of me and took a little nap. He woke up and I knew he was drinking. Then he got up and operated on my arm. I had no problems. He did a good job, even if he had a few drinks. It didn't bother me.

They opened it up and took out a couple bullets. They removed that shrapnel too. He really went over me. They opened the wounds up, cleaned them out real good, then they packed them. They left them like that for three or four days before they sewed them up. I think they were worried about hemorrhagic fever at that time because anytime you got hit with shrapnel, it pushes the clothes into the wound and there were so many rats around to carry hemorrhagic fever.

RICHARD HEMLIN I can't recall any big feelings when the war ended. We were just drained then. Nobody really trusted it. Everybody was in; nobody said, "Are you a Republican? Are you a Democrat? Are you a liberal?" Nobody said a damn thing. "Are you a Catholic? Are you Jewish or what?" I mean, we were too busy, we were all Americans. When you send somebody to war, I mean, you're giving them fifty years and maybe a lifetime of memories. You better have a good cause. It wasn't a good war, but it was a just war. It did the job. We paid a very high price.

DICK NOOE They waited a long time; they stitched up my legs and everything but they weren't real truthful with me, the doctors. They kept telling me I was going to get more sight back and more sight back and I didn't. Then I was discharged from there. I was discharged from the Marine Corps and there was a captain on the discharge board and he said, "Sergeant, you're blind." He said, "You're going to be blind the rest of your life. So you might as well get adjusted to it." I was so angry at him. But you don't slug a captain. He was the only guy that was really truthful with me. I look back on that now and I think God bless him that he just laid it out the way it was.

I'd been discharged from the service, so then I went to a VA hospital in Chicago. They did a bunch more work on me. They did a lot of plastic surgery on my face. I had a nose operation there because my nose had been busted. I was fitted with a plastic eye there. They told me at Heinz, "It's going to be by far the best for you if you go to a blind rehabilitation center right now. Don't go home and sit on your fanny, because you may never get off your fanny and get on with your life." So I did. I went right to a blind rehab center and that was very, very sound advice. That's where I met my wife-to-be. She was a volunteer with the Red Cross. That's where I met her. She'd come into the blind center about once a week and just be there to talk. We started going out — we weren't supposed to, it was against the rules, but we snuck out. That's where I got my self-respect back and I knew...I was always one to do this and do that and get involved in a lot of different things. After that blind rehab center, I just knew I would make it. My mother had said, God bless her, she said, "Well, you can just come home and live with us the rest of your life." I knew when I got out of that blind center that that wasn't the way it was going to be. I was going to do my thing. They taught me how to travel with a cane and brail and typing; daily living skills of various kinds. They expected a lot.

RICHARD HEMLIN We did our job. Eisenhower turned it around. Had we not held the line, who knows? You look at it like South Korea is our tenth or eleventh largest trading partner and North Korea is just bleeding. We were trying to smash them into the ground. It was a limited war, but it was a real solid victory. I mean, the mission was not accomplished. The whole job was to take up the peninsula; it was denied. South Korea grows to be as stable as

Marilyn Monroe visited U.S. troops in Korea a few months after the armistice was signed. *Richard Hemlin*

it is. I'm proud; all of us were, but there was apathy when we got back. It was like they were saying, "Where have you been? What happened?" I wasn't ready for the routine. So it took me a while to try and get my legs under me.

It's embarrassing but noises and quick movements...I didn't know anything about post-traumatic stress. I never checked out anything. I didn't go the VA. It was like, "That's it, get up and fight through it." The nerves and the thoughts have been hit pretty hard. I can close my eyes and I can still see the fins on the mortar, but it's a lot better. My wife has done a masterful job helping me.

DICK NOOE I ended up going to Washington University in St. Louis and that's where I got my master's degree in social work. I worked in a mental health outpatient clinic in Topeka, Kansas, and then in a psych hospital. My wife wanted to get closer to home. She was from Chicago. We zeroed in on Wisconsin. I ended up at Winnebago County Mental Health Clinic. Off and on, I'd see vets there. I'd see Vietnam vets. I've had a subcontract with the VA for the last thirteen years.

You can put flashbacks on the continuum from just thinking about things to a combination of thinking and feeling to actually dissociating and kind of hallucinating. Mine were never that bad, but I'd flash back. Have a combination of thoughts and feelings. Like if I hear something on TV, I still do that. I'll never get over it completely. Those thoughts will always be there. What's happened, as a result of me being in therapy and just working, is that with these flashbacks, they're gone very quickly. I have some startle responses. In fact, the older I get the worse they seem to get. I don't like loud noises. I've got a chronic sleep problem. I'm sure it's related back to what happened to me. You betcha, I can hear myself in some of these vets.

14 Big Switch

"Ask any Korean veteran, there were no parades like there were after World War II. There was apathy, and apathy hurts." — Cliff Borden

By the time the Korean War came to its official end on July 27, 1953, approximately 7,200 American soldiers had been taken prisoner by North Korea and China. Because many of the men were captured during the first sixth months of the war — when North Korea and China made their initial advances down the peninsula — they had been held captive for almost three years before their release. After China entered the war, most American POWs spent their captivity at a series of camps close to the Yalu River along the border between North Korea and China. While the Chinese camps were somewhat open and let the prisoners mingle, they separated ranked men from privates and spent extensive time trying to indoctrinate U.N. prisoners. Along with indoctrination, physical threats, and psychological interrogation, U.N. prisoners of war had to contend with freezing Korean winters, combat wounds, and shortages of food and medical care. China allowed the International Red Cross to visit the prisoners, but only if accompanied by representatives from both the North Korean government and the Chinese Red Cross. At the suggestion of the International Red Cross, the two sides exchanged many of these sick and wounded prisoners through Operation Little Switch, which began on April 20, 1953; the U.N. command turned over approximately 7,500 Chinese and North Korean prisoners in exchange for 684 U.N. POWs. The small scale of Operation Little Switch meant that returning U.N. soldiers were processed through medical facilities; U.N. Command did not create a special processing site for returning soldiers.

Little Switch represented the beginning of the end of the war. When the Chinese and North Korean governments agreed to the operation, they also suggested that truce talks be reopened at Panmunjom. Within several months, the two sides resolved their differences to agree on a cease-fire, to take effect at 10:00 p.m. on July 27. For months, the issue of prisoner

Armistice
July 27, 1953

**CHINA
(MANCHURIA)**

U.S.S.R.

Vladivostok

Tumen R.

Rashin

Chongjin

Hyesanjin

Yalu R.

Chosin

Iwon

Sinuiju

Hungnam

NORTH KOREA

Sea of Japan

Wonsan

Korea Bay

★ Pyongyang

Armistice line

Tongchon

Panmunjom
(Truce Village)

Iron Triangle

SOUTH KOREA

Kaesong

38th Parallel

Chunchon

38th Parallel

Ongjin

Seoul ★

Armistice line

Inchon

Osan

Taejon

Pohang

Yellow Sea

Kunsan

Taegu

Sunchon

Pusan

Strait

Mokpo

Kohung

JAPAN

Korea

Under U.N. control

Under Communist control

0   50   100 Miles

0   50   100 Kilometers

UW–Madison, Dept. of Geography, Cartography Lab

repatriation had delayed the settlement: while China and North Korean insisted that all prisoners return to one of these two states, the United Nations argued that prisoners should be allowed to choose their country of return, rather than being forced to go back to China or North Korea. Because many men in the Chinese Army had fought on the Nationalist side in the Chinese Civil War (which had only ended in 1949) against the Communists, many Chinese soldiers did not want to return to the People's Republic of China. When surveys of POWs confirmed that many did not want to return to China or North Korea, both Communist states became concerned about losing face; negotiations broke off several times over this issue. However, fears that the United Nations would extend and continue the war ultimately led China and North Korea to conclude that it was not worth holding out on the POW issue. The two states agreed to the U.N. plan.

Reaching a cease-fire not only required an agreement between the U.N. and North Korea and China but also required the support of South Korea, especially President Syngman Rhee. Rhee, angry that the war was ending without a reunited Korea under his rule, had released approximately 25,000 North Korean prisoners in an attempt to stall the dicey prisoner repatriation negotiations, opening the U.N. side to charges of bad faith by China and North Korea. China accepted the United States' explanation that it was not involved in the breakout; by threatening to leave Rhee out of the final settlement, but also promising extensive postwar aid, the American government was able to gain Rhee's approval for a settlement.

Operation Big Switch, in which the two sides exchanged the remaining POWs, began in August 1953. Through Operation Big Switch, approximately 75,000 North Korean and Chinese POWs were exchanged for almost 13,000 U.N. POWs, the majority of whom were South Korean and American. The returning American POWs first arrived at "Freedom Village," a special POW return site near Panmunjom. After a short medical and psychiatric examination, most were moved to the Army Replacement Depot at Inchon where they were given access to showers, fresh linens, and supplies provided by both the military and the Red Cross. Prisoners from both sides who chose not to be repatriated were sent to a temporary camp at Panmunjom. At the temporary camp, a five-member Neutral Nations Repatriation Commission, chaired by India, allowed a representative of the POW's home nation to interview the prisoner. After the interview ended, the former POW could choose whether he wanted to return home or go to a neutral nation. Approximately 22,000 Chinese and North Korean prisoners chose not to return home; most of these Chinese prisoners went to Taiwan, which was still held by the Chinese Nationalist government. Twenty-one American POWs made the same decision, shocking many Americans and heightening fears of brainwashing and Communism in the heyday of McCarthyism. For POWs on both sides, Operation Big Switch represented the end of a long and harrowing ordeal, yet due to the unpopularity of the war in the United States, many former soldiers, including POWs, were not publicly celebrated for their contributions.

Cliff Borden, Madison (Army, Eighth Regiment)
Darrell Krenz, Madison (Army, 24th Infantry Division)
Dale King, Colgate (Army, Fifth Artillery)

CLIFF BORDEN We were a year into the war and I was a sophomore at Bucknell University in Pennsylvania. I was not too good a student. [I] decided to look around and see if [I] could find a choice in the service and not be drafted into the infantry. I tried them all out, went through recruiters, and on campus there were recruiters for the Army Security Agency, which is communications intelligence. I went down to the basement of the post office of Lewisburg, Pennsylvania, and Sergeant says to three or four of us, "You guys don't want to be in foot-flogging infantry. You want to be with guys like yourself, who have a couple years of college. You'll start out as a private, but you'll go to school, and if you go through the school, you will get a military occupational specialty and a security clearance, which will pretty much guarantee that you will not be up in front lines should you be assigned or deployed to Korea." The war was raging, so that's what I did. I went to Fort Knox, Kentucky, for Armored Infantry Basic, took my advanced individual training at Fort Devon, Massachusetts, in radio traffic analysis, and graduated from the school.

I went to Korea in March of 1953. We filled the needs at the time, in this case in the intelligence headquarters. I was a typist typing up the intelligence summaries, which were then sent through the chief intelligence officer, who then forwarded them on to Eighth Army Intelligence downtown. The intelligence gleaned from these intercepts was used in part as a basis for determining enemy attacks. When the enemy would be coming

Cliff Borden, center, with friends. *Cliff Borden*

up the hill with a plane or blowing the bugles, we could anticipate these massive frontal assaults from the Chinese Communists or the North Koreans. This was a very important job. We were providing information to save American lives.

DARRELL KRENZ We started with over 800 and only 283 of us got out in Big Switch. We got turned over to the Chinese and I really have to say, they were a little better for us. They gave us all the rice we wanted to eat. I think they'd really started negotiating, because a lot of my friends were POWs under the Chinese and they weren't very good to them. They would stick you in a hole in the ground if you did something bad; I guess you had to suffer for it. I was in the hole for a couple of days but...I didn't do anything bad; I just didn't salute the guard was all.

The Chinese gave us some cotton padded uniforms. The whole time, we were marching through the mountains and living up there in that cold place and I still had no shoes. I just had rags and stuff around me and then if someone died...Finally it caught up to all of us where we all would have some kind of a shirt and stuff. They made us go to school. Seven days a week we had to go down to this one building and listen to them talk about how good the Communist government was and how bad ours was. I even read a book: *The Grapes of Wrath*. They thought at the time that this was the way America was. They used to take us across into Manchuria for wood hauling. We'd have to get a log and bring it back so their guards could boil their rice. If you didn't bring back a big enough log they made you go back again. I remember some of the guards, they didn't have the right clothes either. One of ours who was in charge of us, his ears just got like big elephant ears, frozen.

Little Switch came by and we thought, "Boy, now we're going to go home." They just took some of the people and the wounded. It was some time before we had Big Switch again. One of my best friends, he lives in North Carolina now, he was so sick. I don't think any of us would have lasted more than a couple of more months, especially another winter.

DALE KING At the Mining Camp or the Bean Camp or Pleasant Valley, whichever you want to call it, the interrogation began. We lived in school buildings, next to a large field where they gave us daily education. That lasted for perhaps a month and a half. Capitalism is no good and the only way to go was to be a Communist, so everybody shares and shares alike and all that kind of stuff. It was endless, day after day, they'd beat us over the head. They had a song they would ask us to sing. It was the Communist national song. We had a person who was very clever and musically inclined who gave us words that we would understand, so we created our version which was: "Now take the red flag down from the pole and shove it up Joe Stalin's hole. The working class can kiss my ass, I got the foreman's job at last." The Chinese guards smiled knowing that we had fulfilled our duty but not knowing what we had done. It was very good.

The camp was quite large. There were probably as many as eight hundred people there. Our food was very limited. On the march and in this camp, our food consisted mainly of sorghum and a little birdseed. We had very few vegetables and no meat. I became very ill in that camp and had to go to what they called a hospital. The hospital consisted of some Korean huts in a row. When I checked in, there were two of us in a room. The gentleman next to me was probably even younger than I was. He wasn't very coherent. He was on his way out. In fact, he only lived one day or two days at most. They took off his hat and his head was all full of lice. Mass of lice in his head. I cannot believe what he looked like. They hauled him out. When you're in that hospital for dysentery, they give you what's called "the water diet." It's supposed to improve your condition by not having any solids. They boil up a couple of teaspoons of rice in a huge barrel and give it to you. There was virtually no nutrition available.

I survived. As I got better, they sent me back to my unit. Shortly after that, the sergeants were broken away from the rest of the camp in order not to have any organizational structure within the camp. They figured the sergeants were interfering with the operations of their education. We were sent to the northernmost of the camps. At that camp, education was continued. The interrogation started to be a lot more than it was in the first camp. Asking about, "How big is your unit? What did you do in the unit? What do your relatives do?" Things like that. They'd ask what you had done when you were a civilian back home. If you wanted to get them all riled up, you'd tell them that you owned your own car. They would go off the wall to think that American people would have their own cars. Nobody in China had cars at that time. There was a lot of dissension between the interrogators and the interviewees. We could be factual and they'd still get mad at us because of the difference in what we had as Americans versus what they had as Chinese soldiers. It was the truth but not well received.

After some period of time, maybe three or four months there, we got some inkling that there would be something good. The first switch was where the very sick and those who had difficulty of various sorts medically were exchanged for some Chinese prisoners. That's what was called Little Switch. One good thing about it was, right next to our camp they had a supply depot. Apparently one of the fellows that was let go was aware of it. It wasn't but a couple of days after this exchange before the old bombers all came in and just blew the heck out of it. The planes came in the middle of the day. The planes came over, waved their wings at us, and slammed it.

CLIFF BORDEN We went up to witness Operation Big Switch, which was the big prisoner exchange which was a part of the armistice settlement, the armistice having been signed at Panmunjom on the 27th of July, 1953. I had a chance to see the operation, to take photos. I've always been a serious amateur photographer taking 35-mm and I even changed places with an MP when they would send the truck with prisoners from Koje-do. Across the Imjin River, they would put them onto an MP [Military Police] collection point for prisoners; they would have a two-and-a-half-ton truck. Prisoners

The "Bridge of No Return" crossed the demilitarized zone between North and South Korea. After the armistice, it was used for the prisoner exchange at Operation Big Switch. It was so named because once a released prisoner chose to cross the bridge, there was no going back. *Courtesy U.S. Army*

Cliff Borden on his way to Freedom Village in North Korea, the site where returning and repatriated POWs were processed before crossing into South Korea. *Cliff Borden*

were visible; they took the canvas down. Every other vehicle would be a jeep with MPs with shotguns, riding shotgun as they say, to make sure the prisoners didn't jump off en route. Then it was a distance of perhaps ten miles up to the point of the demilitarized zone. There was a bombed-out bridge that had been repaired — it was called the "Bridge of No Return" — that separated North Korea from South Korea in the middle of the DMZ. What I did when I went up there and changed places with an MP, I grabbed his pistol belt and his pistol and his helmet and went up there as part of the shotgun guard. I could then take my camera and shoot pictures of the Communist Chinese and North Korean Freedom Village, their Freedom Village where their repatriates would be processed. This was actually in North Korea, technically, so I had one shot at that and this of course was an opportunity I was not about to deny myself.

I don't know how legal it was, but I just went ahead and did it anyhow. Nobody was going to argue with the GIs and I was not armed because you couldn't be armed in the demilitarized zone. Unless you were an MP. The Chinese or Korean guards and the United States MPs dressed in appropriate uniforms and they took turns at the Peace Pagoda, where the peace treaty was signed. There was another temporary building in which they conducted talks and they resolved differences, day-to-day arguments they had over relatively minor matters. If the Communists had a complaint they would call a meeting; if we had a complaint we would call a meeting. They still do that, but now they have permanent buildings that sit on the line.

DALE KING My release was in Big Switch with about sixteen hundred others from all the eight camps. We knew they were acting a little funny before the Little Switch went on, and we knew that something was happening before they told us that there was going to be a total exchange of prisoners. There was nothing in anybody's mail that could tell us because they looked at everything. Before you could receive mail, they went over it totally. I received my first letter from my mother when she thought I was alive. I was ready to rotate back when I was taken prisoner. I only had another couple of weeks to go. All these people that rotated back to the United States... But the letters that [my mother] sent; everybody whose name I wrote on a back of a photo that she had, she wrote to. And one of them said that he had heard that I was in prison camp. Now this could have happened because there were people that were left behind because they didn't want to take care of them all, that might know or have seen me or might have heard

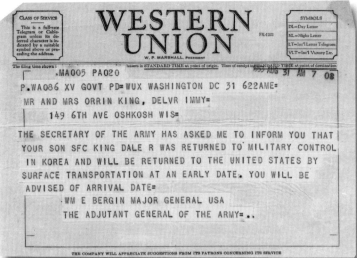

about it. But she wrote a letter to me which indicated she knew I was alive. That was when I was in a hospital and wasn't caring so much whether I lived or died. Quite frankly, at that time I was really down. I looked at this letter and said, "Oh hell, I don't want to die on her twice." Because when she got the missing-in-action letter, I knew that she had problems. The thought of her having to hear that I was dead made it so I perked up a little bit and decided maybe I'll keep on going. It was not a pleasant adventure, but the camaraderie

The telegram Dale King's mother received informing her of her son's release as a POW. *Dale King*

between our people was great. As I say, I go to a meeting once a year now and, as my wife would tell you, "You guys are alike. You have a good sense of humor and you just let it run off your back." I think that's the way it was. It had to be that way; otherwise you wouldn't survive. If you said "Give up," you were gone.

Darrell Krenz, fourth from right, in the hospital after his release as a POW. *Darrell Krenz*

My mother only received three letters from me as long as I was prisoner due to my resentment against what you had to put on the outside of the envelope: the Chinese Committee for World Peace Against American Aggression. They wouldn't send the letter if you didn't say something nice about what was going on in the camp.

DARRELL KRENZ They got us together and put us on trucks and we were going down. It was quite a ways away, overnight. During the morning, we were going down the road and we only had the back open a little bit where we could see once in a while, and we kept seeing something lying along the side of the road all the time. But the two guards, they wouldn't let us do much. All of a sudden the guard lifted up the thing. We're still going across this big bridge and all kinds of flags across the bridge and all of a sudden here were American flags. Then we knew we were home. What was lying alongside of the road, the guys were all taking their cotton padded uniforms off and throwing them away. They didn't want anything more to do with them.

A couple of times I said, "I'm not moving; I'm not going to do this. I'm going to die anyway; why prolong it?" There was always something that sparked a "Come on, let's go." I didn't have a good life when I was a kid. I was going days and days without food, the way our family did. I weighed 180 pounds when I went to Korea. When I come out I was 102. If I saw someone else giving up, I'd say "Hey, you can't be doing that." I'd just go grab him and say, "Come on, let's go walk around; let's do something." I just kept on going and finally got out.

CLIFF BORDEN I was an observer of a history-making activity. It was an emotional time particularly when you saw the Chinese trucks, which were a little smaller than a two-and-a-half-ton U.S. Army truck, carrying our prisoners and you could see them hanging out of the sides, waiting. They just couldn't wait to get to freedom, and I have some pictures taken across the rice paddies of these people coming across, these fellow soldiers who've been to prison, many as long as three years. Fifty percent of our prisoners were in the first six months of the war. A lot of these people had spent a long time in captivity; a lot had died in captivity, been tortured.

There is a letter to my mother, which I read years later, that I had written a few days right after, telling of the experience I had going into a room where the television media and newspapers were assigned in the Freedom

Trucks used during Operation Big Switch to bring POWs to freedom. *Cliff Borden*

Village compounds. I wasn't supposed to be in there but went in there anyhow and they brought out this young man. I have the letter to my mother explaining how the young man broke down after much questioning. He was real cool and answered all the questions, until the last one when the guy said, "If you had a choice right now what you really wanted, what would it be?" His lips quivered — I was very close — and he said, "I want to go home. I want to go home." He just broke down, totally broke down emotionally, and a lieutenant colonel gently led him away and the cameras shut down and that was the end of the interviews for the day. It was a very, very emotional experience.

DALE KING After we crossed the Big Switch, well, we went back on the *Charles Black*. We were met, first of all, by a full colonel who welcomed us back. Just before that was a sight that you could not believe: Chinese going north and Koreans were disrobing and throwing the boots and the suits that they got from us and all their clothes off and throwing them in the road. We were crossing and they were throwing their clothes off and we were coming down. They were well taken care of. They were just proving that they still thought their system was better than [ours] and trying to antagonize. It was kind of funny in a way because we knew better. We got down there, got off, and they gave us a meal and the Red Cross gave us some additional supplies.

DARRELL KRENZ I jumped off the truck. The flap went up and then a couple of Marines came over and said, "We'll help you off the truck." And I said, "I don't need your help." I still had some pride in me. I jumped off the truck onto my face. I thought I was stronger than I was. I looked over there and saw the American flag. I went over there and I put my arms around that pole and I couldn't keep control of myself at all. I just hung on to that thing. Pretty soon an officer come over and says, "Come on now, son. You're home now." I said, "OK. I'm home."

DALE KING There was a little bitty PX so we could get cigarettes if we wanted them. They had cameras and watches that you could buy. They gave us an instant four dollars a day for rations missed, so we had cash in our pocket. I bought a camera and a watch there because they took away the Rolex that I had. We just stayed there for a while until they had arranged the boat, the *General Black*, which took us back. They transported us by helicopter to another encampment at Inchon. Then they bused us from the encampment to the boat. My parents met me in San Francisco. My younger brother was along with them, and my uncle lived in San Francisco, so we got together with him, then we drove back to Wisconsin.

Oshkosh hosted a parade to celebrate Dale King's release after twenty-eight months in a North Korean POW camp. *Dale King*

DARRELL KRENZ I didn't do anything for many years after I came home. I wouldn't even let my wife wear a red dress. She'd better not have any rice or anything like that in the house. Since I got in the Legion and the VFW [Veterans of Foreign Wars] and started going to these reunions, it's gotten a lot easier. I know three years ago I tried to give a talk at the Legion down there when we had Memorial Day and I was just breaking down all the time. It's gotten a lot better. There are still some points where I start thinking a little bit too much about it and then I go do something else right away. It'll never go away. I mean, it's been over fifty years, you know, and I still think about it. You just got to say, "It's never going away." There was so much happening, so much death. It was terrible.

CLIFF BORDEN When I got home, it was just after the war. I got home in March. I had a sixty-day leave. I was two years in Far East command, so I was given a post-combat area leave. I was proud of being a soldier. I lived under the shadow of the greatest generation, the World War II guys we looked up to. World War II was constantly on our minds. I was eleven years old when Pearl Harbor was attacked, and I was fifteen years old when VJ-Day came and the Japanese surrendered. The military always had a fascination for me, and still does. I still consider the major portion of my life and my being is being a soldier. I was proud of the fact that we had saved the South Korean people. I wasn't afraid to wear my uniform. In those days it was like the uniform worn in Europe in the ETO [European Theater of Operations] by the World War II veterans — Ike jacket and wool trousers. The only thing different was the fact that I was wearing Korean ribbons instead of wearing Pacific or Theater ribbons from World War II. I was wearing Korean ribbons. I went downtown and I walked into the malt shop. There were people there that I had known before the war, before I went to college. They said, "Cliff Borden, where have you been?" They didn't know I was in the Army. They'd gone to college and graduated and so on and they were in there, having a malt in the afternoon.

When they found out that I had given up my studies and joined the Army, that I wasn't drafted but had volunteered to go to Korea, they were not very complimentary to me. They called me a fool for having done this. A World War II veteran kicked me out of one of the major veterans' organizations' posts when I went to try to join. He said, "Get out of here, kid. You lost America's first war!" They considered that we lost it, because it wasn't a total victory like theirs had been. Theirs had been a "popular war." The citizenry from all walks of life backed it. This was absent in Korea. So when we got home it was thankless at best to drop your life and go in and serve and be in harm's way and maybe come home dead in a box. At best it, it was a losing cause, because we only ended up with a stalemate. We ended up back essentially on the 38th parallel. Without the time it takes to evaluate history, it takes decades to put things in proper perspective. In 1954, when I came back to my home of New Providence, New Jersey, that perspective was not there. This apathy for the returning veterans has been shared by many. If you ask any Korean veteran, there were no parades like there were after World War II. There was apathy, and apathy hurts.

Epilogue: Father and Son

"I remember looking at the orders and thinking, 'My dad was in Korea.' I remember calling him up and saying, 'I'm going to Korea!' There was a slight pause on the phone and he said, 'Tell me what it's like.'" — Paul Braatz

The armistice that ended the Korean War did not establish an official peace between North and South Korea; today, the two Koreas remain divided by a demilitarized zone (DMZ), one of the most heavily guarded places in the world. Many Korean families separated by the war never met again. Though the two countries remain technically at war, many Korean citizens bear little ill will toward one another and continue to hope for reunification. Indeed, in 1998, South Korean President Kim Dae Jung began his "Sunshine Policy," which sought a peaceful coexistence with North Korea, though reunification still remains a stated goal of South Korea. The Sunshine Policy increased political contact between South and North Korea and included cooperative business ventures, humanitarian aid from South to North, and contact between family members. In 2000, President Kim won the Nobel Peace Prize as a result of the Sunshine Policy. Still, the future between these two states — ethnically identical but politically and ideologically polarized — remains unclear.

Despite the devastation wrought by the war, South Korea has gone through major changes, establishing a vibrant economy and a strong multi-party democracy. North Korea, however, continues to be a closed, enigmatic, single-party state, led by Kim Jong-il, son of Korean War–era leader Kim Il-sung, who led North Korea until his death in 1998. Though Korea remains divided between North and South, the dream of a united Korea that led to such a deadly, destructive, and frustrating war remains a strong hope today.

The end of the Korean War did not mean the end of the close relationship between the United States and South Korea. South Korea has remained an important ally of the United States, existing on the front lines of the Cold War and continuing to play a major role in American defense in the region. The United States has thus maintained a series of military bases in South Korea, many of which it still holds today. Since the end of the war in 1953, thousands of American men and women have served in South Korea, watching over the demilitarized zone between North and South Korea. Marine Paul Braatz is a living example of the continuing presence of the U. S. military in Korea; the son of Korean War veteran Art Braatz, Paul followed in his father's footsteps when he served in Korea in the mid-1990s. Their story is told below.

Paul Braatz, Monona (Army, 501st Military Intelligence Brigade) Arthur Braatz, Monroe (Marines, Fifth Regiment)

PAUL BRAATZ I knew that Dad had served in the military and as kids growing up we knew that he was a Marine. I had some inkling that he was in Korea. Exactly what he did and where, I really didn't know a whole lot about. We really didn't know what much until we were up at Boy Scout camp. We were on the rifle range and you've got your little .22s set up and you get three rounds to put in the paper targets. It was pretty exciting for thirteen- and fourteen-year-olds. Dad was up there and he always just kind of stood in the back. He was a Scout Master keeping an eye on things. They said, "Art, why don't you go ahead and take some shots?" "Oh no, that's OK. I don't have my glasses." "Oh come on, come on." We're all kind of egging him on. He said, "OK, OK." So he gets down without his glasses and proceeds to put three .22 rounds out of a well-used little rifle right in the dead center of the bull's eye. We were all wide-eyed and he goes, "Well, I spent some time in the Marine Corps as a small-arms instructor." We were kind of like, "Oh." That's when the realization kind of hit and that kind of went together with the fact that underneath the couch in the family room were some pictures of Dad in the military. I started putting two and two together and sure enough he had fought as a Marine in Korea. We had to kind of string that together a little bit. There wasn't a lot that he spoke about, but when that realization was there, that kind of sent a different perspective on where Dad comes from.

Art Braatz stands in flak jacket and helmet near the main line of resistance during armistice negotiations. *Art Braatz*

ARTHUR BRAATZ I was drafted into the Corps. During my senior year here at the UW, I knew that I was going to be in the draft status. I had applied for a Navy commission and by the time my application got in, my draft number was too close and the Navy could not accept me.

I was a small-arms instructor back at a recruit depot for a number of months and then things really got rough in Korea, so I was in the retraining command and eventually shipped over to Korea. I arrived in Korea in October of 1952 and was assigned to Baker Company, First Battalion, Fifth Marines. I became company clerk for most of my time in Korea. As company clerk, it was my responsibility to make sure we knew the location of everybody that had been evacuated. There were quite a large number who were wounded and evacuated. This took quite a bit of doing. For several weeks I wound up contacting the military hospitals in the area for IDs on anybody that had been evacuated that day. Some were evacuated to hospital ships between Korea and Japan. I was with that until it was time for me to return to the States.

In July 1953, I boarded ship. The highlight of that trip was coming back under the Golden Gate Bridge in San Francisco. It was announced that the truce had been signed in Korea. It was quite an exhilarating moment, one that I will never forget. The 27th of July, 1953. Apparently it had been announced on shore at the same time because there were cars up on the bridge and so forth honking for dear life. It was one of those exciting moments; for us personally it was almost comparable to the announcement at the end of World War II, the big celebrations. We were all elated that it had been signed and yet in a way there was a little bit of regret — the fact that we couldn't have been there to be part of it at the time that it took place. I had spent quite a bit of time in a bunker on the main line of resistance closest to the access at the Panmunjom Corridor. From where we were, if we had had a good pair of field glasses, which we were allowed to use at certain times, we could actually see into the truce sight.

PAUL BRAATZ After I graduated from college, I came to the conclusion that it was necessary to serve. I thought about the Marines. I actually looked at everyone, but really the Army gave me a greater choice. They said, "We will actually give you the ability to choose." Based on my education, they said, "You might even be eligible to learn a language." So when I enlisted in the military then, I was given a choice of a number of languages. I remember my top three options were Polish, Arabic, and Korean. I looked at Polish and

Paul Braatz was stationed south of Seoul and recalls Korea as a "busy, dynamic country." Paul is pictured, top row, center.
Paul Braatz

I said, "That doesn't have much of a use." Arabic at the time didn't mean anything to me and I thought Korean would be interesting. There was a lot going on in the Asian theater; it was an interesting area of the world.

The orders came that I was being sent to Korea. I remember the word went right by me and then I stopped and went, "Wait a second. Korea. I'm going to Korea." I remember looking at the orders and thinking, "My dad was in Korea." I remember calling him up and saying, "I'm going to Korea!" There was a slight pause on the phone and he said, "Tell me what it's like."

ARTHUR BRAATZ I never imagined forty years later that my son would go there. At the time he went into service I never thought that would be a

Art and Paul Braatz took snapshots of the same terrain in Korea forty years apart. Art's photograph, top, was taken in 1953 shortly before the armistice was signed. *Art Braatz, Paul Braatz*

possibility and yet he went into the service with the idea that he would be in military intelligence. As soon as he was assigned to DLI [Defense Language Institute] and studying Korean I said, "Well, maybe you'll get over there and see some of the country that I had seen." But until that developed, I'd never given that a thought of it being even a remote possibility. He saw some of the area where we had been. It was interesting to compare notes with him about what has changed and what hasn't in the time since. I hadn't even seen most of his pictures until today. I didn't even realize he had them. I think we just started comparing notes. It was very rewarding to hear that he had seen some of the same terrain and that physically it's the same but structurally the country has changed fantastically.

PAUL BRAATZ It was very interesting. The whole area was just shattered and it was interesting to see the rebirth and the growth, especially in the South. They'd fly into the Inchon airport, and my first trip over there, I flew in at night. I remember looking out the window and it was pitch black. I was used to seeing cities and things like that and I realized that I was looking out into the North Korean side. Absolutely not a light anywhere, and when the plane banked and turned, you were looking at South Korea, brightly lit up, very active. You could see the cars going down the highway. That was an eye-opening experience as I was coming in at night realizing that these are two very different worlds that I'm moving into here.

I was stationed south of Seoul, and the country pretty much progressed, as you would think any country would. I mean the farmers were in the fields; there was traffic on the highways. It's a very busy, dynamic country. When you started progressing north of Seoul, though, there was a different tension. When you watched and looked along the highways, they were mined. You could see along the bridges there were these huge concrete blocks that were actually charged so that in the event that there was some type of incursion from the North, these blocks would be blown and the roads would be blocked. You looked at the rice paddies and there were tank traps throughout the rice paddies and every hill had a concrete bunker. Seoul's just a matter of minutes, with today's military, from the demilitarized zone. There was a definite different tension level the closer you got to the DMZ and the farther north you traveled from Seoul. There was still tension there. At that point I think the troop strength was approximately forty-three thousand U.S. troops, and quite frankly we always thought of ourselves as a speed bump. If anything did happen, we weren't going to be

Paul Braatz's present day photograph of the "Truce Village" of Panmunjom, where the 1953 armistice was signed. It now exists as a neutral meeting place inside the demilitarized zone separating the two countries. *Paul Braatz*

in the game very long. We were just there to kind of slow things down until something could be brought in to support us.

When it finally settled in that I was in Korea, it was a continuation of what Dad had served in. He was sent over there for a reason. There was some aggression and he went over there and was part of it helping stop some aggression — the North and the Chinese coming down into the South. Here I was thirty-six, forty years later, coming back as a part of that. There was a huge feeling that made it more valuable to me. Dad was over there. I was speaking to him about having pulled guard duty in a bunker that overlooked Panmunjom and the DMZ. I remember calling him and saying, "You know, I went up to the DMZ at Panmunjom." And he goes, "Really? That's where I served. I served as a guard. I looked over the Truce Village and it was in a bunker up there." And I went, "Oh man." It really kind of put it home that that's where he stood watching while the truce talks were actually going on. That really struck a chord.

ARTHUR BRAATZ I often wonder as I read news reports from time to time, when or if there will ever be a peace accord. You hear of all of the financial and starvation woes in North Korea and wonder if eventually they're going to get to their knees and finally say, "OK, we give up." I hope that will happen for the benefit of the entire world.

PAUL BRAATZ From what I have seen of the Korean people, they are very dynamic and ingenious. You would hope that they could bring themselves together because it's been a divided country for a long time and there's really no reason that they're two peoples. They should be one people.

Appendix I
WISCONSIN VETERAN BIOGRAPHIES

Dale H. Aleckson
Army, 24th Corps
Mosinee

Dale Aleckson served with the U.S. Army for eighteen months, from June 1947 to December 1948. He was stationed in Seoul, South Korea, with the Judge Advocate General's Office. After his discharge in 1948, he attained an MS in school finance and worked as a public school finance manager in West Allis–West Milwaukee. He raised three children with his wife, Donna.

Donald F. Arne
Marines, Seventh Regiment
Oshkosh

After joining the service in January 1951, Don Arne worked as a medical corpsman with the Seventh Marine Regiment for four years. After his discharge from the Marines, he had four children with his wife, Gail, and worked in promotional marketing sales until 1992.

Clifford C. Borden Jr.
Army, Eighth Regiment
Madison

Cliff Borden served in the Army Security Agency in Okinawa, Japan, and Seoul, South

Cliff Borden
James Gill/Wisconsin Public Television

Korea, from 1951 to 1954. He has thirty-five years of combined service in the Army, the Army Reserves, and the Army National Guard. In addition to a host of other civilian careers, including work as radio news reporter and television news anchor, Cliff has worked for the Wisconsin Department of Veterans Affairs

221

as the public informations officer. He serves as the vice president of public relations for the Korean War Veterans Memorial Association of Wisconsin, Inc. He and his wife of forty-nine years, Sally, have four sons and one daughter. They live in Madison, Wisconsin.

Arthur Braatz
Marines, Fifth Regiment
Monroe

Arthur Braatz served for two years in Korea in the Fifth Marine Regiment. After the war, he worked as an accountant and was active as a Boy Scout volunteer. He and his wife, Arlayne, have four children and live in Monroe, Wisconsin. Art's son, Paul Braatz, served in Korea fifty years after the armistice was signed.

Paul Braatz
Army, 501st Military Intelligence Brigade
Monona

Paul Braatz went to Korea with Army intelligence more than fifty years after his father, Art, returned from the Korean War. He is currently an Army reservist who has served in Iraq and lives in Monona, Wisconsin.

John Breske
Marines, First Regiment
Elderon

John Breske served in the U.S. Marines with the First Regiment from 1952 to 1954. He was awarded the Silver Star for injuries he sustained in combat in Korea on the last night before the Korean armistice agreement was signed. After the Marines, he worked as a barber and a ginseng grower and raised two children. He lives in Elderon with his wife, Peggy.

Alice Dorn
Air Force, 801st Air Evacuation Squadron
Middleton

Alice Dorn

Alice Dorn enlisted in the United States Air Force Nurse Corps in December 1952. As a flight nurse, she was based with the 801st Medical Air Evacuation Squadron and provided in-flight medical care for soldiers injured in Korea who were headed to Japanese hospitals for care. After the war, she worked in public health nursing in Dane County,

Alice Dorn
James Gill/Wisconsin Public Television

Wisconsin. She is married to Harold Dorn, with whom she raised three children. She lives in Madison.

Arthur J. Gale
Air Force, 49th Fighter-Bomber Wing
Onalaska

Arthur Gale served four years in the Air Force as a fighter jet technician with the 49th Fighter-Bomber Wing. He graduated from Dunwoody College of Technology in 1958. After working for Lackore Electric Motor Sales & Repair, he started his own refrigeration business, which his three sons now run. Gale lives with his wife, Peggy, in Onalaska.

Robert B. Graves
Army, First Raider Company
Spring Green

Robert Graves

Robert Graves served as an Army Raider in the Korean War from September 1950 to April 1951. Graves graduated from UW–Madison in 1956 with a degree in landscape architecture. He served as an apprentice to Frank Lloyd Wright, working on his later designs before Wright's death in 1959. His work in landscape architecture includes golf courses throughout the United States. Robert and his wife, Derry, raised four daughters and one son.

Robert Graves
James Gill/Wisconsin Public Television

Donne C. Harned
Air Force, 35th Fighter-Interceptor Wing
Blue Mounds

After serving in the South Pacific as part of the Merchant Marine in World War II, Brigadier General Donne C. Harned enlisted in the U.S. Air Force in June 1948 as an aviation cadet. He was commissioned a second lieutenant in July 1948. In June 1950, he volunteered for Korea and flew more than one hundred combat missions. General Harned also served as a forward air controller directing air strikes. Altogether, Harned gave thirty-two years of service to his country. He has five children with his wife, Parnee. They live in Blue Mounds.

Lee R. Haspl
Army, 25th Division
Madison

Lee Haspl

Lee Haspl was born in Prague in what is now the Czech Republic. Haspl emigrated to the United States while still in his teens. He was drafted into the Korean War in 1950 and served two years in the U.S. Army in the 105-mm Howitzer outfit of the 25th Division. In July 1952, Haspl arrived a private and two years later, he left the Army a sergeant first class. Forgoing the chance to become master sergeant, he chose instead to return to Milwaukee to marry. He and his wife, Sandra, have two daughters. They live in Madison.

Lee Haspl
James Gill/Wisconsin Public Television

Richard V. Hemlin
Army, Seventh Division
Madison

Richard Hemlin served two years with the U.S. Army in the Seventh Division, G Company, during the Korean War. During the spring of 1953, he fought in two of the bloodiest battles of the war at Pork Chop Hill, April 16–19 and July 6–11, 1953. After the war, Hemlin worked in marketing and sales and owned a small business. He and his wife, Lila, have three daughters, Christen, Jill, and Pamela. They live in Madison.

Ray Hendrikse
Marines, First Division
Monona

Ray Hendrikse

Ray Hendrikse served four years with the First Marines. He participated in the Inchon landing in September 1950 and fought in the battle at the Chosin Reservoir in December 1950. He worked as a forestry products and utilization specialist after the war. Hendrikse has three children with his wife, Ruth, and lives in Monona.

Ray Hendrikse
James Gill/Wisconsin Public Television

Cornelius Hill
James Gill/Wisconsin Public Television

Cornelius Hill

Army, 24th Division
De Pere

Cornelius Hill enlisted in the Army with guardian consent at the age of sixteen. He served with the Fifth Regimental Combat Team of the 24th Division. He was present at the Yalu River when Chinese troops crossed the border into North Korea. He lives in De Pere.

John E. Hotvedt

Navy, VC-61 Composite Squadron
Amherst Junction

John Hotvedt is a decorated former U.S. Naval Aviator with twenty-five years of service. In World War II, he flew Hellcats on photo missions. In Korea, he flew VC-61s on prestrike reconnaissance and poststrike damage assessment. After his service, he worked in real estate. He is married to Audrey and has three daughters and one son. He lives in Amherst Junction.

Valder John
James Gill/Wisconsin Public Television

Valder W. John
Army, 24th Infantry Division
Green Bay

Valder John is a veteran of both the Korean and Vietnam Wars with twenty-six years of service in the U.S. Army. In Korea, he served with the 24th Infantry Division. He was taken prisoner at Taejon in July 1950 and is a survivor of the Sunchon Tunnel Massacre, for which he received the Purple Heart. John is a member of the Oneida Indian Nation. In recognition of his military service and sacrifice, the Oneida named him an honorary Chief Warrior of the Consolidated Tribes of North American Indians. After Vietnam, he

worked for the Department of Veterans Affairs in hospital administration. He raised four children with his wife, Linda. They live in Green Bay.

Robert W. Kachel
Marines, First Regiment
La Crosse

La Crosse's Bob Kachel worked in intelligence with the First Marine Regiment during the Korean War, and after the war he became an electrician. He has four children with his wife, Mary.

Chester Kesy
Army, Seventh Division
Mosinee

Chet Kesy served in the U.S. Army for seven years. During the Korean War, he served with the Seventh Division and worked afterward as a pipefitter. He is the father of eight children. He lives with his wife, Joyce, in Mosinee.

Robert Kimbrough
Marines, First Regiment
Madison

Robert Kimbrough served with the First Marine Regiment in Korea from June 1951 through December 1953. He was a platoon leader for the Second Platoon, C Company. Kimbrough was

Robert Kimbrough

Robert Kimbrough
James Gill/Wisconsin Public Television

Dale King
James Gill/Wisconsin Public Television

awarded the Purple Heart and the Bronze Star. He retired from the military as a full colonel in 1976. He is an emeritus professor of English literature and taught classes at UW–Madison from 1959 to 1991. He and his wife, Phyllis Rose, live in Madison.

Dale R. King

Army, Fifth Artillery
Colgate

Dale King served with the Fifth Regimental Combat Team in Korea. He was taken prisoner for twenty-eight months, moving between three camps, the last of which was Camp 4

in Wiwon, North Korea, on the Yalu River. He was part of Operation Big Switch when, after nearly two and a half years of imprisonment, he was exchanged on August 29, 1953. King graduated from UW–Madison in 1957. He was hired by Cutler-Hammer as a cost accountant and retired as vice president of finance. He purchased Lakeland Overhead

Dale King

Door Corporation in Stevens Point. He was an alderman for the City of Greenfield for ten years and the council president for four years. He is the father of seven children and two stepchildren. He lives in Colgate.

Donald A. Kostuck
Army, 25th Infantry Division
Schofield

Don Kostuck served with the U.S. Army for twenty-nine years of active service and three years in the Army Reserves. During this time, he served nineteen years overseas, thirteen years in Asia and six years in Germany and Norway. He served with the 25th Division in Korea and as a first sergeant and sergeant major in the Vietnam War. Among his honors are two Purple Hearts, the Combat Infantry Badge, the Bronze Star, nine Good Conduct Medals, and the Korean Service Medal with five combat stars. He served as the director of Emergency Government for Marathon County in Wausau for fifteen years. He and his wife, Ann, have one son and live in Schofield.

Darrell J. Krenz
Army, 24th Infantry Division
Madison

Darrell Krenz enlisted with the 101st Airborne in January 1949 but transferred to the 24th Division soon after in order to go overseas. He went to Korea July 3, 1950, and was on the front lines until July 20, when he was taken prisoner at Taejon. He remained a prisoner of war for the duration of the conflict and was

released as part of Operation Big Switch in August 1953. He worked for the Otis Company as an elevator technician for thirty-four years. He and his wife, Marchita, raised four children. They live in Madison.

Eui Tak Lee
James Gill/Wisconsin Public Television

Eui Tak Lee
Army, 25th Division
McFarland

A native Korean, Eui Tak Lee grew up in South Korea and was forced to change his name and abandon his native language under Japanese occupation. He witnessed the establishment of the Republic of Korea through free election.

Lee joined the Tactical Liaison Office with the 25th Division in 1952. He emigrated to the United States after the war and lives in McFarland, Wisconsin.

DuWayne Lesperance
Army, 25th Infantry Division
La Crosse

During the Korean War, DuWayne Lesperance played trumpet with the 25th Infantry Band. In addition to performance responsibilities, Lesperance also manned the .30-caliber machine gun for the Army Band. After the war, he worked in welding and construction, as well as in factory and office work. He went back to school part-time, and in 1969 received a master of fine arts from Washington State University. He taught Art History at UW–La Crosse for twenty-six years. He still enjoys making art and playing the trumpet and percussion. He lives in La Crosse.

Roger D. Lewison
Army, 24th Infantry Division
Sparta

Roger Lewison is a veteran of both the Korean and Vietnam Wars. He has more than twenty years of service in the Army. In Korea, he was platoon leader to A Company, Sixth Medium Tank Battalion, 24th Infantry Division. He is a life member of a number of organizations that include the Veterans of Foreign Wars, the Military Order of the Purple Heart, Vietnam Veterans of America, and the Korean War Veterans Association. Lewison was voted Outstanding Veteran of the Year by the Wisconsin State Council of Vietnam Veterans of America

in 2002. Roger and his wife, Carol Ann, have three daughters and live in Sparta.

Jim McConnell
Army, 32nd Infantry Division
Superior

Jim McConnell served with the U.S. Army for twenty-two years. As part of the 32nd Infantry, he was at the Chosin Reservoir in December 1950. He and his wife, Betty, raised one daughter. They live in Superior.

James J. Mendyke Sr.
Army, 45th Division
Stevens Point

Jim Mendyke enlisted in the Army in June 1951 and served with the 45th Division in Korea. After the military, he worked for Sentry Insurance Company in Stevens Point for forty years. He and wife, Joan, have six children and are the proud grandparents of seventeen grandchildren.

Dick C. Nooe
Marines, Fifth Regiment
Neenah

Dick Nooe served with the Fifth Marine Regiment during the Korean War. He lost his sight from injuries caused by Chinese grenades while serving as sergeant in charge on Outpost Esther three days before the armistice was signed. Nooe attended graduate school and became a psychotherapist. He was named Blinded Veteran of the Year in 1966 and National Big Brother of the Year in 1977. He and his wife, Sara, have been

Dick Nooe
James Gill/Wisconsin Public Television

married for more than fifty years and live in Neenah, Wisconsin. They raised two children.

Julius W. Ptaszynski
Army, Eighth Division
Wausau

Julius Ptaszynski served two years in Korea with the U.S. Army Medical Corps as a medical technician. After the service, he worked for Woolworth's, managed and owned three Ben Franklin Variety Stores, and managed the Boy Scouts of America Scout Shop. He and his wife of forty-six years, Marlene, live in Wausau. They have three children and five grandchildren.

Elroy Roeder
Army, Second Infantry Division
Rothschild

Elroy Roeder served with the Second Infantry Division during the Korean War. He fought in the battle of Heartbreak Ridge in September and October 1951. He lives in Rothschild.

LeRoy E. Schuff
Marines, Fifth Regiment
Neenah

LeRoy Schuff served with the U.S. Marine Corps for seventeen years. He landed at Inchon with the First Marine Division on September 15, 1950. He was wounded in action September 24 near Seoul and was hospitalized

LeRoy Schuff
James Gill/Wisconsin Public Television

LeRoy Schuff

for five months before returning to Korea. After the service he worked for the Kimberly-Clark Corporation. He earned a BS in industrial education in 1969 and went on to receive an MS in audiovisual communication. He serves as the commander for the Wisconsin Military Order of the Purple Heart. He and his wife, Darline, have been married forty-five years. They have three children and seven grandchildren.

Stewart E. Sizemore
Army, 24th Infantry Division
Lake Geneva

As a Marine who left occupied Japan after World War II to fight in Korea, Stewart Sizemore has twenty years in service to the U.S. Army and Marines. In Korea he served as a machine gunner with L Company, 34th Regiment, 24th Division. He and his wife, Diana, raised three children and live in Lake Geneva.

Stanley B. Smith
Army, Fifth Division
Superior

Stan Smith served in Korea with the Army's Fifth Regimental Combat Team. While on ambush patrol, Smith received a gunshot wound that entered at the base of his neck and exited the right shoulder, narrowly missing both his jugular vein and his spinal column. After working in construction, Smith

Stewart Sizemore
James Gill/Wisconsin Public Television

returned to school to become a registered medical technologist. Parents to four children, Stan and his wife, Dorothy, live in Superior.

Robert R. Strand
Army, First Cavalry Division
Iola

Robert Strand enlisted in the Army and went to Korea with the First Cavalry. Shortly after his arrival, he became ill with hemorrhagic fever and spent four months in the hospital in Sapporo, Japan, and one month in rehabilitation in Tokyo. After the war, Strand taught business to high school students and worked as an accountant. He has three children with his wife, Stella. They live in Iola.

Valedda Wilson

Air Force, Nurse Corps
Green Bay

Valedda Wilson served seven years and eleven months with the Air Force Nurse Corps. After service, she worked as a certified registered nurse in anesthesiology. She raised three children and lives in Green Bay.

William O. Wood

Army, Seventh Division
Racine

W. O. Wood enlisted in the Army in 1948. He fought in the invasions at Seoul and Inchon with B Battery, 49th Field Artillery Battalion, moving north to the Yalu River and then back down to Hungnam. He was awarded the Bronze Star for "outstanding courage and daring" in heroic action near Pungsan in November 1950. He met Chet Kesy in Japan in 1949 when they were both boxing. Kesy and Wood met again when they participated in *Wisconsin Korean Stories* and reminisced about the war, boxing, and the medals they received. Wood and his wife, Joyce, have two sons. They live in Racine.

W. O. Wood
James Gill/Wisconsin Public Television

APPENDIX II
THE HONOR ROLL

Natives of Wisconsin Who Died in Hostile Action (Including Missing and Captured) in the Korean War, 1950–1957*

DWM = died while missing   DWC = died while captive   KIA = killed in action   DOW = died of wounds

AIR FORCE

NAME	RANK	HOMETOWN [†]	TYPE	DATE OF DEATH [‡]
Thomas C. Baker	Staff Sergeant	La Crosse	DWM	February 28, 1954
David Bruzelius Jr.	Sergeant	Monroe	DWM	September 24, 1951
Richard B. Caldwell	Staff Sergeant	Wauzeka	DWM	February 28, 1954
Louis D. Holland	Captain	New Richmond	DWM	December 31, 1953
Jerome Karpowicz	Sergeant	Crivitz	DWM	May 18, 1954
Howard J. Landry	First Lieutenant	Wisconsin Rapids	DWM	March 3, 1952
John R. Pentecost Jr.	First Lieutenant	Lancaster	DWM	February 3, 1953
Douglas M. Smith	First Lieutenant	Oshkosh	DWM	March 17, 1954
Robert R. St. Mary	Airman First Class	Campbellsport	DWM	February 24, 1954
Edward J. Stoll	Staff Sergeant	Milwaukee	DWM	January 31, 1954
Jerome A. Volk	First Lieutenant	Milwaukee	DWM	November 20, 1951

ARMY

NAME	RANK	HOMETOWN	TYPE	DATE OF DEATH
Wilbert V. Adamick	Sergeant	Lafayette	KIA	July 9, 1953
Willis L. Akins	Private	Milwaukee	DWC	July 11, 1950
Donald O. Albert	Private	Dodge	DWM	August 30, 1951
Verle S. Albertson	Private	Polk	KIA	August 29, 1951
Elmer J. Albrecht	Private First Class	Manitowoc	KIA	September 6, 1950

*Source: Korean War Casulty File, 1950–1957 (machine-readable record), Records of the Office of the Secretary of Defense, Record Group 330.

[†]Army lists county; Air Force, Navy, and Marines list town or place.

[‡]For persons who died while missing or captured, the date of casualty is the date died or declared dead (e.g., date of a finding of death), not the date declared missing or captured.

ARMY

NAME	RANK	HOMETOWN	TYPE	DATE OF DEATH
Jack D. Alexander	Private First Class	Marinette	DWC	July 12, 1950
Donald P. Allan	Private First Class	Milwaukee	KIA	September 1, 1950
Leslie R. Amann	Corporal	La Crosse	KIA	January 3, 1951
Wayne R. Amelung	Private	Ashland	KIA	July 27, 1950
Gale C. Anderson	Private First Class	Brown	KIA	October 8, 1951
Robert D. Anderson	Private First Class	Dane	DWM	December 2, 1950
Norbert O. Anderson	Private First Class	Milwaukee	DWC	February 14, 1951
Loris W. Anderson	Private First Class	Rock	KIA	July 20, 1950
Donald E. Anderson	Corporal	Ashland	KIA	March 7, 1951
John W. Anderson	Private First Class	Rock	KIA	July 16, 1950
Eugene L. Angell	Private First Class	Richland	DWC	July 16, 1950
Eugene J. Arcand	Private First Class	Brown	KIA	December 9, 1950
Ray L. Arpke	Corporal	Sheboygan	DWC	December 1, 1950
Donald J. Ayen	Sergeant First Class	Dane	DWC	December 1, 1950
Raymond W. Backhaus	Private First Class	Washington	KIA	November 19, 1952
Donald L. Baer	Private First Class	Racine	DWM	July 20, 1950
David J. Baermann	Corporal	Milwaukee	KIA	December 6, 1950
Benjamin B. Baldwin	Master Sergeant	Milwaukee	KIA	May 18, 1951
Keith D. Ballwahn	Private First Class	Vernon	KIA	January 3, 1951
Durrell Balthazor	Private	Outagamie	KIA	November 3, 1952
James J. Banczak	Private First Class	Langlade	KIA	April 4, 1951
Ernest W. Barnes	Private	Milwaukee	KIA	August 15, 1950
Charles J. Baron Jr.	Private	Iron	DOW	September 3, 1950
Wallace E. Barr	Private First Class	Grant	KIA	July 20, 1950
Bruce O. Barton	Private First Class	Columbia	KIA	September 21, 1950
Marlin F. Basina	Private First Class	Shawano	KIA	February 4, 1951
Kennet Baskerville	Private First Class	Milwaukee	KIA	April 26, 1952
Gerald A. Bauer	Private	Eau Claire	DWC	April 25, 1951
Gerald Baumgartner	Private	Taylor	KIA	May 16, 1953
Richard Baumgartner	Corporal	Milwaukee	KIA	May 11, 1952
Jefferson Beaver	Sergeant	Dunn	KIA	September 2, 1950
Clarence W. Becker	Corporal	Rock	KIA	September 1, 1951
Robert L. Belille	Corporal	Sawyer	KIA	December 7, 1950
Earl L. Belk	Private First Class	Walworth	KIA	September 14, 1951
Richard A. Bell	Corporal	Washington	KIA	July 24, 1950
Ralph Bender	Private First Class	Sheboygan	DWC	December 2, 1950
Maurice Benson Jr.	Private First Class	Lafayette	KIA	January 1, 1951
William A. Benthien	Sergeant	Manitowoc	KIA	May 21, 1951
Karl Bera	Private First Class	Langlade	KIA	October 9, 1951
William A. Bernier	Sergeant	Winnebago	KIA	April 26, 1951

ARMY

NAME	RANK	HOMETOWN	TYPE	DATE OF DEATH
Matthew R. Berres	Corporal	Milwaukee	KIA	March 30, 1953
Frederick Bertrang	Private First Class	Eau Claire	DWM	July 20, 1950
Robert A. Best Jr.	Private First Class	Milwaukee	DWM	December 2, 1950
James C. Bilty	Private	Milwaukee	KIA	May 19, 1951
George T. Bissell	Sergeant First Class	Dane	DOW	July 14, 1953
Hawk A. Black	Corporal	La Crosse	KIA	November 26, 1950
Robert R. Blair	Private First Class	Rock	KIA	July 19, 1950
Theodore Blaisdell	Private	Rusk	KIA	October 15, 1952
Paul J. Blasczyk	Private First Class	Manitowoc	KIA	July 12, 1951
Ferdina Blechinger	Private First Class	La Crosse	KIA	May 17, 1951
Wilbert G. Block	Sergeant	Green	KIA	February 5, 1952
Russell R. Blodgett	Private First Class	Dane	KIA	June 17, 1952
Robert F. Blohowiak	Second Lieutenant	Brown	KIA	August 11, 1952
John T. Blume	Private First Class	Barron	DOW	March 14, 1953
Roy S. Boach	Private First Class	Oneida	KIA	February 13, 1951
Howard Bogenschild	Private	Milwaukee	KIA	November 5, 1950
Marcus H. Bongard	Private	Jefferson	KIA	September 24, 1950
Maxmilli Borkowski	Private	Milwaukee	KIA	June 16, 1951
Loren C. Bortz	Private	Columbia	KIA	July 11, 1950
Lloyd J. Bosben	Private First Class	Oneida	KIA	July 15, 1950
Ronald L. Boyce	Private First Class	Sheboygan	KIA	August 4, 1950
Carroll G. Brandt	Private First Class	Langlade	DWM	November 30, 1950
Lyle H. Brandt	Corporal	Kewaunee	DOW	September 17, 1950
Morris W. Breezee	Private First Class	Dunn	KIA	September 8, 1950
Donald P. Bringe	Private First Class	Milwaukee	DWC	July 14, 1950
Jessie Brown	Corporal	Milwaukee	KIA	March 23, 1951
Juelynn O. Brown	Private	Dunn	KIA	September 3, 1950
Raymond H. Brown	Corporal	Fond du Lac	KIA	December 2, 1950
Edward J. Bucholtz	Master Sergeant	Fond du Lac	DWM	November 29, 1950
Buddy E. Buckmaster	Private First Class	Barron	KIA	December 2, 1950
Leroy M. Buechel	Private	Calumet	KIA	February 17, 1952
Wayne F. Bullis	Private	Racine	KIA	August 16, 1950
Earl G. Bumpas	Private First Class	Milwaukee	KIA	September 1, 1950
Herbert H. Burdick	Private First Class	Winnebago	KIA	June 2, 1951
Joseph S. Burzynski	Sergeant First Class	Kenosha	DOW	July 14, 1952
Thomas T. Caldwell	Corporal	Shawano	DOW	December 4, 1950
Henry B. Carlson	Private	Sawyer	KIA	October 29, 1952
Antonino Chiarello	Private	Milwaukee	KIA	August 2, 1950
Everell V. Clanin	Private First Class	Milwaukee	KIA	January 3, 1951
Edward H. Collins	Sergeant	Adams	DWC	December 1, 1950

ARMY

NAME	RANK	HOMETOWN	TYPE	DATE OF DEATH
Victor J. Condroski	Private First Class	Milwaukee	KIA	April 25, 1951
Stanle Conhartoski	Corporal	Iron	KIA	February 3, 1951
Clarence A. Cooper	Private First Class	Washington	DWM	November 28, 1950
Frederick Corbine	Private First Class	Sawyer	KIA	June 24, 1953
Lamoine V. Cormican	Private First Class	Chippewa	DOW	July 16, 1950
Robert A. Couey	Private First Class	Sawyer	KIA	July 24, 1950
Reginald J. Coutant	Corporal	Columbia	KIA	April 3, 1951
Clare E. Cowee	Private First Class	La Crosse	KIA	August 31, 1951
Eugene R. Creuziger	Private First Class	Racine	KIA	September 16, 1951
Dominik Cupryniak	Private	Milwaukee	DOW	September 5, 1950
Harold J. Dagnon	Private First Class	Shawano	KIA	December 2, 1950
Delford M. Dalberg	Corporal	Grant	KIA	September 14, 1950
George G. Damico	Private First Class	Barron	KIA	September 27, 1950
Louis T. Damitz	Sergeant	Marinette	KIA	August 27, 1951
Richard Dansberry	Private	La Crosse	DWC	February 4, 1951
Earl L. Dansberry	Sergeant	La Crosse	DOW	May 19, 1951
Denton K. De Long	Private First Class	Pierce	DOW	May 18, 1951
Leslie J. De Luca	Private First Class	Milwaukee	DWC	July 16, 1950
Billy R. De Voll	Private First Class	Rock	KIA	January 7, 1951
James D. Delaney	Private First Class	Iowa	KIA	November 4, 1952
Frederick J. Dempcy	Private First Class	Milwaukee	DWM	November 30, 1950
Philip V. Deragon	Private First Class	Ashland	KIA	May 19, 1951
John F. Dewey	Private	Rock	KIA	September 10, 1951
Charles R. Di Ulio	Private First Class	Iron	KIA	February 22, 1951
Charles A. Dickman	Private	Monroe	DWM	July 12, 1950
Jack L. Dinkel	First Lieutenant	Eau Claire	KIA	June 24, 1951
Richard F. Dodmead	Private First Class	Clark	KIA	June 15, 1952
Charles Drengberg	Private	Door	DOW	November 29, 1950
Thomas W. Duffy	Corporal	Manitowoc	KIA	February 13, 1951
Donald J. Dulac	Private First Class	Eau Claire	KIA	October 13, 1951
Donald L. Dupont	Private First Class	Jackson	DWM	December 2, 1950
Lyle R. Dupont	Corporal	La Crosse	KIA	April 25, 1951
Donald F. Ebert	Private	Waukesha	KIA	October 28, 1951
Melvin H. Ebert	Private	Fond du Lac	KIA	September 23, 1951
Delbert V. Edgette	Captain	Douglas	KIA	January 14, 1951
Harold M. Edgington	Sergeant First Class	Walworth	KIA	September 8, 1950
Bernard J. Einum	Corporal	Dunn	KIA	February 12, 1951
Kenneth C. Eirich	Sergeant	Sheboygan	KIA	August 9, 1950
Vernon C. Eliason	Private First Class	Chippewa	KIA	September 4, 1950
Tellus H. Elkins	Private First Class	Milwaukee	DOW	June 14, 1952

ARMY

NAME	RANK	HOMETOWN	TYPE	DATE OF DEATH
Lawrence W. Erdman	Sergeant First Class	Marathon	KIA	May 18, 1951
Daniel G. Erste	Private	Milwaukee	DWM	December 6, 1950
William G. Ewing	Private	Iowa	KIA	October 30, 1951
Donald P. Faldet	Private	Jackson	KIA	July 16, 1950
Leo F. Falvey	Private	Manitowoc	KIA	September 16, 1950
Harold O. Fay	Private First Class	Dane	KIA	March 7, 1953
Marvin J. Fenske	Private	Outagamie	KIA	October 15, 1952
Lawrence Ferkovich	Sergeant	Ashland	KIA	September 19, 1951
George H. Finstad	Corporal	Trempealeau	KIA	September 6, 1950
James R. Fisher	Corporal	Fond du Lac	KIA	November 29, 1950
John J. Fitzgerald	Private First Class	Milwaukee	DWC	January 4, 1951
Thomas L. Flaherty	Private First Class	Douglas	KIA	March 9, 1951
Ervin J. Flauger	Private First Class	Shawano	DWC	November 30, 1950
Michael E. Foley	Private First Class	Racine	KIA	January 29, 1951
Walter A. Fonder	Private First Class	Brown	KIA	August 3, 1950
Henry L. Ford	Private	Vernon	KIA	September 22, 1950
Robert M. Ford	Private First Class	Price	KIA	December 5, 1950
Robert F. Fox	Private First Class	Milwaukee	KIA	April 10, 1952
Louis M. Frank	Sergeant First Class	Racine	KIA	February 7, 1951
Jack L. Frater	Private	Portage	KIA	June 17, 1952
Aloysius J. Freund	Sergeant	Fond du Lac	DWC	July 16, 1950
John W. Freymiller	Private	Grant	KIA	July 18, 1953
Jerrold Fronzowiak	Private First Class	Dodge	KIA	October 9, 1951
Robert R. Funke	Sergeant	Milwaukee	DWM	November 2, 1950
Robert H. Gaedeke	Corporal	Milwaukee	KIA	June 1, 1951
Joseph E. Gallitz	Corporal	Waukesha	KIA	June 14, 1953
Valentine R. Gannon	Private	Chippewa	KIA	July 28, 1952
Ralph E. Garbisch	Sergeant	Milwaukee	KIA	February 5, 1951
Arvil R. Garner	Private	Milwaukee	KIA	July 30, 1950
Eugene A. Gawlik	Private	Milwaukee	KIA	July 16, 1950
Robert F. Geiger	Private First Class	Green	KIA	September 21, 1952
Morris C. Gensch	Corporal	Green Lake	KIA	April 8, 1952
Robert A. Gerlach	Private	Milwaukee	DOW	September 18, 1950
Donald L. Gerrits	Private First Class	Outagamie	KIA	September 19, 1950
John P. Gershewski	Private First Class	Milwaukee	KIA	July 15, 1953
Francis Gilbertson	Corporal	Green	KIA	August 8, 1952
William A. Gilson	Corporal	Oneida	KIA	October 30, 1950
Charles J. Gitzlaff	Private First Class	Milwaukee	DOW	June 30, 1951
Edwin Goede Jr.	Private	Rock	KIA	July 11, 1950
Rueben J. Goerl	Private First Class	Shawano	KIA	February 13, 1951

ARMY

NAME	RANK	HOMETOWN	TYPE	DATE OF DEATH
William O. Goetz	Private	Milwaukee	KIA	May 5, 1952
Wallace E. Goff	First Lieutenant	Dane	KIA	August 22, 1950
Donald A. Goggins	Private	Milwaukee	KIA	April 22, 1953
James Goldsworthy	Private First Class	Rock	KIA	October 27, 1951
Harry J. Gonia	Private First Class	Winnebago	KIA	September 23, 1950
Robert J. Gora	Private	Milwaukee	KIA	October 9, 1951
Harold L. Gorman	Private First Class	Manitowoc	KIA	September 6, 1950
Kenneth J. Gorman	Sergeant	Waupaca	DWC	February 12, 1951
Norbert J. Gorman	Private First Class	Dodge	KIA	July 31, 1950
Paul A. Graber	Corporal	Shawano	KIA	May 18, 1951
Rodney F. Graff	Private	Douglas	KIA	July 14, 1953
Wilbur L. Grass	Private First Class	Grant	KIA	September 16, 1950
Ronald J. Grassold	Private First Class	Milwaukee	KIA	April 18, 1953
Laverne A. Gruber	Corporal	Sauk	KIA	November 2, 1950
Henry T. Gruna	Corporal	Marathon	KIA	June 11, 1952
Oswald Grunig	Corporal	Fond du Lac	KIA	June 21, 1952
Raymond Gunderson	Private First Class	Milwaukee	DWC	November 10, 1950
Russell Haakenson	Corporal	Vernon	KIA	October 13, 1950
Neal W. Haferman	Private First Class	Wood	KIA	July 29, 1950
Lawrence Halvorson	Sergeant	Barron	KIA	July 20, 1950
Robert H. Hamm	Private	Rock	KIA	November 30, 1950
Carl P. Hammer	Corporal	Monroe	DOW	November 5, 1950
Joseph E. Handl	Corporal	Manitowoc	KIA	February 4, 1951
Melvin O. Handrich	Sergeant First Class	Waupaca	KIA	August 26, 1950
Harlan T. Hanson	Private First Class	Columbia	KIA	April 22, 1951
Raymond W. Hanson	Corporal	St. Croix	KIA	October 14, 1951
Daniel W. Hanus	Private	Shawano	KIA	October 19, 1952
Donald P. Hardinger	Private First Class	Wood	DWM	July 6, 1953
David J. Hargrave	Sergeant	Barron	KIA	September 3, 1950
Lamar F. Hassel	Private First Class	Lincoln	KIA	August 1, 1950
Richard Hawkes	Second Lieutenant	Bayfield	KIA	July 29, 1950
Earl W. Hedrington	Private	Milwaukee	DOW	May 20, 1951
Donald O. Heesen	Private	Washington	KIA	September 24, 1951
Merlin A. Heinecke	Sergeant	Washington	DWM	December 2, 1950
Dale A. Heise	Private First Class	Oconto	KIA	September 19, 1951
Charles Helgerson	Private First Class	Eau Claire	KIA	April 23, 1951
Orline W. Heling	Private	Shawano	KIA	April 17, 1953
Donald Hendrickson	Private First Class	Rock	DWM	December 6, 1950
Norman Henricksen	Corporal	Milwaukee	KIA	July 11, 1950
Wallace B. Hermann	Corporal	Trempealeau	KIA	April 29, 1952

ARMY

NAME	RANK	HOMETOWN	TYPE	DATE OF DEATH
Claude R. Hess	Private First Class	Outagamie	KIA	December 12, 1950
Paul F. Heuss	Corporal	Lincoln	KIA	September 13, 1950
Kenneth C. Hilgart	Corporal	Price	KIA	June 29, 1951
Donald L. Hitz	Private First Class	Dunn	DWM	July 22, 1950
Harold L. Hodge	Captain	Adams	KIA	December 6, 1950
Henry E. Hohne	Private	Kewaunee	KIA	November 14, 1951
John H. Holmes	Private First Class	Manitowoc	KIA	February 4, 1951
Eugene R. Honel	Private First Class	Monroe	KIA	October 18, 1951
William J. Hoolihan	Private	Outagamie	KIA	July 16, 1950
Arth Hopfensperger	Private First Class	Outagamie	KIA	November 28, 1950
Dani Hopfensperger	Sergeant First Class	Outagamie	KIA	September 11, 1950
William Hotchkiss	First Lieutenant	Rock	KIA	July 16, 1950
Oliver Hottenstein	Corporal	Shawano	KIA	July 24, 1950
Eugene O. Houle	Private First Class	Outagamie	KIA	October 3, 1951
Harvey J. House	Private	Sawyer	KIA	July 25, 1950
Bernard L. Howe	Private First Class	Lafayette	KIA	July 11, 1950
Joseph A. Howell	Private First Class	Grant	DWM	November 28, 1950
Ronald D. Huebner	Private First Class	Rock	KIA	October 13, 1950
Glenn Huff	Corporal	Milwaukee	DWC	November 25, 1950
Gene M. Ingram	Private	Oneida	KIA	July 16, 1950
Ralph V. Jackson	Corporal	Richland	DWM	November 30, 1950
Douglas G. Jackson	Private	Barron	KIA	July 16, 1950
Arthur F. Jacob	Private First Class	Milwaukee	DWM	September 16, 1950
Richard Jahnke	Private First Class	Milwaukee	KIA	August 17, 1950
John R. Jalas	Private	Milwaukee	DWM	July 18, 1952
John C. James	Private First Class	Eau Claire	DWC	November 30, 1950
Roland J. Jarvey	Corporal	Oconto	KIA	February 13, 1951
Donald C. Jaskulske	Private First Class	Racine	KIA	September 14, 1950
Kenneth L. Jensen	Private	Rock	KIA	August 1, 1952
Donald P. Jentzsch	Private	Taylor	KIA	September 29, 1952
T. T. Johnsbury	Corporal	Waushara	KIA	February 6, 1951
Ervin M. Johnson	Sergeant First Class	Trempealeau	DWC	February 13, 1951
Phillip B. Johnson	Corporal	Kenosha	KIA	September 18, 1950
Vernon G. Johnson	Corporal	Jackson	DWC	December 1, 1950
Norman H. Johnson	Corporal	Fond du Lac	KIA	August 11, 1950
Edmund R. Johnson	Private First Class	Jackson	KIA	September 6, 1950
Marvin J. Johnson	Private First Class	Oneida	DWM	February 13, 1951
Gordon R. Johnson	Private First Class	Jackson	KIA	September 5, 1950
John R. Jonesiv	Private First Class	Racine	DWM	April 25, 1951
Kenneth L. Jones	Private First Class	Waukesha	KIA	July 20, 1950

ARMY

NAME	RANK	HOMETOWN	TYPE	DATE OF DEATH
George A. Jorgensen	Private First Class	Milwaukee	KIA	August 8, 1951
Raymond E. Jose	Private First Class	Marinette	KIA	August 11, 1950
Hilary W. Justman	Private First Class	Fond du Lac	KIA	November 7, 1952
Joe Kaczmarczyk	Private First Class	Taylor	KIA	September 19, 1951
Joseph C. Kainz	Corporal	Pierce	KIA	May 7, 1952
Ernest Kaminski	Private First Class	Portage	KIA	July 13, 1951
David B. Kampa	Private First Class	La Crosse	KIA	August 12, 1950
Daniel F. Kamps	Second Lieutenant	Outagamie	KIA	July 27, 1950
Gordon W. Kanter	Corporal	Milwaukee	KIA	June 27, 1952
Clyde W. Kappus	Sergeant First Class	Eau Claire	KIA	May 18, 1951
Ross W. Katzman	Private	Walworth	DWC	May 17, 1951
John F. Kelleher	Private	Rock	KIA	July 16, 1950
Gerald J. Keller	Corporal	Richland	KIA	July 14, 1952
Gilbert A. Kemnitz	Sergeant	Milwaukee	DWC	February 14, 1951
Vernon L. Kesler	Corporal	Wood	KIA	January 26, 1951
Rufus L. Ketchum	Sergeant	Burnett	KIA	December 6, 1950
James E. King	Private	Manitowoc	KIA	July 22, 1950
Daniel W. Kirkland	Private	Milwaukee	KIA	July 12, 1950
David R. Kittleson	Private First Class	Milwaukee	KIA	November 29, 1950
Charles R. Klatt	Private First Class	Winnebago	KIA	November 28, 1950
Melvin R. Klein	Private First Class	Washington	KIA	February 12, 1951
Laverne R. Klevgard	Private First Class	Buffalo	KIA	March 24, 1953
Charles J. Kling	Captain	Eau Claire	KIA	February 16, 1953
John Klunk	Sergeant First Class	Sheboygan	KIA	February 4, 1951
Forrest N. Knich	Corporal	Milwaukee	KIA	July 31, 1950
Francis D. Knobel	Private First Class	La Crosse	DWM	December 12, 1950
Harry A. Knoke	Private First Class	Forest	KIA	November 26, 1950
Roy E. Knopp	Private	Milwaukee	KIA	November 1, 1950
Jerome W. Knorr	Corporal	Marathon	KIA	July 4, 1952
Ralph E. Knuth	Private	Eau Claire	KIA	September 4, 1951
Paul E. Kochanski	Private	Milwaukee	KIA	September 12, 1950
Glenn E. Kohn	Private	Dodge	KIA	July 24, 1953
Harvey A. Kolberg	Private	Florence	KIA	November 7, 1952
Jack Korakian	Corporal	Racine	KIA	January 23, 1952
Leonard Koscielak	Private First Class	Milwaukee	DWM	September 1, 1950
Donald Kosmecki	Private First Class	Milwaukee	KIA	July 24, 1953
Chester F. Kotowicz	Sergeant	Milwaukee	KIA	June 13, 1953
Jerome W. Kottmer	Private First Class	La Crosse	DWM	November 30, 1950
Stanely F. Kountney	Private	Iron	KIA	May 31, 1951
Clarence E. Krei	Private First Class	Marinette	DWM	November 29, 1950

ARMY

NAME	RANK	HOMETOWN	TYPE	DATE OF DEATH
Eugene Kressin	Private	Milwaukee	KIA	November 6, 1952
Walter B. Kretlow	Private First Class	Milwaukee	DWM	December 2, 1950
George A. Krizan	Sergeant First Class	Milwaukee	KIA	February 15, 1951
Stanley Krukowski	Private First Class	Barron	DWC	January 1, 1951
Janis Krumins	Private First Class	Milwaukee	KIA	June 14, 1953
Jerome M. Krumpos	Corporal	Brown	KIA	August 31, 1950
Raymond Krzyzaniak	Sergeant First Class	Rusk	DWC	January 21, 1951
Roland W. Kubinek	Captain	Vilas	DWC	December 1, 1950
Melvin L. Kuehl	Private First Class	Dodge	KIA	July 31, 1952
Wayne A. Kuehn	Sergeant	Milwaukee	DWM	November 30, 1950
Roger R. Kuhlman	Second Lieutenant	Eau Claire	KIA	September 12, 1950
Fave R. La	Private First Class	Marathon	KIA	July 3, 1952
Robert J. Lahey	Second Lieutenant	Outagamie	KIA	February 15, 1951
Lee W. Langeberg	Sergeant First Class	Fond du Lac	KIA	September 4, 1950
Lyle M. Langlitz	Sergeant First Class	Winnebago	DOW	February 4, 1951
James M. Lansing	Corporal	Winnebago	KIA	September 20, 1950
John H. Lantry	Private	Milwaukee	KIA	October 13, 1952
Edward R. Lashok	Private First Class	Winnebago	KIA	November 26, 1950
John Lasiuk Jr.	Private	Milwaukee	DWM	November 2, 1950
Donald L. Laughran	Corporal	Rock	KIA	February 14, 1951
Frank C. Lavora	Private	Milwaukee	KIA	September 23, 1950
Lazaros Lazarou	Corporal	Racine	KIA	October 25, 1951
Donald Lee	Private	Milwaukee	KIA	September 21, 1952
Robert G. Lenz	Private First Class	Rock	DWM	July 16, 1950
John J. Lepp	Corporal	Brown	DWM	October 15, 1952
Vincent Libassi	Sergeant	Marinette	KIA	August 3, 1950
Dale E. Lind	Corporal	Dane	KIA	April 23, 1951
Erwin A. Lindemans	Private First Class	Barron	KIA	April 23, 1951
William J. Lingle	Corporal	Langlade	DWC	November 30, 1950
Charles P. Link	Private First Class	Milwaukee	KIA	October 17, 1951
Laverne J. Loether	Private First Class	Monroe	KIA	May 18, 1951
Leslie V. Lokker	Sergeant	Rusk	DOW	September 5, 1950
John W. Longwitz	Sergeant	Oneida	KIA	October 17, 1950
Thomas H. Loomis	Private	Milwaukee	DWC	December 2, 1950
Mannie L. Loshaw	Private	Oneida	DOW	October 14, 1952
Robert C. Luedtke	Private	Marinette	KIA	October 14, 1952
Kenneth Lundberg	Private	Oneida	DWM	July 31, 1950
Gerald D. Madel	Sergeant	Winnebago	DWM	July 8, 1953
Andrew W. Mahon	Private First Class	Kenosha	DWM	November 30, 1950
Richard W. Mahr	Private First Class	Monroe	KIA	October 14, 1952

ARMY

NAME	RANK	HOMETOWN	TYPE	DATE OF DEATH
Arthur Majeske Jr.	Private	Milwaukee	DWC	July 12, 1950
Frank M. Malczewski	Private First Class	Milwaukee	DWC	November 30, 1950
Robert Malkiewicz	Corporal	Milwaukee	KIA	August 18, 1950
Bernard Marquardt	Sergeant First Class	Milwaukee	KIA	March 7, 1951
Frank O. Mars	Sergeant	Milwaukee	KIA	July 16, 1950
Harold L. Marsh	Sergeant First Class	Winnebago	DWC	July 20, 1950
Odvin A. Martinson	Second Lieutenant	Manitowoc	KIA	July 6, 1951
Robert L. Mastin	Private First Class	Eau Claire	KIA	May 18, 1951
Henry E. Matton Jr.	Private First Class	Barron	KIA	November 11, 1950
Harley D. May	Corporal	Brown	KIA	March 15, 1951
Carl E. McLaflin	Sergeant First Class	Rock	KIA	February 12, 1951
James McClenathan	Corporal	Douglas	KIA	May 29, 1951
Michael W. McClone	First Lieutenant	Waupaca	KIA	September 3, 1950
Donn A. McFarlane	Private First Class	Eau Claire	KIA	January 13, 1951
James C. McGuire	Corporal	Winnebago	KIA	July 11, 1950
William M. McGuire	Sergeant	Rock	KIA	August 29, 1951
Paul L. McKittrick	Private	Richland	KIA	October 31, 1950
Bruce D. McKown	Sergeant First Class	Dane	KIA	September 26, 1952
Andrew G. McLeod	Private First Class	La Crosse	DOW	August 6, 1952
John J. McMahon	Corporal	Columbia	KIA	October 5, 1951
Richard O. McNitt	Private	Jefferson	KIA	October 3, 1951
Carl E. McPherson	Sergeant	Milwaukee	KIA	February 28, 1951
Franklin W. McVay	Lieutenant Colonel	Eau Claire	KIA	August 4, 1951
Jerome D. Mechler	Private	Waupaca	DOW	September 4, 1950
Fredrick Mehlhorn	Private First Class	Shawano	KIA	August 28, 1952
Jacob J. Meier	Corporal	Milwaukee	KIA	October 9, 1950
Ervin S. Melcher Jr.	Private	Outagamie	KIA	March 15, 1951
Kennet Mellenthien	Private	Dodge	KIA	August 30, 1951
Charles W. Melton	Private First Class	Washburn	KIA	July 24, 1950
Frank Mercurio	Private	Milwaukee	KIA	September 29, 1951
Gerald F. Merrill	Corporal	Barron	KIA	January 16, 1951
Allen C. Mertes	Private First Class	Washington	KIA	November 4, 1950
Robert L. Mervicker	Sergeant	Oneida	KIA	September 1, 1950
Frederick R. Meyer	Sergeant	Milwaukee	KIA	September 19, 1950
Joseph W. Mick	Private First Class	Monroe	DWM	November 2, 1950
Robert C. Mielke	Private	Kenosha	DWC	July 20, 1950
Hugh J. Mikkelsen	Sergeant	Winnebago	KIA	May 30, 1951
Arthur K. Mikulik	Private	Iowa	KIA	February 6, 1951
Wilhelm Milbrandt	Private First Class	Dane	KIA	February 4, 1951
John G. Miles	Private First Class	La Crosse	KIA	September 20, 1950

ARMY

NAME	RANK	HOMETOWN	TYPE	DATE OF DEATH
Gerold M. Miller	Private First Class	Milwaukee	DWM	December 2, 1950
Robert F. Miller	Corporal	Waupaca	DWC	November 29, 1950
Jerome A. Misuraco	Corporal	Iron	KIA	October 30, 1950
John H. Mitchell	Master Sergeant	Kenosha	KIA	September 12, 1950
Truman O. Moen	Corporal	Trempealeau	KIA	August 9, 1952
August A. Molina	Private	Milwaukee	KIA	July 20, 1950
Jack D. Monnot	Private First Class	Langlade	KIA	September 25, 1950
Rondo J. Monroe	Private	Barron	KIA	October 31, 1952
Thomas P. Moore	Private First Class	St. Croix	DOW	June 11, 1953
Austin Morgan	Private	Shawano	KIA	September 22, 1950
Edward M. Morrison	Private	Ashland	KIA	July 6, 1950
Durlin J. Morse	Private	Adams	DWM	December 2, 1950
Robert C. Morse	Private First Class	Langlade	KIA	July 11, 1950
Murel R. Mott	Private	Clark	DWC	July 20, 1950
Donald E. Mrotek	Private First Class	Manitowoc	KIA	September 5, 1950
Edward J. Mueller	First Lieutenant	Sheboygan	KIA	April 2, 1953
Edwin H. Mueller	Private First Class	Marathon	KIA	September 25, 1951
Robert G. Naatz	Corporal	Rock	KIA	January 21, 1953
Joseph J. Neitzer	Private First Class	Forest	KIA	July 4, 1951
Thomas E. Nelson	Private First Class	Ashland	KIA	July 9, 1953
Dion L. Neman	Private	Milwaukee	KIA	October 19, 1951
Alvin M. Nemitz	Private	Brown	KIA	July 18, 1953
Edward D. Nethery	Corporal	Lafayette	KIA	May 18, 1951
Rhinold Neumiller	Sergeant	Kenosha	KIA	September 1, 1950
Harlan R. Nevel	Corporal	Grant	DOW	March 18, 1953
Charles W. Newberry	Sergeant	Vilas	KIA	February 22, 1953
Tommy Newell	Private First Class	Taylor	KIA	August 15, 1950
Myron E. Newman	Sergeant	Green	KIA	June 29, 1952
Russel H. Nielsen	Sergeant	Racine	KIA	November 15, 1950
Gerald D. Norder	Master Sergeant	Green	KIA	May 29, 1951
Leon Norton	Private First Class	Milwaukee	KIA	October 16, 1952
Donald W. Novacek	Private	La Crosse	DWC	February 13, 1951
Edward D. Nowaczyk	Private First Class	Milwaukee	KIA	September 30, 1951
Erwin R. Nussbaumer	Private First Class	Milwaukee	DWM	May 18, 1951
Ronald R. Oakley	Corporal	Outagamie	DWM	December 3, 1950
Russell M. Odberg	Private First Class	Polk	KIA	April 23, 1951
William T. Ohara	Private First Class	Milwaukee	DWC	July 16, 1950
Otto A. Ohme	Corporal	Milwaukee	DWC	November 30, 1950
Richard C. O'Keefe	Corporal	Dane	KIA	July 23, 1953
Darrell Olds	Corporal	Dane	KIA	February 4, 1951

ARMY

NAME	RANK	HOMETOWN	TYPE	DATE OF DEATH
Robert A. Olson	Corporal	Oneida	KIA	May 25, 1951
Charles M. Olson	Corporal	Calumet	KIA	May 22, 1951
Richard O. Olson	Second Lieutenant	Dane	KIA	May 9, 1953
Charles Ostrander	Corporal	Portage	DWM	December 1, 1950
Albert Ostrowski	Private	Milwaukee	KIA	August 1, 1952
Clifford L. Otis	Private First Class	Dane	KIA	September 1, 1950
Glen R. Owen	Private First Class	Manitowoc	KIA	February 14, 1951
Michael H. Paczocha	Private First Class	Milwaukee	DWM	November 28, 1950
Joseph T. Pahle	Corporal	Milwaukee	KIA	October 7, 1952
Robert G. Pallesen	Private	Racine	DWC	July 14, 1950
James A. Panosh	Private First Class	Manitowoc	DWM	September 7, 1952
Darrell J. Parsons	Private First Class	Calumet	DOW	November 24, 1952
William D. Partin	Private	Waukesha	KIA	March 26, 1951
Alfred Paschelke	Private First Class	Milwaukee	DWC	November 26, 1950
Edwin E. Patten	Private	Chippewa	DWM	November 30, 1950
Wayne H. Paulsen	Private First Class	Chippewa	KIA	July 17, 1951
Robert J. Paun	Private First Class	Clark	KIA	October 20, 1952
Duane N. Peaschek	Corporal	Sheboygan	DWM	February 13, 1951
Richard E. Pease	Private First Class	Adams	KIA	September 3, 1950
Rudolph Pellegrini	Private	Outagamie	DOW	August 16, 1950
Louis C. Pepera	Private First Class	Marinette	DWC	November 27, 1950
Clarence D. Perrin	Corporal	Juneau	KIA	April 26, 1951
Clifford A. Persons	Private	Douglas	KIA	October 25, 1951
George W. Peterburs	Captain	Milwaukee	KIA	November 2, 1950
Russell F. Peters	Sergeant	Rock	DOW	January 12, 1952
Bruce A. Peterson	Corporal	Milwaukee	KIA	March 30, 1951
Dean V. Peterson	Private	Buffalo	KIA	July 20, 1950
John W. Pettit	Sergeant	Crawford	KIA	December 1, 1950
Ralph R. Pfeiffer	Private First Class	Fond du Lac	KIA	October 11, 1951
Desmond Pierce	Master Sergeant	Sheboygan	KIA	December 9, 1950
Frederick E. Pierce	Private First Class	Rock	KIA	July 20, 1950
Leon Piwoni	Corporal	Clark	DWM	November 28, 1950
Robert J. Poczekaj	Corporal	Milwaukee	KIA	September 5, 1950
Robert E. Polzine	Private First Class	Milwaukee	DWC	December 1, 1950
Robert L. Poppe	Private First Class	Sheboygan	KIA	October 14, 1952
Myron L. Potter	Private	Waushara	KIA	April 25, 1951
Harold L. Powell	Private First Class	Ozaukee	KIA	August 21, 1952
Merritt L. Pratt	Sergeant First Class	Langlade	KIA	November 2, 1950
Edward J. Pratt	Sergeant	La Crosse	DWM	November 2, 1950
Leonard Purkapile	Private First Class	Grant	DWM	November 28, 1950

ARMY

NAME	RANK	HOMETOWN	TYPE	DATE OF DEATH
William H. Quale	Private	Racine	KIA	September 4, 1950
Robert Quiroz	Private First Class	Milwaukee	KIA	September 26, 1950
Myron F. Radank	Private First Class	Milwaukee	KIA	December 2, 1950
Robert P. Raess	Private First Class	Iowa	DWM	September 1, 1950
James D. Ramel	Private	Fond du Lac	KIA	September 1, 1950
Robert M. Rauen	Private First Class	Milwaukee	KIA	June 24, 1953
Gerald L. Ray	Private	Vernon	KIA	July 9, 1953
Mitchell Red Cloud Jr.	Corporal	Jackson	KIA	November 5, 1950
Norm Reichenberger	Private First Class	Winnebago	KIA	January 1, 1951
Edward L. Reick	Private	Waukesha	KIA	June 26, 1952
Francis R. Reiswitz	Private First Class	Marinette	KIA	February 5, 1951
Donald G. Renstrom	Sergeant	La Crosse	DWM	February 14, 1951
Leander J. Rettler	Sergeant	Washington	KIA	July 3, 1952
Eugene C. Rhode	Sergeant	Oneida	KIA	June 14, 1953
Eugene E. Rhyner	Private First Class	Chippewa	KIA	December 19, 1950
Harold P. Rice	Master Sergeant	Monroe	KIA	September 5, 1950
Clarence E. Rickl	Corporal	Wood	KIA	July 31, 1951
Reginald F. Riviere	Corporal	Milwaukee	DOW	April 12, 1951
Gerald G. Robinson	Corporal	Langlade	KIA	October 13, 1950
Francis J. Rochon	Private First Class	Douglas	DWM	September 1, 1950
Randolph R. Rogers	Private	Dane	KIA	February 12, 1951
Walter W. Roggow	Private First Class	Waupaca	DWC	December 1, 1950
Charles W. Rollins	Private	Price	KIA	June 13, 1952
Raymond J. Rosbeck	Private First Class	Washington	DOW	September 22, 1952
Douglas W. Rose	Private First Class	Marathon	KIA	October 4, 1951
Gerald V. Rossiter	Private	Dunn	DWM	July 29, 1950
William F. Roy	Private First Class	Bayfield	KIA	January 12, 1952
Ernest R. Roye	Private	Bayfield	KIA	November 20, 1952
Robert G. Rucinski	Private First Class	Marinette	KIA	June 10, 1951
William H. Rueger	Private First Class	Langlade	KIA	June 9, 1951
Ronald P. Ruka	Sergeant	Pierce	KIA	July 17, 1953
Robert A. Ryan	Private First Class	Dane	KIA	June 11, 1952
William H. Ryman	Private First Class	Grant	DWM	December 10, 1950
Richard Salvatore	Private	Kenosha	KIA	October 20, 1951
Floyd A. Sandlin	Private	Douglas	KIA	July 25, 1950
Neil M. Sather	Corporal	Vernon	KIA	July 20, 1950
Gerald H. Saxton	Private First Class	Marinette	KIA	August 12, 1950
Paul R. Schanhofer	Corporal	Monroe	KIA	February 10, 1951
Douglas F. Schauf	Private	Walworth	KIA	May 18, 1951
Verno Schermerhorn	Sergeant	La Crosse	KIA	July 31, 1952

ARMY

NAME	RANK	HOMETOWN	TYPE	DATE OF DEATH
Alphonse R. Schmitt	Private	Marathon	KIA	October 4, 1951
Andrew Schneider	Sergeant	Milwaukee	KIA	July 8, 1953
John C. Schneider	Corporal	Milwaukee	KIA	October 19, 1952
Arley B. Schneider	Corporal	Milwaukee	KIA	August 12, 1950
William G. Scholze	Private	La Crosse	KIA	July 27, 1950
Richard L. Schott	Private	Milwaukee	KIA	July 27, 1950
Floyd M. Schroeder	Sergeant First Class	Juneau	DWM	June 11, 1952
Gordon T. Schroeder	Private	Milwaukee	DWM	September 3, 1950
Maynard Schroeder	Private	Oconto	DOW	June 14, 1953
Clair C. Schuknecht	Private First Class	Milwaukee	KIA	July 27, 1950
Bertram E. Schultz	Private First Class	Shawano	KIA	July 20, 1951
Richard J. Schultz	Private First Class	Manitowoc	DWC	November 2, 1950
John Schwed Jr.	Private	Fond du Lac	DWM	October 25, 1951
Harold G. Schwemer	Corporal	Milwaukee	KIA	July 4, 1952
Eugene C. Schwend	Private First Class	Green	KIA	February 13, 1951
Lawrence H. Scott	Private First Class	Sauk	DWC	November 30, 1950
Bernard E. Scovell	Sergeant	Dunn	KIA	February 13, 1951
Raymond W. Seegert	Sergeant	Winnebago	KIA	January 12, 1952
Robert W. Seidel	Corporal	Fond du Lac	KIA	June 12, 1952
Deloy G. Semingson	Private First Class	Eau Claire	KIA	September 1, 1950
Charles H. Senz	Private First Class	Winnebago	DWM	December 2, 1950
Donald D. Shaw	Private First Class	Ashland	KIA	July 4, 1952
James H. Sheldon	Corporal	Eau Claire	KIA	November 20, 1952
Charles Shifflett	Corporal	Milwaukee	KIA	August 8, 1952
Thomas W. Short Jr.	Corporal	Dane	KIA	October 21, 1951
Ernest V. Simonson	Private First Class	Vernon	DWC	February 12, 1951
Gerald T. Sinz	Private	Dunn	KIA	August 17, 1950
John O. Skaug	Private	Vernon	DWM	July 9, 1953
George M. Skogstad	Private	Trempealeau	KIA	December 15, 1952
Joseph Skwierawski	Corporal	Milwaukee	DWC	November 2, 1950
Carl C. Slade	Private First Class	Dodge	KIA	November 17, 1952
Richard J. Slater	Private	Barron	KIA	February 8, 1951
Louis E. Slusarski	Sergeant First Class	Portage	KIA	October 10, 1951
James W. Smaglik	Private First Class	Buffalo	KIA	February 4, 1951
Richard E. Smelcer	Private	Richland	KIA	September 14, 1950
Allen W. Smith	Private First Class	Portage	DWC	February 12, 1951
Harvey E. Smith	Private First Class	Milwaukee	KIA	September 20, 1950
Clarence W. Smith	Private	Chippewa	KIA	September 12, 1951
George C. Smith	Private First Class	Milwaukee	KIA	May 19, 1951
Adolph E. Snarski	Corporal	Iron	KIA	October 20, 1950

ARMY

NAME	RANK	HOMETOWN	TYPE	DATE OF DEATH
Ralph Soderstrom	Private	Milwaukee	KIA	May 18, 1951
Milnor L. Solberg	Sergeant	Sawyer	DWM	December 2, 1950
Edward J. Solway	Private First Class	Brown	DWM	May 18, 1951
John Soman	Private First Class	Marathon	KIA	August 11, 1950
Dean R. Sorenson	Private First Class	Racine	KIA	July 23, 1952
Francis B. Spaeth	Corporal	Monroe	KIA	October 13, 1951
Jack J. Stai	Sergeant	Eau Claire	KIA	May 17, 1952
Joseph W. Stapleton	Private First Class	Iowa	KIA	June 9, 1951
Kenneth R. Stark	Private First Class	Columbia	KIA	January 15, 1951
Ronald C. Stec	Corporal	Kenosha	KIA	March 25, 1951
Robert J. Stein	Private First Class	La Crosse	KIA	August 18, 1950
Harold Steinhilber	Private	Lafayette	KIA	September 17, 1951
Lawrence F. Stenzel	Private	Marathon	KIA	September 21, 1951
Russell L. Stephens	Private	Green Lake	DWC	November 30, 1950
Jerome H. Stoffel	Sergeant	Washington	DWM	July 9, 1952
Richard T. Stone	Sergeant First Class	Dane	KIA	September 25, 1950
Thomas Stretsbery	Private First Class	Juneau	KIA	August 30, 1951
Arthur H. Stroud	Corporal	Milwaukee	KIA	November 30, 1950
Francis E. Stutlien	Private First Class	Jackson	DWC	February 12, 1951
Jerome A. Sudut	Second Lieutenant	Marathon	KIA	September 12, 1951
Leonard J. Sullivan	Private	Iron	KIA	August 11, 1950
Robert D. Sumter	Private	Milwaukee	KIA	April 17, 1953
Laverne A. Sutliff	Corporal	Burnett	KIA	April 17, 1953
Franklin T. Swartz	Corporal	Kenosha	KIA	November 21, 1951
Edward Swiechowski	Private First Class	Winnebago	KIA	March 1, 1952
Stanley Szymanski	Private	Brown	KIA	October 18, 1951
Harold G. Tacke	Private First Class	Milwaukee	KIA	July 16, 1950
Melvin E. Taggart	Private First Class	Outagamie	KIA	July 25, 1952
Jack H. Taktakian	Private First Class	Racine	KIA	August 3, 1952
Richard D. Tatro	Private	Langlade	KIA	July 16, 1950
Claude E. Tennant	Private	Racine	DWM	February 15, 1951
Willard N. Tessin	Sergeant	Sheboygan	DWC	December 1, 1950
Joseph Thomas	Private First Class	Price	KIA	July 12, 1950
Arlie O. Thompson	Corporal	Monroe	KIA	May 29, 1951
Duane Thompson	Corporal	Dunn	DWM	November 30, 1950
Jerry A. Thompson	Private First Class	Portage	DWC	November 30, 1950
Spencer J. Thompson	Corporal	Milwaukee	KIA	September 19, 1951
Joseph A. Thomson	Corporal	Milwaukee	DOW	November 29, 1950
John B. Thorn	Corporal	Sauk	KIA	March 19, 1953
Wallace L. Timm	Private	Jefferson	KIA	June 15, 1952

ARMY

NAME	RANK	HOMETOWN	TYPE	DATE OF DEATH
Luis P. Torres	Private First Class	Waushara	DWM	September 1, 1950
Edward J. Travis	Sergeant	Milwaukee	DOW	October 12, 1951
Gregory W. Triggs	Private First Class	Dane	KIA	July 26, 1950
John Truter	Private First Class	Racine	DWM	November 30, 1950
Lawrence G. Turczyn	Private	Milwaukee	KIA	July 12, 1950
Eugene C. Turner	Private First Class	Marathon	KIA	October 6, 1952
Richard M. Urmanski	Corporal	Marathon	KIA	January 1, 1951
Nicholas Valentine	Sergeant	Grant	DWM	December 6, 1950
Wiilliam O. Van Pelt	Private First Class	Polk	KIA	September 16, 1950
Gordon Vandenbush	Corporal	Oconto	KIA	August 12, 1950
Steve J. Vertcnik	Private First Class	Milwaukee	KIA	August 23, 1950
Carl F. Vorbeck	Private First Class	Milwaukee	KIA	September 20, 1950
William H. Vorpagel	Private	Lincoln	KIA	August 13, 1950
Anthony Vranic	Private First Class	Sheboygan	DWM	August 11, 1950
Roman J. Waldkirch	Private First Class	Washington	KIA	September 16, 1951
Robert B. Walker	Captain	Grant	KIA	September 24, 1950
Paul A. Wall	Sergeant First Class	Crawford	KIA	June 2, 1951
Robert C. Walsh	Private First Class	Rock	DWC	November 4, 1950
Harold T. Warp	Corporal	Adams	KIA	September 24, 1950
Valent Warrichaiet	Private First Class	Oneida	KIA	July 9, 1953
Dillon E. Warthan	Private First Class	Monroe	DWC	November 30, 1950
Melvin G. Washburn	Private	Winnebago	KIA	July 20, 1950
Raymond H. Weiland	Private	Milwaukee	KIA	April 11, 1953
Clarence H. Weiss	Private First Class	Sauk	DOW	April 9, 1952
Jack Weister	Private First Class	Ashland	DWC	February 11, 1951
Edward H. Welsch	Private	Manitowoc	KIA	September 20, 1950
Wilbert Wendricks	Private First Class	Brown	KIA	July 26, 1950
Roman L. Weninger	Private	Washington	KIA	January 26, 1951
Frank J. Wenzel	Corporal	Milwaukee	KIA	November 22, 1950
Rodney D. Wenzel	Private	Wood	KIA	October 14, 1952
Alan R. Werndli	First Lieutenant	Dane	DOW	October 16, 1952
Melvin P. Wester	Sergeant	Ozaukee	KIA	October 14, 1952
Raymond Wewason	Corporal	Forest	KIA	September 21, 1950
Delbert J. Whalen	Corporal	Lafayette	DWM	July 8, 1953
Kenneth J. Whalen	Master Sergeant	Pierce	KIA	September 26, 1950
Elwin I. Whaley	Major	Waukesha	DWC	February 13, 1951
Rudolph A. White	Private First Class	Juneau	KIA	August 18, 1950
Theodore W. Wieseke	Private First Class	Milwaukee	KIA	July 7, 1953
Douglas C. Wilson	First Lieutenant	Grant	KIA	December 18, 1950
Leroy H. Winans	Private First Class	Oconto	KIA	March 22, 1952

ARMY

NAME	RANK	HOMETOWN	TYPE	DATE OF DEATH
Bruce J. Woda	Corporal	Milwaukee	KIA	March 7, 1951
Siegfried A. Wolf	Master Sergeant	Waukesha	KIA	October 31, 1951
Donald C. Wolff	Corporal	Dane	KIA	February 11, 1951
Harvey J. Wood	Corporal	Ozaukee	DWM	November 30, 1950
James J. Woodmansee	Sergeant	St. Croix	KIA	March 7, 1951
Fred B. Worzala	Corporal	Milwaukee	KIA	September 15, 1950
John R. Wulf	Private First Class	Wood	KIA	June 21, 1952
David H. Wustrack	Sergeant	Fond du Lac	DWM	February 13, 1951
Lawrence M. Yaeger	Private	Outagamie	KIA	September 3, 1952
Donald T. Yasko	Private First Class	Racine	KIA	October 1, 1952
Arthur A. York	Private First Class	Waushara	DWM	November 26, 1950
Donald R. Young	Private First Class	Wood	KIA	February 12, 1951
Robert C. Young	Private	Vernon	KIA	October 31, 1952
Eugene C. Zahm	Private	Milwaukee	KIA	October 16, 1952
Thomas E. Zarada	Private First Class	Taylor	KIA	June 26, 1951
Donald E. Zentner	Private First Class	Lincoln	KIA	April 30, 1951
Thomas E. Zimmer	Corporal	Milwaukee	DWM	December 6, 1950
Myles W. Zimmerman	Corporal	Green	DWM	July 13, 1953
Jack E. Zipfel	Private	Milwaukee	DOW	March 17, 1952
Ronald M. Zirbel	Private First Class	Dodge	DWM	July 31, 1950
Roland H. Zurfluh	Private	Wood	KIA	July 16, 1950

MARINES

NAME	RANK	HOMETOWN	TYPE	DATE OF DEATH
Ward O. Bard	Staff Sergeant	Milwaukee	KIA	November 8, 1950
Roger P. Becker	Corporal	Green Bay	KIA	September 30, 1951
Clarence L. Bentley	Corporal	Middleton	DOW	June 16, 1951
Orle S. Bergner	Second Lieutenant	Abbotsford	KIA	October 22, 1951
Michael B. Betthauser	Private First Class	Tomah	KIA	November 2, 1950
Richard L. Bower	Private First Class	Plymouth	KIA	December 3, 1953
Edward W. Breutzmann	Corporal	Milwaukee	KIA	September 23, 1952
John C. Brossard	Private First Class	Columbus	KIA	July 26, 1952
Jack L. Brushert	Lieutenant Colonel	Eau Claire	KIA	December 7, 1953
Boris R. Christ	Private First Class	Milwaukee	KIA	December 12, 1952
Stanley R. Christianson	Private First Class	Mindoro	KIA	September 29, 1950
Donald G. Christopherson	Sergeant	Fond du Lac	KIA	December 2, 1950
John P. Clark	Private First Class	Solon Springs	KIA	November 21, 1950
Michael E. Cooley	Private First Class	New Holstein	KIA	December 15, 1952
Bobby D. Correll	Private First Class	Franksville	KIA	May 17, 1951

MARINES

NAME	RANK	HOMETOWN	TYPE	DATE OF DEATH
Henry Deiss Jr.	Private First Class	Richland Center	KIA	October 27, 1950
James K. Doran	Corporal	Madison	KIA	April 24, 1951
Robert L. Droysen	Private First Class	Racine	KIA	September 23, 1950
Kenneth R. Duhr	Corporal	Richland Center	KIA	November 28, 1950
Kenneth E. Dvorak	Private First Class	Milwaukee	KIA	December 11, 1950
James K. Eagan	Lieutenant Colonel	Muscoda	DWC	November 29, 1950
Leland E. Ehrlich	Sergeant	Dousman	KIA	December 7, 1950
Theodore C. Ellis	Private First Class	Green Bay	KIA	November 27, 1950
Melvin L. Eye	Private First Class	Mills	KIA	September 29, 1950
James T. Fiedler	Private First Class	Green Bay	KIA	June 1, 1951
David R. Flood	Private First Class	Superior	KIA	November 28, 1950
Bert J. Gasford	Private First Class	New Richmond	KIA	December 27, 1952
Gerald C. Graveen	Private First Class	Milwaukee	KIA	September 14, 1951
Ronald W. Greeb	Private First Class	Milwaukee	KIA	May 15, 1951
James T. Griswold	Private First Class	Randolph	KIA	January 30, 1953
Richard B. Hanson	Private First Class	Kenosha	DOW	March 22, 1953
Richard E. Henderson	Private First Class	Oshkosh	KIA	September 13, 1951
Douglas L. Hewlett	Corporal	Waterford	KIA	September 28, 1950
James E. Iverson	Corporal	La Crosse	KIA	November 30, 1950
Adrian D. Janiszewski	Private First Class	Milwaukee	KIA	March 22, 1953
Raymond E. Jesko	Private First Class	Milwaukee	DOW	December 10, 1950
Walter Jung	First Lieutenant	Milwaukee	KIA	May 18, 1951
Arthur R. Kazmierczar	Sergeant	Milwaukee	KIA	August 18, 1950
Edward Kiedrowski	Private First Class	Eland	KIA	June 15, 1952
Kenneth J. Kohlbeck	Corporal	Manitowoc	KIA	November 27, 1950
Edward Kokott	Private First Class	Arcadia	KIA	January 8, 1952
Daniel B. Kott	Private First Class	Milwaukee	KIA	April 24, 1950
Harvey E. Kudick	Private First Class	Kawaunee	DOW	October 6, 1952
Adrian Kurowski	Sergeant	Green Bay	KIA	November 28, 1950
John E. Laborg	Private First Class	Ashland	KIA	March 17, 1953
Charles H. Larsen	Gunnery Sergeant	Tomah	KIA	December 7, 1950
Earl W. Lester	Private First Class	Dallas	KIA	August 10, 1952
Norman P. Looker	Private First Class	Kenosha	KIA	November 17, 1951
Stanley W. Maedke	Private First Class	Marinette	KIA	September 22, 1950
Jerome M. Mangner	Private First Class	La Crosse	KIA	March 26, 1954
Gilbert P. Mantey	Corporal	Milwaukee	KIA	August 18, 1952
Robert G. McCormick	Sergeant	Madison	KIA	March 28, 1953
Thomas C. McCullen	Sergeant	Fond du Lac	KIA	October 7, 1952
Clifford S. Meronk	Private First Class	Hatley	KIA	August 7, 1952
Norbert J. Misorski	Private First Class	Milwaukee	DOW	May 28, 1952

MARINES

NAME	RANK	HOMETOWN	TYPE	DATE OF DEATH
David D. Mueller	Sergeant	Milwaukee	KIA	February 13, 1953
James W. Nelson	Captain	Unknown	KIA	December 14, 1953
Bruce W. Payton	Private First Class	Bristol	KIA	December 1, 1950
Gordon A. Peterson	Private First Class	Iola	KIA	October 29, 1952
Allen L. Phillips	Private First Class	Union Grove	KIA	February 23, 1953
Richard G. Reese	Private First Class	Jonesville	KIA	December 2, 1950
Gerald H. Roark	Private First Class	Milwaukee	DOW	April 6, 1953
Richard B. Roznowski	Private First Class	Green Bay	KIA	September 12, 1951
Duane N. Ruld	Private First Class	Hayward	KIA	May 28, 1951
Raymond F. Schmidt	Private First Class	Markesan	KIA	October 6, 1952
Phillip W. Seeley	Private First Class	Boscobel	DWM	November 2, 1952
Maynard A. Selvog	Corporal	Cambridge	KIA	August 27, 1952
Colin Shultz	Private First Class	Hazelhurst	KIA	December 11, 1950
William L. Sittig	Private First Class	Richland Center	KIA	February 13, 1953
Forrest G. Skidmore	Private First Class	Pearson	DWM	July 9, 1953
Eugene R. Sorensen	Private First Class	Milwaukee	KIA	December 2, 1950
Ronald D. Strommen	Private First Class	Janesville	DWM	November 28, 1950
Donald Terrio	Private First Class	Milwaukee	KIA	December 1, 1950
Peter Tilhof	Private First Class	Milwaukee	KIA	November 28, 1950
Chauncey L. Ullman	Private First Class	New London	KIA	November 8, 1952
Leroy Waskiewicz	Corporal	Milwaukee	DOW	September 25, 1950
Albert G. Weber	Corporal	Monroe	KIA	September 29, 1950
Owen C. Wiederhold	Corporal	Marinette	KIA	November 28, 1950
Howard S. Wirth	Private First Class	Milwaukee	KIA	October 1, 1952
William E. Zbella	Master Sergeant	Wausau	KIA	August 6, 1952
George M. Zukowski	Private First Class	Wabeno	KIA	December 29, 1952

NAVY

NAME	RANK	HOMETOWN	TYPE	DATE OF DEATH
Donald E. Adams	Ensign	Milwaukee	KIA	August 14, 1952
William C. Blackford Jr.	Lieutenant	Milwaukee	KIA	July 26, 1953
Orville M. Cook	Lieutenant	Bagley	DWM	May 19, 1954
Vern H. Fuller	Engineman First Class	Menomonie	KIA	October 12, 1950
Wayne A. Krueger	Seaman	Two Rivers	KIA	October 17, 1951
Deane W. Noringseth	Hospitalman	Sparta	KIA	July 12, 1953
William E. Pulliam II	Lieutenant	Milwaukee	KIA	August 3, 1952
Lyle A. Sorensen	Interior Communications	Racine	KIA	October 13, 1952

Bibliography

Blair, Clay. *Forgotten War: America in Korea, 1950–1953*. New York: Times Books, 1987.

Bruning, John R. *Crimson Sky: The Air Battle over Korea, 1950–53*. Washington, DC: Brassey's, 1999.

Carlson, Lewis H. *Remembered Prisoners of a Forgotten War: An Oral History of the Korean War POWs*. New York: St. Martin's Press, 2002.

Chen, Jian. *China's Road to the Korean War: The Making of the Sino-American Confrontation*. New York: Columbia University Press, 1994.

Cumings, Bruce. *Origins of the Korean War*. 2 Vols. Princeton, NJ: Princeton University Press, 1990.

———. *War and Television*. New York: Verso, 1992.

Edwards, Paul M. *A to Z of the Korean War*. Lanham, MD: Scarecrow Press, 2005.

———. *The Korean War*. Westport, CT: Greenwood Press, 2006.

Foot, Rosemary. *A Substitute for Victory: The Politics of Peacemaking at the Korean Armistice Talks*. Ithaca, NY: Cornell University Press, 1990.

Kaufman, Burton I. *The Korean War: Challenges in Crisis, Credibility, and Command*. Philadelphia: Temple University Press, 1986.

Hastings, Max. *The Korean War*. New York: Simon and Schuster, 1987.

Huston, James A. *Guns and Butter, Powder and Rice: U.S. Army Logistics in the Korean War*. Selinsgrove, PA: Susquehanna University Press, 1989.

Langley, Michael. *Inchon Landing: MacArthur's Last Triumph*. New York: Times Books, 1979.

Rose, Lisle A. *The Cold War Comes to Main Street: America in 1950*. Lawrence: University Press of Kansas, 1999.

Stokesbury, James L. *A Short History of the Korean War*. New York: W. Morrow, 1988.

Stueck, William. *The Korean War: An International History*. Princeton, NJ: Princeton University Press, 1995.

———. *Rethinking the Korean War: A New Diplomatic and Strategic History*. Princeton, NJ: Princeton University Press, 2002.

Weintraub, Stanley. *MacArthur's War: Korea and the Undoing of an American Hero*. New York: Free Press, 2000.

Index

About the Authors

As a production assistant for the Wisconsin Public Television documentary produced in partnership with this project, Sarah A. Larsen spent countless hours screening and interviewing the men and women whose stories are told in these pages. In addition to working closely with each veteran, she gathered images for the project, many of which appear here. A graduate of the University of Wisconsin–Madison, Larsen also worked on the production of *Wisconsin World War II Stories: Legacy* with the History Unit of Wisconsin Public Television. While working on that project she compiled the first searchable, electronic list of Wisconsin soldiers killed while serving in the Second World War.

For this volume, Larsen transformed the raw transcripts of veteran interviews into a comprehensive, book-length format. She lives with her husband, step-kids, and Italian greyhound in central Madison.

Jennifer M. Miller has worked as a teacher and lecturer for the University of Wisconsin–Madison History Department from which she received her master's degree in 2005. An expert in American foreign relations in East Asia during the Cold War, she is currently working on a PhD dissertation on American-Japanese relations during the 1950s. She is a member of the Society for Historians of American Foreign Relations, and has been published in *Reviews in History*.

Miller authored the historical chapter introductions for this book. She lives on Madison's East side and travels often to Japan for research.